Practicing in the New Mental Health Marketplace:
Ethical, Legal, and Moral Issues

Practicing in the New Mental Health Marketplace:
Ethical, Legal, and Moral Issues

Edited by
Richard F. Small and Laurence R. Barnhill

American Psychological Association
Washington, DC

Published by
American Psychological Association
750 First Street, NE
Washington, DC 20002

Copies may be ordered from
APA Order Department
P.O. Box 92984
Washington, DC 20090-2984

In the United Kingdom, Europe, Africa, and the Middle East, copies may be ordered from
American Psychological Association
3 Henrietta Street
Covent Garden, London
WC2E 8LU England

Typeset in Century by EPS Group Inc., Easton, MD

Printer: Data Reproductions Corp., Auburn Hills, MI
Cover Designer: Design Concepts, San Diego, CA
Technical/Production Editor: Marianne Maggini

Library of Congress Cataloging-in-Publication Data
Practicing in the new mental health marketplace : ethical, legal, and moral
  issues / edited by Richard F. Small and Laurence R. Barnhill.
      p. cm.
    Includes bibliographical references and index.
    ISBN 1-55798-494-8 (alk. paper)
    1. Managed mental health care.   I. Small, Richard F.   II. Barnhill,
  Laurence R.
  RC465.5.P7   1998
  362.2'0425—DC21   98-15627
                                                                        CIP

British Library Cataloguing-in-Publication Data
A CIP record is available from the British Library.

Printed in the United States of America
First edition

Contents

Contributors

Dana C. Ackley, PhD, Building a Managed Care Free Practice and Peak Performance Consultation, Roanoke, VA

Carol Shaw Austad, PhD, Psychology Department, Central Connecticut State University

Laurence R. Barnhill, PhD, Private Practice and Alliance Behavioral Healthcare, PC, Bloomington, IN

William H. Berman, PhD, Department of Psychology, Fordham University and BHOS, Inc., White Plains, NY

Barbara Eileen Calfee, JD, LSW, Calfee & Associates, Huntsburg, OH

Nicholas A. Cummings, PhD, Nicholas and Dorothy Cummings Foundation, Scottsdale, AZ, and Department of Psychology, University of Nevada, Reno

Shirley Ann Higuchi, JD, Legal and Regulatory Affairs, American Psychological Association, Washington, DC

Billie J. Hinnefeld, JD, PhD, Legal and Regulatory Affairs, American Psychological Association, Washington, DC

Stephen W. Hurt, Westchester Division, New York Hospital–Cornell Medical Center and BHOS, Inc., White Plains, NY

Renee H. Martin, JD, Kalogredis, Tsoules and Sweeney, Ltd., Wayne, PA

Franklin G. Miller, PhD, SASSI Institute, Bloomington, IN

Glenn A. Miller, PhD, SASSI Institute, Bloomington, IN

Thomas C. Morgan, Psychology Department, Central Connecticut State University

Michael J. Murphy, PhD, ABPP, Department of Psychology, Indiana State University

Thomas F. Nagy, PhD, Department of Psychiatry and Behavioral Sciences, Stanford University School of Medicine

Ethan Pollack, PhD, Private Practice, Needham, MA, and Massachusetts School of Professional Psychology, Boston

Sarah Pratt, MA, Department of Psychology, Fordham University

Karen Shore, PhD, Private Practice, Westbury, NY, and National Coalition of Mental Health Professionals and Consumers, Commack, NY

Richard F. Small, PhD, Spring Psychological Associates, Sinking Spring, PA

Michael J. Stutman, JD, Kalogredis, Tsoules & Sweeney, Ltd., Wayne, PA

Thomas E. Sweeney, JD, Kalogredis, Tsoules & Sweeney, Ltd., Wayne, PA

Anthony M. Trachta, MSW, Partners Psychiatry and Mental Health, Boston, MA

Acknowledgments

My interest in ethics and mental health services clearly comes from the influence of my parents, Charles and Phyllis Barnhill. From them I learned to value fairness, help others, and uphold high standards—great guidance for a lifetime. I also have had many excellent teachers and colleagues who have nurtured my curiosity and growth: especially John Snyder, Jerry Rubenstein, John Werner, Marsha McCarty, and Mike Murphy. I particularly want to thank my good friend Frank Miller, who helped me, personally, with this project, as well as the Sharks. My best is for the love of my life, Kristine, and our children, Jason, Luke, and Sarah, who have helped me and held me to the highest standards, whenever they could.

LAURENCE R. BARNHILL

In acknowledging those who have helped me get to the point where I had the confidence to embark on this project, I will invariably omit many important people. Professionally, Sam Knapp, Toni Rex, Tom DeWall, and my "buddies" at the Harrisburg Bureau of Disability Determination have particularly added to my understanding of the interface of clinical, professional, and ethical issues. If it were not for Larry Barnhill's persistence and my family's support, this book would never have happened. And, special thanks to my secretary, Mary Blair, who has been tirelessly pleasant in the face of many difficult tasks.

RICHARD F. SMALL

Practicing in the New Mental Health Marketplace:

Ethical, Legal, and Moral Issues

Introduction

Uncontrolled growth in health-care services has come to an end, probably forever. The continuing expansion of the U.S. economy during the last 50 years allowed a similar (and even more rapid) expansion of health-care programs and benefits. Businesses increased health-care benefits to attract and retain employees, and generous benefits became expected. Payment mechanisms based on fee for service, or UCRs (usual and customary rates), provided little incentive for providers to cut costs. Thus, until recently, cost was not a major consideration in the provision of health-care services.

Most current mental health practitioners completed professional training and entered the field with virtually no instruction in the financial realities of service delivery. The idealism of young professionals who were dedicated to the needs and rights of individual patients was not inconsistent with the health delivery and reimbursement system. Currently, however, economic realities are forcing cost containment to become a major emphasis in health care. Managed care has become one of the major vehicles of cost containment, and business methods have been forcefully introduced into what was previously experienced as a private relationship between professional and client.

Indeed, it is difficult to pick up any health-care periodical, or listen to conversations between health-care providers, without encountering the dreaded words *managed care*. Despite a plethora of articles about financial aspects of managed care—some bemoaning the concept and its implementation, some warning therapists to join groups or lose their jobs, and some warning consumers about HMOs—little has been written about the ethical dilemmas that practitioners face, and must resolve, in our new health-care environment.

This book includes the voices that make up that debate. The controversies define a profession in upheaval and transition. Together we (professionals and clients, lawyers and businessmen, consumer advocates and legislators, and supporters and opponents of managed care) will chart the course of the mental health field into the new century. It is safe to say that no one was ready for the changes, and similarly, no one knows how it will turn out.

It is at such times of uncertainty that ethical and moral questions become more central to human dialogue (Gaylin, 1991). Questions of right and wrong are no longer so easily answered. Is it "wrong" for a clinician to slant a report to a managed care company to obtain needed services for a single mother in poverty who needs help dealing with her children? Is it wrong for managed care companies to refuse to cover 30-day inpatient stays for alcohol problems? Is it wrong for clinicians to use a benefit plan aimed at brief therapy to provide a thorough evaluation, and then blame the insurance company for not covering ongoing treatment? Is it wrong for managed care companies to say their benefit plan covers "up to 20 sessions a year" if they rarely authorize more than 6? Is it wrong for clinicians to change a diagnosis or procedure code when billing a managed care company to protect the patient or to achieve reimbursement? Is it wrong for managed care companies to refuse to cover treatment for personality disorders because "treatment doesn't work?" Is it wrong for a clinician to do the job of utilization review (UR) and limit treatment of patients they have never seen? The majority of practitioners report that their code of ethics does not adequately address these combined clinical–financial issues (Murphy & Phelps, 1997).

One problem is that professional ethics and business ethics are not necessarily identical. This can make it difficult for professionals who have been trained that ethics require that they (a) not use their influence over the client for personal gain, (b) fully disclose advantages and disadvantages of professional practices, (c) encourage free choice by clients, and (d) make paramount the client's well-being rather than the therapist's needs.

In business, on the other hand, the well-being of the business is paramount, including maximizing profits. Although treating customers well may be good business, corporate managers who make decisions that benefit customers at the expense of the corporation may be charged for violating their fiduciary responsibilities. There are no codified ethical constraints, then, against marketing that tells only about advantages and not disadvantages of a product; against legal contracts that control professionals' behavior and even speech; against contracts that limit who consumers can see for services; against business practices such as stalling on payments, agreeing to cover services and later refusing payment; even against handling complaints dishonestly by telling clients that no one else is complaining; against implying to clients that a good therapist could have cured them in six sessions; and so forth. Furthermore, individual practitioners are prohibited by antitrust laws from taking collaborative action because it is seen as anticompetitive, whereas large corporations with assets in the billions of dollars can take over huge segments of the field and set guidelines for practitioners and clients without constraint, generally because they are reducing costs, and hence are considered procompetitive.

The lack of constraints on business activity in health care has thus led to a burgeoning field of legislative activity, recently referred to as *managed care reform*. Many feel that only legislative action (i.e., new laws and regulations) will rein in excesses of the business methods applied to health care, and every state in the union is considering legislation to regulate managed care.

Thus, even the question of right or wrong cannot be answered simply: The emotionality of the situation often leads to conclusions regarding being *morally* right or wrong. If the implication is that certain practices are *ethically* right or wrong, then we are generally dealing with the code of ethics of a profession, and violations can have consequences among the professionals. Being *legally* right or wrong may allow litigation as a means of action against violations or may require advocacy efforts to change the law through legislative processes. Ethical practice in the contemporary environment requires knowledge of all three perspectives: the moral, the ethical, and the legal.

If your practice is changing, or if you are a new professional entering the mental health field, this book will help guide you through some of the most difficult conflicts and dilemmas in professional practice today. Other recent books have helped professionals understand how these marketplace changes have come about (Lowman & Resnick, 1994), detailed new clinical practice patterns for HMOs (Austad & Berman, 1991), explored financial issues (Zieman, 1995), and provided suggestions for how to escape managed care (Ackley, 1997). The profession continues in turmoil, however, in part because the underlying ethical and moral issues have not been sufficiently addressed. This volume focuses on the moral, ethical, and legal issues in the new environment so practitioners and students can understand these conflicts and develop effective responses to the emotional, financial, and professional dilemmas they face in contemporary practice.

The upheaval in the evolving health-care marketplace is the most drastic change in professional practice since the initiation of insurance coverage of mental health services 30–50 years ago. In fact, some commentators (Small, 1996) argue that inclusion of third-party oversight (utilization review) of what had previously been a private process between client and clinician, regardless of who paid for it, may make "psychotherapy," as we have known it, impossible.

In a broader sense, we are participants in what is referred to as *health-care reform*, which is affecting all aspects of health care in our society. Whether by government action or marketplace forces, these changes appear to represent the end of uncontrolled growth of health-care services. It is unlikely that our society will ever again expand health-care programs and benefits without considering their costs, as has been the norm during the last 50 years. In hindsight, the neglect of the financial aspect of health care seems to have been highly irresponsible. Professionals were taught to offer the highest level of care to every individual, regardless of cost. Cost–benefit analyses of these choices were considered impalatable. Third-party payments and a feeling that "the insurance company pays" led to overuse of medical technology and procedures. Similarly, third-party payments allowed therapists to continue treatment if it was beneficial without questioning "Is this really worth $100 a session?"

When practitioners and patients choose services that others uncritically fund, growth seems inevitable. Yet the concept of "rationing" is described as politically untenable, so "managed" health care has demonstrated a way to limit services and reduce the growth rate of health-care costs in a way that has become widely accepted, if frequently decried. Involvement of a third party that requires justification and reduction of services, and that uses business strategies to force discounts in fees and costs, has fundamentally and permanently changed health care.

In our day we have seen the president of the United States (William J. Clinton) pound on a table demanding that we control health-care costs, followed by large-scale mergers and buyouts forming the huge corporations that are actually carrying out health-care reform in the marketplace. Cost increases and professionals' salaries have been reduced substantially, and corporate profits and executive salaries have risen so rapidly as to attract venture capitalists and even organized crime.

Some commentators predict the end of the "cottage industry" of private practice and the initiation of "seamless" integrated health-care delivery systems that are information intensive and cost and outcomes driven. It seems likely that efficacy-based treatment and outcome evaluations will become more standard in mental health practice as we enter the new century. It is hoped that these changes will result in an improvement in the quality and consistency of our services rather than merely trapping consumers and professionals in bloated, insensitive, and profit-focused bureaucracies (Nelson, Clark, Goldman, & Shore, 1989).

While most health care and mental health care may be absorbed into such systems, some of the professional practice of psychotherapy will continue to occur outside such systems and will return to its roots as a private pay fee for service enterprise. There are many conflicting scenarios regarding how mental health services will be provided and paid for. Yet, when the increased acceptance and demand for psychological services in schools, workplaces, the justice system, and so forth is examined, it seems highly improbable that such services will not be demanded and provided. Furthermore, for every person who will take whatever is offered, there is another who will demand quality care. Private practice will not "end" in our field because it can be so low cost and because many consumers want strictly private services. That is, although "economies of scale" may drive most physicians to become part of integrated systems, there will probably never be a system less costly than a therapist in an office with an answering machine.

As practice patterns change, it is inevitable that new ethical issues, conflicts, and dilemmas will arise. In this book, we asked some of the leaders in the profession to address such questions as the following: What are the new emotional, financial, values, and ethical conflicts that professionals face? What are the new ethical dilemmas experienced by professionals functioning as clinicians, reviewers, entrepreneurs, managed care executives, and so forth? What roles can professionals play to reduce abuses in the managed care industry? How do clinicians deal with anger and helplessness, loss of autonomy, increased financial pressure, unnecessary review, wasted time holding on 800 phone lines, and so forth? How do we protect clients from deceptive and unethical marketing practices? How do we protect health care from excess profit seeking? How should mental health professionals respond to "gag" clauses and obscure indemnification clauses in contracts? What are ethical and appropriate responses to denial of benefits? How do we prevent overuse and underuse of our services? How can we support each other to aim at high standards and eliminate poor practices whether in managed care or clinical practice?

The authors address these questions from multiple perspectives and thus provide mental health professionals with moral, ethical, and legal tools to (a) guide their own contacts with clients and institutions, protect themselves legally, and feel good about their work; (b) assert and teach high ethical standards to fellow professionals, students, and the public; and (c) effectively challenge institutions, businesses, and other professionals who may push unrealistic or inappropriate expectations on providers and consumers.

The volume is divided into two parts. In the first part, Practice Issues, the authors address the fundamental issues of ethics and morality in social policy and professional practice. First, Barnhill's survey research shows the varying ways psychologists respond when they experience ethical, legal, or moral conflicts such as protecting their clients versus complying with managed care contract expectations. The survey results show that if clinicians perceive themselves or their clients as being exploited or treated unfairly, they do respond, and ethical questions become even more complicated. Next, Murphy explains historical and practice trends and some of the basic tensions involved in the process of funding mental health services; in other words, how we got here and why. Cummings, Shore, and Austad and Morgan explore widely differing beliefs and emotional responses regarding the clash of business and professional ethics. Cummings, one of the originators of managed mental health care, shows why it was inevitable and needed and details moral questions and training issues for practitioners working with managed care. Shore takes the opposite perspective, protesting harmful practices of managed care, exploring moral issues of good and evil, and offering alternatives to managed care. Austad and Morgan explore the social equity concerns of allocating a limited resource for the public in the most efficient, equitable, and effective way possible. They point out that we are likely to have managed care until we can come up with a better system.

The increasing importance of outcomes research is addressed by Pratt, Berman, and Hurt, who assert that ethical practice requires gathering outcome data. Pollack describes the dilemmas of professionals in the middle—those who are practicing in the new role of reviewers in for-profit managed care companies. Nagy explores the rapidly expanding role of psychologists in medical care settings and shows how ethical guidelines apply to behavioral medicine practice. Miller and Miller introduce the potential ethical and social policy conflicts in the burgeoning and high profile area of addictions screening and add the perspectives of institutional consumers of addictions screening, together with ethical guidelines for practitioners.

In the second part, Business and Legal Issues, the authors explore these increasingly essential aspects of the context of clinical work and ensure that the reader will understand contemporary legal and business matters in the new marketplace. Reviews by attorneys Sweeney, Stutman, and Martin, Higuchi and Hinnefeld, and Calfee present the most up-to-date information on legislation, case law, and regulatory parameters affecting practitioners. Sweeney, Stutman, and Martin focus on contract law and case law precedents that determine the responsibilities of practitioners when benefits are limited by managed care—this is essential for all clinicians. Higuchi and Hinnefeld offer a comprehensive overview of the new business arrangements that organize and fund clinical practice, offering a guide through the maze of the new business arrangements. Calfee, a clinical social worker as well as an attorney, highlights key risk management principles. Ackley discusses ethical and marketing issues in practicing outside of managed care. Finally, Trachta provides a personal reflection on the impact of capitation on professional practice by contrasting his experiences with private sector capitation to the rapidly expanding area of capitation of services in the public sector.

LAURENCE R. BARNHILL
RICHARD F. SMALL

References

Ackley, D. (1997). *Breaking free of managed care*. New York: Guilford Press.

Austad, C. S., & Berman, W. H. (1991). *Psychotherapy in managed health care: The optimal use of time and resources*. Washington, DC: American Psychological Association.

Gaylin, W. (1991). *On being and becoming human*. New York: Penguin.

Lowman, R. L., & Resnick, R. J. (Eds.). (1994). *The mental health professional's guide to managed care*. Washington, DC: American Psychological Association.

Murphy, M. J., & Phelps, R. (1997, March). *Managed care's impact on independent practice and professional ethics*. Paper presented at the American Psychological Association Midwinter Convention, St. Petersburg, FL.

Nelson, L. J., Clark, H. W., Goldman, R. L., & Shore, J. E. (1989). Taking the train to a world of strangers: Health care marketing and ethics. *Hastings Center Report, 19*, 36–43.

Small, R. (1996, August). *Ethics and managed care*. Paper presented at the 105th Annual Convention of the American Psychological Association, Toronto, Ontario, Canada.

Zieman, G. (Ed.). (1995). *The complete capitation handbook*. Tiburon, CA: CentraLink/Jossey-Bass.

Part I

Practice Issues

1

Defining the Issues: Survey Research in Ethics and Managed Care

Laurence R. Barnhill

The increased involvement of business practices in psychological services is bringing about major changes in professional practice. The changes are rapid, multifaceted, pervasive, and threatening to providers and consumers, altering the very nature and structure of professional mental health treatment. For better or worse, and whether we like it or not, the massive influx of business strategies and procedures has become an increasingly significant influence on our field. How are these changes affecting practitioners? What clinical, financial, and ethical dilemmas do they face? Also, how are they responding?

Changes in Psychological Services as a Result of Increased Business Involvement

This chapter is a report of a preliminary effort to explore the nature of these changes and how they are affecting our field from the point of view of practicing psychologists. In a brief literature review I discuss the causes of these changes, as well as their larger context, and show how and why managed care has become so dominant. The impact of cost-containment strategies, and the emotional, attitudinal, and behavioral responses of mental health professionals, are then examined, in part by a survey exploring these issues. The results indicate that this new environment places practitioners in situations beyond their training which are loaded with emotional and financial pressures and that they are provided with little professional consensus about how to respond to these pressures. To formulate appropriate ethical standards to guide us through this period of profound transition in our field, we need to understand how practitioners feel about the changes and what they are doing in response to their dilemmas.

Marketplace Changes

It is easy to argue that changes were coming anyway and that they were inevitable. Indeed, many of the changes address long-standing problems in the field that have evolved over the last 30 years (Broskowski, 1991). For example, one of the early concerns of managed mental health-care managers, as well as corporate purchasers, was "treatment plan by benefit design." That is, mental health treatment would often last just as long as the benefit maximum, which seemed wasteful, if not ethically questionable (Wyatt, 1995). Cummings (chapter 3, this issue) criticized "therapeutic drift," or unnecessarily protracted treatment, as another questionable practice that concerned benefits managers, if not the profession. Other issues, including cost figures showing mental health services increasing more than twice as fast as medical-surgical costs (most of the increase is accounted for by proprietary inpatient programs for adolescents and substance abuse rather than increases in outpatient costs), all needed to be addressed (Broskowski, 1991).

Certainly it has been rare in professional circles to advocate drastically increased efficiency of services. The groundbreaking study *The Treatment of Families in Crisis* (Langsley & Kaplan, 1968) was unique in the era by calculating financial savings produced by preventing hospitalization. It was generally ignored by the professions and for-profit hospitals alike, though the principles are now widely applied by managed care (Cummings, 1988). Similarly, warnings that we need to define our services more specifically or someone else will do it for us have tended to fall on deaf ears. Now someone has done the work of defining our services for business customers in a way that shows a profit for them, thus initiating the "free-market" era (Austad & Berman, 1991).

The influence of increased free-market forces has produced a decline in the rate of increase of costs of mental health services, and, in some cases, there is an actual decline in cost. Resources are being diverted from inpatient services to outpatient services (Savitz, 1995). More clients who could appropriately benefit from short-term therapy are receiving it. In some cases, there is increased access for more consumers, even if the benefit is more limited. Consumer satisfaction is a more explicit goal. In spite of the problems involved, there are ways that managed care has had salutary effects on health-care services in general and psychological services in particular (Cummings, 1995).

It may also be important for mental health professionals to realize that these changes are part of larger changes in health care in general, as well as in the global economy, and are not just about mental health care in particular. In the *New England Journal of Medicine*, Kassirer (1995) warned physicians about the same process, "market-driven health care creates conflicts that threaten our professionalism" and that this is "not an abstract dilemma.... [Physicians may] be forced to choose between the best interests of their patients and their own economic survival" (p. 51).

Likewise, cost reductions and increased market competition in mental health are not just an aspect of health-care cost containment, specifically. Increased global competition has many sectors of the economy downsizing and focusing on cost reduction and increasing efficiency. Business executives, union leaders, government and civic leaders, and professionals outside of our field tend to shrug off our complaints and fears—they generally feel that they are all facing the same kinds of economic problems and do not see why mental health should be different. Lower cost, better defined, and less mysterious mental health services make sense to them. (Just ask your friends and relatives.)

In short, the fundamental structure underlying the delivery of mental health services has changed. It is natural that many professionals feel these effects personally, but such reactivity may obscure or distort our perspective about the issues involved and about what needs to be done.

Managed Care and Business Practices

Most mental health professionals learned to practice in an environment that was not so dominated by business practices, and they are not prepared to respond effectively to these changes. In order for us to cope effectively with a new force, it is necessary to understand it. Managed care organizations (MCOs) have gained power by legal and business methods that puzzle and frighten providers untrained in such matters. Contracts that include obscure indemnification clauses requiring clinicians to assume responsibility and liability for mistakes of the MCOs threaten providers with unfair economic risk shifting. "Gag clauses," which forbid providers from criticizing the company, telling clients that they disagree with the company's judgment of medical necessity, or telling clients about alternative treatments that might be of benefit to the client but not part of the health plan, emphasize the lack of autonomy and power of the individual provider. Similarly, terminating providers from approved panels for too frequent appeals or other unspecified causes can lead to fear, anger, and helplessness on the part of the provider (Higuchi, 1994).

Efforts to limit the power of the corporations are blocked by antitrust laws because the corporations are seen as procompetitive (i.e., they have driven down prices). These laws prevent professionals from collective action (which could be seen as illegal boycotts) and further reinforce the transfer of power from professionals to profit-making business entities.

Marketing practices are another business influence that may seem shocking or scandalous to many of us who entered the field with a primary focus on helping others. Flooding markets with advertising about free evaluations by for-profit mental health facilities diverts clients from professional and personal referral networks, confuses clients about what to expect from mental health professionals, and expends large sums in advertising instead of providing services. Managed care "products" sold to companies often mislead consumers as to their actual benefits. Many plans state a benefit of 20 outpatient sessions a year, though they may only approve 6 sessions. The clinician is left to explain the problem to the client (using the limited time available for treatment). MCO executives and corporate human resources managers who advance their careers by demonstrating cost reductions generally claim that beneficiaries have been informed, but it is a rare client who understands their benefit plan. One legislator recently threatened to require the insurance industry to "speak English" (Rushing, 1996).

Other business practices such as discounting prices to capture market share and put competitors out of business have been acceptable for department stores and gas stations but are considered out of bounds in professional practice. Recruiting pitches to "come work for us or we'll put you out of business" emphasize the power of the use of market and legal forces. Such competitive and secretive practices, accepted in business, are new in health care and are often seen as questionable, inappropriate, or unethical (Morreim, 1988; Shore, 1995). Practitioners also experience emotional conflict and ethical questions when they see services reduced, MCO profits increase, and seven-figure MCO executive salaries (Karon, 1995).

Cost Containment

Certainly of all the changes in the "new marketplace," cost-containment procedures are the most intrusive to the practicing clinician. The introduction of cost-containment strategies has had a direct impact on the nature, quality, and quantity of services consumers receive, as well as on the relationship between provider and client. Utilization review, the emphasis on brief therapy, exclusions of "untreatable diagnoses" (such as personality disorders or conduct disorders), exclusions of marital therapy, contracts that allow only crisis intervention, "witholds" that are returned to providers if cost-containment goals are met, and a variety of other procedures impinge on what was previously a private agreement between professional and client (and sometimes an indemnity insurance plan that functioned as a financing and claims administration system). Case management procedures that waste providers' time on 800 numbers and require large amounts of uncompensated paper work to get approval for a few sessions result in rationing care by reducing the amount of available hours for service delivery.

Other cost-containment practices affect clients more directly. When third-party payers seek to interview clients to assess medical necessity, or just deny services leading clients to have to appeal for needed services, clients are sometimes put in a position of persuading someone that they are sick enough to require treatment. This is rarely in the client's best interest. Or similarly, if a client is told that his or her panic disorder, grief reaction, somatoform problem, and so forth should be cured in six or eight sessions, then the client may feel shame and failure if he or she is not better by then ("I tried therapy, I failed"), anger at the therapist for not curing him or her in the allowed time frame, or both (Ackley, 1997). Further problems occur when a new health plan comes in with a different panel of providers and expects the client to switch providers in midtreatment. This is likely to be more of a problem in mental health services than in many medical plans because the therapist–patient relationship is such an integral part of the treatment.

Response of Mental Health Professionals

Emotional and Attitudinal Issues

Just as it is important to understand the new forces influencing our profession, it is important to examine how practitioners have responded. Emotional reactions to the changes in the market and profession are often intense (Haas & Cummings, 1991; Newman & Bricklin, 1991; Shore, 1995). Incentives seemed less intrusive and more benign in the past, whereas now the market has brought economic forces, which have heightened the perception of fear and greed, into the picture (S. Callahan, 1995). Trying to stay rational and objective can be a challenge (D. Callahan, 1996). Two particular areas of controversy and emotional reactiveness include reactions to change and reactions to capitation.

1. Reactions to these changes vary considerably, with some professionals embracing the new market (including the emphasis on brief therapy, case management, efficacy-based treatment, and entrepreneurial activity) and thinking of traditionalists as "dinosaurs." Opponents of such changes fear loss of autonomy and inadequate treatment and decry turning the mental health profession into products to be marketed, as well as the waste involved in advertising and unnecessary review procedures (Cantor, 1995).

2. Reactions are also varied regarding the profit motive in capitation and other ways of making money beyond fee for service, usually by reducing costs (and generally, services). Most professionals understood and accepted the economics of fee for service, making money for a unit of work or a salary. Making money off of the work of other professionals or profiting from cost savings is new for most providers and sometimes feels alien to the values that brought them into the field (Haas & Malouf, 1989).

On the other hand, mental health professionals functioning as MCO managers see their role as preserving a rational mental health benefit for consumers by providing targeted interventions and controlling waste, sometimes over the protests of providers who may be guided by their own self-interest. They point out that the public would generally rather have optical and dental benefits if they could choose. Therefore, it is incumbent on mental health programs and providers to justify services to individual and business consumers in clearly defined ways, as well as to cut costs, in order for our field to survive. They, too, feel like the good guys (Cummings, 1986).

Advocacy for Patients

At the heart of the health professions is the responsibility to serve the best interest of the patient (Crawshaw et al., 1995). New business arrangements often seem to put other entities in charge of determining the need for, amount, type, and course of treatment. Such third-party payers include MCOs, employee assistance programs, corporations, unions, government, and so forth, and if practitioners do not please these customers, they are likely to lose access to the members of the organizations involved (Freeman, 1995). Nevertheless, our primary responsibility is to the individual client (Lazarus, 1995). This was recently reiterated by the Council on Ethical and Judicial Affairs of the American Medical Association (1995).

The American Psychological Association's (1992) Code of Ethics emphasizes "clarifying to all parties" the nature of the relationships involved (e.g., when a third party is paying for services for a client and has expectations about the treatment as well as expectations about information about the client and the treatment; Canter, Bennett, Jones, & Nagy, 1994). The Code discusses protecting clients from harmful influences that the psychologist can control but does not discuss issues of managed care or other market changes specifically (Newman & Bricklin, 1991). It seems safe to assume that the Code will need to address issues involved in the marketplace changes explored here either with some revisions to it or with some relevant commentary and guidance. (See Bersoff, 1995, for limitations in ethics codes.)

Recent discussions about balancing professional responsibilities with cost-containment methods tend to focus on the issue of "quality of services." This seems a potentially useful issue to balance the intense focus on cost reduction. However, broad concepts such as quality of service do not provide clinicians with adequately clear ethical guidelines when confronted with the reality of a client who needs more service than is provided in the benefit plan. Clearly, obtaining knowledge about the system, informed consent issues, appeal procedures, and so forth is one way to be competent and reasonable in the managed care environment (Bennett, Bryant, VandenBos, & Greenwood, 1990).

However, the reality is that there are strong temptations to "game the system" in order to help or protect the client (Haas & Cummings, 1991; Morreim, 1991). The conflicting forces are real, and the resulting ethical dilemmas are complex. In a concrete sense, many clinicians report that they often underdiagnosed for indemnity insurance (to protect the client) but feel pressure to overdiagnose, or at least find a diagnosis that will be covered, with managed care plans (Kovacs, 1996). When faced with a conflict over protecting the patient or honoring the letter of the contract with the managed care company, many clinicians decide to do what will help the patient.

Survey Research on Ethics, Values, and Attitudes Regarding Managed Care and Mental Health Services

To gain an understanding of the ethical posture that practitioners are adopting in regard to the growing influence of business practices in professional psychology, I am in the process of developing a survey that explores potentially controversial topics including rationing, patient advocacy, managed care, brief therapy, the role of business methods and the profit motive, and behavioral dilemmas involved in contemporary ethical conflicts. The questions address issues in the literature (Barnett, 1992; Barton & Barton, 1984; Elpers & Abbott, 1992; Geraty, Hendren, & Flaa, 1992; Green, 1990; Rinella, 1986) as well as those raised in focus groups of psychologists. The survey questions are listed in Appendix A.

Preliminary data have been gathered from 92 psychologists solicited from meetings at the American Psychological Association (APA) 1995 Convention (N = 31) and the Indiana Psychological Association 1994 Convention (N = 61). These data are being used to refine the instrument for further research designed to illuminate psychologists' responses to ethical and value dilemmas that result from the growing influence of business on professional psychology. The pilot data are presented here to provide a preliminary view of the issues that are emerging and to show how various groups of practitioners are responding to them. Some of the questions have been used in further survey work for APA Division 42, Independent Practice (Murphy & Phelps, 1997).

The mean age of the respondents was 45.5 years, and the mean years in practice was 15. Sixty-five percent were men, and 35% were women. This is similar to the overall APA profile mean age of 50 years, mean years of practice of 18, and a gender ratio (men:women) of 55:45 (American Psychological Association [APA], 1996a). It is also similar to the Murphy and Phelps (1997) study of 442 members (APA Division 42) with a mean age of 52 years, mean years of practice of 19, and a men:women ratio of 62.5:37.5.

All of the participants were practitioners: Seventy-three percent were in full-time practice, whereas 27% were in part-time practice. Ninety percent provided independent fee for service as well as insurance reimbursed services, 66% participated in PPOs, 59% in various other managed care plans, and 40% in HMOs. This compares to Murphy and Phelp's (1997) figure of 89% of practitioners participating in any type of managed care arrangement.

Practice settings included 36% in solo practice, 30% in group practice, 24% in institutional clinical settings (hospitals, rehabilitation facilities, clinics, and counseling centers), whereas the other 10% varied among academics, researchers, pastoral counselors, and so forth. The Division 42 sample is more weighted to solo practice, with 89% in solo practice, 18% in group practice, 30% in institutional clinical practice, and 10% in academics (participants could list more than one; Murphy & Phelps, 1997).

Sixty-five percent of practitioners reported that managed care cases made up less than 40% of their practice, and only 11% of practitioners reported that managed care made up 60% or more of their cases. Murphy and Phelps (1997) reported that a mean of 40% of cases was covered by managed care in 1996, with a mode of 50% of cases. Median net total income was $67,000, with 38% reporting over $75,000 and 41% reporting under $60,000. This is similar to the APA study on salaries of psychologists (APA, 1996b), though the data are not organized comparably.

Survey Questions and Results

Survey Items

Most of the items ask practitioners to rate agreement or disagreement on a 5-point scale (strongly agree, agree, neutral, disagree, or strongly disagree) to such items (the following are abbreviated, see Appendix A for the complete wording) as: "Restrictions in services are inevitable" (No. 1), "Focus on the client's best interests is compromised when therapists get a profit from reducing services" (No. 7), "Therapists prefer longer term therapy because it is easier" (No. 8), "Copayment makes clients work harder" (No. 10), "If you can solve a problem briefly, it is unethical to extend the treatment" (No. 11), "I believe managed care organizations keep clinical information confidential" (No. 13), and "Utilization review [UR] has reduced unnecessary hospitalization and reoriented priorities to outpatient care" (No. 15).

Some items ask behavioral questions to find out the frequency (never, sometimes, or often) with which practitioners "modify diagnoses or CPT [current procedural terminology] codes to protect the client" (No. 5), "modify diagnoses or CPT codes to obtain reimbursement" (No. 6), "terminate clients before they wanted because they had received maximum benefits from treatment" (No. 9) and for what reasons a practitioner would "give up advocating for additional benefits for a client" (too hard, didn't know how, or not want referrals to stop; No. 20).

Descriptive Statistics

See Appendix B for the mean scores for each item. Several trends can be seen in the responses to the survey.

Strong concerns about fiscal responsibility. The highest percentage of agreement was with the statement that clients work more efficiently in therapy with copayments (No. 10), with 91% agreeing and only 6% disagreeing. Some respondents noted that this had been established by research and felt that copays were useful to demonstrate commitment and to discourage the curious or lazy. The second highest rate of agreement was with the idea that it is unethical to extend treatment if you can solve a problem briefly (No. 11), with 85% agreeing versus 9% disagreeing.

A clear majority of 71% agreed that it is unethical to bill for an hour if the work was finished in a half hour and the rest of the time was filled with "chitchat," whereas 16% disagreed (No. 18). While there was a consensus on this item, some respondents objected to the characterization of such conversation as chitchat, saying that relationship building and taking breaks was also important in therapy and that these factors necessitated bits of "open" time. One respondent worried that there was a developing expectation to constantly "hurry" therapy, which would be a poor model for clients on how to live (see also O'Rourke, Snider, Thomas, & Berland, 1992).

With regard to whether restrictions on mental health care are inevitable, the majority (52%) agreed or strongly agreed (No. 1). The distribution of responses was bipolar, however, with a large number (40%) disagreeing. While acknowledging that restrictions seemed necessary, some who disagreed believed that it might very well be a false economy: Because mental health services save money through medical cost offset, and also save money on public welfare and jail expenses, it may therefore be a good idea economically to have unrestricted access to them ("In California," 1994).

Suspicions and criticisms of managed care in general and of capitation specifically. Seventy-eight percent agreed that therapists profiting from reducing services compromised the ethical constraint of focusing on the client's best interests, whereas 13% disagreed (No. 7). Business ethics in general were seen as in conflict with health-care ethics by 54% of respondents, whereas 20% disagreed (No. 17). Noted considerations included misleading and expensive advertising, inappropriate contract elements such as gag clauses, dropping panel providers for making appeals, and large executive salaries (see also Fins, 1992). A similar number of respondents endorsed the most inflammatory item, that MCOs were "parasites," with 55% agreeing and 17% disagreeing (No. 3). Some felt that such language was inappropriately biased, though others reported appreciation for capturing some of the emotional reality of the new market (see also Fox, 1995).

Only about half of the respondents (48%) believed that UR reduced unnecessary hospitalization and reoriented priorities to outpatient care (No. 15), in spite of the credible and impressive data MCOs present regarding reduction in inpatient expenses (e.g., from 70% inpatient and 30% outpatient expense to 30% inpatient and 70% outpatient in 10 years; Savitz, 1995).

Even fewer respondents believed that MCOs keep clinical information confidential, with less than a quarter agreeing (24%). Most were neutral about the question, with 36% disagreeing (No. 13). A much higher (62%) percentage of APA Division 42 members reported in the Murphy and Phelps (1997) study that they did not believe that managed care companies kept clinical information confidential.

Advocacy for patients and services. A majority of clinicians emphasized the desire to protect services for clients. Most (67%) agreed that they preferred to err on the side of too much treatment rather than too little (No. 2), and a similar (63%) amount disagreed that longer term therapy was preferred because it was easier and more comfortable (No. 8). Even more agreed (78%) that the client's best interest would be compromised if the therapist could profit from reducing services (No. 7). Clinicians then must balance these advocacy concerns with their fiscal responsibility issues noted in the first section of this chapter.

Behavioral indicators. Because ethical dilemmas are played out in concrete behaviors, the survey included questions designed to determine which course of action the respondents would take in specific situations (Items 4, 5, 6, 9, 19, and 20). Perhaps the most significant behavioral issues relate to practitioners' willingness to modify diagnoses and CPT codes to meet the needs of their clients and themselves. In this sample, a surprisingly low percentage (10%) of clinicians said that they never modified diagnosis or CPT code for client reimbursement (No. 4), whereas a similarly low percentage (12%) said that they never modified diagnosis or CPT code to protect the client's confidentiality or future employment or insurance prospects (No. 5). That over 85% of these practitioners would modify (or have modified) such codes at least rarely is one of the most intriguing findings of the study. To look further, 60% agreed that they would modify sometimes or more often for the client's reimbursement or protection. In a replication, Murphy and Phelps (1997) found that 75% of their sample agreed that "psychologists make changes in diagnosis to protect patients."

With regard to obtaining their own reimbursement (No. 6), a larger number of respondents (27%) would never modify for their own reimbursement, and only 35% would modify sometimes or more often. See the *Gaming the system* section in Discussion and Conclusions for further discussion and possible hypotheses to explain these data.

Comparative Tabulations

The data were also examined to determine if responses were affected by gender, age, income level, practice setting, and amount of managed care involvement. The observations are suggestive and may serve as sources of hypotheses, but they do not fit criteria for the testing of statistical significance.

Gender differences. While the genders were more alike than different on this survey, some trends suggestive of differences are shown in Table 1. In many cases, male practitioners seemed to be more accepting of business-oriented issues, whereas female practitioners seemed more idealistic. For example, more women psychologists agreed that business customs are antithetical to mental health ethics (47–68%, No. 17; see Table 1), and more women agreed that focus on the client's best interests can be compromised when therapists profit from reducing services. Men, on the other hand, reported greater frequency of terminating clients before they were ready because they had reached maximum benefit from treatment. Also, more male practitioners agreed that length of treatment is affected by when the benefits run out.

Men seemed to be more accepting of aspects of managed care practice than women practitioners. More male than female practitioners trusted that MCOs kept information confidential, and the former were more likely to agree that UR has reduced unnecessary hospitalization. Some men also

Table 1. Gender Difference in Survey Responses

Item no./abbreviated questions	Agreement (%)	
	Men	Women
4. Never change diagnosis for client's reimbursement?	7	13
5. Never change diagnosis for client's protection?	9	16
7. Client compromised when therapists profit?	74	87
8. Long-term therapy comfortable?	35	9
9. Terminate clients after maximum benefit?	62	52
12. Length of treatment affected by benefits?	40	23
13. MCOs confidential?	30	13
15. UR reduced hospitalization?	53	42
17. Business customs not psychological ethics?	47	68
20B. Not know how to appeal?	2	25

Note. MCOs = managed care organizations; UR = utilization review.

endorsed the idea that longer term therapy is done because it is easier and more comfortable, whereas few women agreed.

Men might be more willing to challenge MCOs: Only 2% reported that they had given up advocating for benefits because they did not know how to appeal, whereas 25% of women endorsed that response. Perhaps the reason that this percentage for men is so low is that men are less willing to admit that they do not know how to appeal!

As far as behavioral indicators, women are about twice as likely as men (8–14%) to report that they never change diagnosis or procedure code for client's reimbursement or protection. However, it is interesting to note that as far as changing diagnosis or procedure code for their own reimbursement, the genders were the same: Thirty-three percent would do it sometimes or more often.

Age differences. Age and years of experience were strongly correlated with negative attitudes about the new business environment and opposition toward managed care and capitation, as seen in Table 2. Almost all of the most senior practitioners agreed that the profit motive compromised the client's best interests, whereas a smaller majority of the less experienced clinicians agreed. In a similar vein, most of the oldest providers agreed that business customs are incompatible with health-care ethics, whereas only about half of the youngest agreed. Similarly, most of the older practitioners agreed that MCOs are parasites, whereas only about a third of the youngest agreed.

On the other hand, more senior practitioners seemed more accepting of certain market realities than their younger colleagues. More experienced clinicians agreed more that restrictions in services were inevitable than less experienced ones. Experienced providers also agreed more that UR had reduced hospitalization, and older clinicians also believed that MCOs kept information confidential more than younger practitioners.

It is interesting to note that older clinicians reported greater likeli-

Table 2. Age Difference in Survey Responses

Item no./abbreviated questions	Agreement (%)	
	Younger, less experienced, or both	Older, more experienced, or both
1. Restrictions inevitable?	47	61[a]
3. MCOs parasites?	37	60[b]
4. Change diagnosis for client reim? (sometimes or more)	47	66[a,b]
5. Change diagnosis for protection? (sometimes or more)	49	71[b]
7. Client compromised when therapists profit?	63	94[a]
13. MCOs confidential?	17	32[b]
15. UR reduced hospitalization?	33	56[a]
17. Business customs antithetical to psychology?	47	70[b]
19A. Change diagnosis for adolescent?	42	68[b]
20A. Give up advocating, too hard?	50	31[b]
20C. Give up advocating, MCO stop referral?	6	18[b]

Note. MCOs = managed care organizations; UR = utilization review.
[a]Comparison is based on years of experience, compared by quartiles. [b]Comparison is based on age, compared by quartiles.

hood of changing diagnosis or CPT code for the client's reimbursement (No. 4), for protection of the client (No. 5), and to obtain services in the case example of the adolescent conduct disorder (No. 19A). However, no difference was found between age groups on changing diagnosis or CPT code for the provider's reimbursement (33% of all groups reported changing sometimes or more often).

One other intriguing difference between age groups is worth noting. Younger practitioners noted that they were more likely to give up advocating for more benefits for a client because it was "too hard." On the other hand, the youngest practitioners were the least concerned that an MCO would stop sending referrals if they keep advocating.

Income level. Higher income practitioners tended to have attitudes more accepting of business influences on practice in general and on their own income specifically, as seen in Table 3. The biggest difference between income groups was that higher income groups believed that UR had reduced unnecessary hospitalization and that length of treatment was affected by benefits.

There was also a consistent tendency for higher income groups to endorse attitudes that would favor practice income. For example, higher income groups agreed more that they would prefer to err on the side of too much treatment rather than too little. They also agreed less than lower income groups that it is unethical to bill for the full hour if part of the session was chitchat, that it is unethical to extend the treatment if you

Table 3.   Income Level and Survey Responses

	Agreement (%)	
Item no./abbreviated questions	Lower income	Higher income
1. Restrictions inevitable?	67	47
2. Prefer err too much treatment?	57	73
3. MCOs parasites?	46	64
5. Change diagnosis to protect clients? (sometimes or more)	34	70
7. Client compromised when therapists profit?	82	69
11. Unethical to extend treatment after solve problem?	90	80
12. Length of treatment affected by benefits?	22	51
15. UR reduced hospitalization?	33	66
18. Unethical to bill for full hour, with chitchat?	77	58
19B. Pro bono for adolescent?	44	64
20A. Give up advocating, too hard?	33	44
20B. Give up advocating, not know how?	33	3
20C. Give up advocating, MCO stop referral?	11	24

Note.   MCOs = managed care organizations; UR = utilization review.

can solve a problem briefly, and that profit for reducing services compromised ethical constraints.

Higher income groups were more likely to give up advocating for additional benefits because they did not want the MCO to stop sending referrals and because it was "too hard." Lower income groups were more likely to give up because they "didn't know how."

While higher income groups may have shown an interest in their own pocketbook, they also espoused idealistic tendencies and support for clients and services. Upper income groups were more likely to disagree that restrictions are inevitable and agree more that MCOs are parasites. They were more likely to change diagnosis or CPT code to protect the client than lower income groups, but not for their own or the client's reimbursement. Higher income groups also reported being more likely to provide pro bono services on the case example.

Practice setting. There was a good distribution of three groups of practitioners: 36% solo, 30% group, and 24% clinic practitioners. The solo practitioners, unsurprisingly, distinguished themselves by their opposition to managed care practices. Table 4 shows differences between solo practitioners and others for these items. For example, solos agreed that MCOs were parasites more than group and clinic practitioners, and they also agreed more that business customs were incompatible with health-care ethics.

Solo practitioners generally refused to see benefits to UR, agreeing that UR has "improved the consistency of treatment plans" less than clinic and group providers. Remarkably, they also agreed little that UR has reduced unnecessary hospitalization. Only 19% of solo practitioners agreed,

Table 4. Practice Setting and Survey Responses

Item no./abbreviated questions	Agreement (%)	
	Solo practitioners	Group and clinic practitioners
2. Rather err too much?	78	65
3. MCOs parasites?	75	50
4. Change diagnosis—protect client?	72	58
9. Maximum benefit—kick out?	35	56
11. Unethical to string it out?	74	92
15. UR reduce hospital?	19	69
16. UR improve treatment plan?	39	58
17. Business ethics not psychology ethics?	66	50
18. Unethical to chitchat?	59	75
	Group practitioners	Solo and clinic practitioners
4. Change diagnosis—client reimbursement?	44	70
12. Length depends on benefits?	52	27
13. MCOs confidential?	30	19
19A. Adolescent case—change diagnosis?	44	62
20A. Give up advocating, too hard?	50	35
20C. Give up advocating, referrals?	23	10
20D. Give up advocating, not needed?	31	15

Note. MCOs = managed care organizations; UR = utilization review.

whereas a much greater percentage of group (82%) and clinic (52%) practitioners agreed that unnecessary hospitalization was reduced. Clearly these are substantial differences in perspective.

Solo practitioners emphasized a focus on the client more than other groups and also advocated for practice features that could aid clients and make their professional lives more reinforcing. They were more likely to change diagnosis or CPT code to protect the client. Solos were more likely to err on the side of too much rather than too little treatment compared with other groups, and they terminated clients who had achieved maximum benefit from treatment before they wanted less often (35% vs. 56%). Solos also agreed less often that it is unethical to bill for a full hour if 20 minutes was chitchat and less often that it was unethical to extend the treatment beyond solving a problem.

Of the three practice settings, group practitioners seemed to be the most accepting and cooperative regarding the new marketplace practices, as seen in the bottom half of Table 4. They agreed most that the length of treatment is affected by the benefits and were more likely to agree that MCOs kept information confidential. Group practitioners were the least willing to change diagnosis or CPT code to get reimbursement for the client and were also least willing to change diagnosis for the case example.

Group practitioners were more likely to stop advocating for services because they did not want the MCO to stop sending them referrals and because the client "really didn't need more." Actually, group practitioners stopped advocating more often for all reasons, including that it is "too hard," perhaps suggestive of the resignation that many clinicians experience in working with increasing amounts of managed care.

Full- versus part-time practice. Full-time practitioners were more likely than part-time clinicians to believe that business customs were incompatible with health-care ethics and likewise that MCOs were parasites, as seen in Table 5. However, full timers were more likely to trust that MCOs kept information confidential, whereas part timers were more skeptical.

With regard to clinical practices, full-time practitioners were more likely to endorse items that would be compatible with running a business: They were more likely to err toward too much rather than too little treatment, agree that length of treatment is affected by benefits, and agree less that it is unethical to bill for a full hour if some of the time was chitchat.

Correlates of managed care affiliation. It is not surprising that practitioners with higher percentages of managed care in their practices hold attitudes that are more compatible with business and managed care methods, as seen in Table 6. High-percentage managed care participants were much more likely to agree that providers tend toward long-term therapy because it is more comfortable than low-percentage managed care participants. High-percentage MCO participants also agreed more that restrictions are inevitable, that length of treatment is affected by the benefits, that UR has reduced unnecessary hospitalization, and that it is unethical to extend treatment beyond solving a problem. They disagreed more that business customs are antithetical to health-care ethics.

However, high-percentage managed care participants may also have ways of coping with the pressures of the system in that they are more likely to change the diagnosis or CPT code for the client's reimbursement, and to protect the client, though groups once again do not differ on how often they change diagnosis or CPT code for their own reimbursement.

Table 5. Full- Versus Part-Time Practice

	Agreement (%)	
Item no./abbreviated questions	Full time	Part time
2. Rather err too much?	77	42
3. MCOs parasites?	60	46
12. Length of treatment affected by benefits?	39	21
13. MCOs confidential?	30	8
17. Business customs antithetical to psychology?	60	42
18. Unethical to bill for full hour, with chitchat?	66	79

Note. MCOs = managed care organizations.

Table 6. Amount of Managed Care Participation

	MCO partici- pation (% agreement)	
Item no./abbreviated questions	High	Low
1. Restrictions inevitable?	67	49
4. Change diagnosis for client reimbursement?	82	58
5. Change diagnosis for client?	72	55
8. Long-term therapy comfortable?	56	22
11. Unethical to extend treatment?	93	80
12. Length of treatment affected by benefits?	48	27
15. UR reduced hospitalization?	56	44
17. Disagree that business customs antithetical to psychology?	64	33
18. Unethical to bill for full hour, with chitchat?	53	85
20A. Give up advocating, too hard?	44	34
20B. Give up advocating, not know how?	10	23
20C. Give up advocating, MCO stop refer?	44	11

Note. MCO = managed care organization; UR = utilization review.

High-percentage managed care participants also do not agree as often that it is unethical to bill for the full hour if some of the time is spent chitchating.

Few high-percentage managed care participants reported not knowing how to advocate for additional client benefits compared with a lower percentage of managed care respondents. However, the higher percentage participants were more likely to report that they did not advocate for more benefits because it was too hard and most significantly because they did not want to stop receiving MCO referrals.

Discussion and Conclusions

Several major themes emerge from the data related to changes in practice in the new mental health marketplace.

Capitation

One is a controversy about the effects of capitation. The majority of mental health practitioners believe that making a profit from reducing services is wrong. These practitioners generally believe in efficiency and avoiding unnecessary services, but they are concerned that the financial incentives in capitation compromise the ethical constraint of focusing on the client's best interests.

Supporters of capitation note, however, that capitation has advantages over other systems because each component of the health-care systems can benefit. "Incentives" can be "aligned" if (a) payers, including business and government, benefit from a controlled budget for a fixed amount or cost for mental health services; (b) individual consumers benefit from keeping service costs low, even if the benefit is limited; (c) managed care companies benefit by making profits when keeping costs down and customer satisfaction up; and (d) (some) providers can benefit by maintaining a steady referral flow, even if they must discount fees and minimize services. Furthermore, if providers become capitated themselves, then they can make their own decisions about treatment allocation rather than have outside parties decide (Alter, 1995).

It is difficult to argue with the contention that mental health providers should learn to work within a budget. Supporters of managed care and market-based reform are clearly greeted by business and government decision makers with more acceptance than practitioners who oppose any limits on mental health services (Dubin, 1995). Most practitioners, however, at this time believe that the dangers of capitation outweigh the possible benefits.

Confidentiality

A second area of controversy addressed is the area of confidentiality. In the past, confidentiality has been seen as a necessity for mental health services. Consumers and providers are beginning to grasp that things have changed, and the issue is becoming increasingly controversial (Lewin, 1996). Less than a quarter of respondents agreed that MCOs keep clinical information confidential. Because much of the information is now turned over to national data banks, one health-care attorney declared that "confidentiality is over" (Petrila, 1995). Explanations are left to the clinician, necessitating greater effort to establish informed consent (Appelbaum, 1993).

Several respondents observed that many more clients were being denied health, disability, or life insurance coverage following use of their managed mental health-care benefits. Even an insurance manager reported that his superior announced at a sales meeting that "we don't take anyone who's been on Prozac" (personal communication, 1995). Certainly one way insurance companies can increase profit is to have people decide that it is in their best interest not to file claims (Shore, 1996). Efforts to protect confidentiality, however, seem to be gathering momentum as at least one state, Massachusetts, recently enacted legislation preventing "redisclosure" beyond the MCO without an additional consent signature. The belief that clinicians may need to protect their clients from inadequate confidentiality practices that lead to discrimination against them is clearly one justification for "gaming the system"—as discussed in the *Gaming the System* section.

Changing Practice Patterns

Beyond these two controversies, probably the main overall trend indicates a change in practice patterns and perceptions between older and younger practitioners, as well as between solo and group practitioners. Because older and more experienced practitioners were more negative about and opposed to managed care, one hypothesis could be that younger practitioners do not yet understand the problems involved. Perhaps a more likely explanation would be that the youngest providers are already used to something that the more experienced practitioners feel is a violation of long-standing professional standards. As the new generation of practitioners face a different set of experiences and expectations than their seniors, a "changing-of-the-guard" phenomenon seems likely.

Differences between solo and group practitioners may indicate a similar trend. Both older practitioners and solo practitioners tend to focus more on the client than on the MCO. For example, both older and solo practitioners prefer more treatment rather than less, fewer terminations against the client's wishes, more likelihood of changing a diagnosis to protect the client or to obtain services, and so forth. Group and younger practitioners are generally more comfortable with managed care and business influences on practice, more likely to believe that UR had reduced unnecessary services, and are more likely to give up advocating for services because it was "too hard." Also, group practitioners are more likely to give up advocating because of concern about losing MCO referrals. This latter tendency increases for practitioners who have a high percentage of managed care patients in their practices.

Values affecting practice seem to be in the process of changing as managed care becomes more dominant, the younger generation enters the field, and more practice is done in groups. The danger that focus on the client may be lost in the midst of changes in financial incentives, and practice structures, seems real and needs additional research.

Gaming the System

The large number of providers who report that they change diagnosis or procedure codes for client protection or reimbursement, at least rarely, requires some discussion. Such a trend could affect the integrity of clinical statistics, and it too needs further research.

One possible conclusion is that if practitioners perceive themselves as being pushed too far, they will game the system to protect their clients and to a lesser extent themselves. One vantage point was highlighted by one respondent with the comment that clients coming in for therapy are "all depressed, aren't they?" Another respondent defined the conflict in the following way: "I care more for my clients than for the unfair rules of a greedy corporation." Another mentioned feeling troubled that marital therapy was often not covered, so she often felt forced into naming one person as the patient and giving a diagnosis, which often skewed perception of a relationship problem.

Several respondents challenged the implication that they were gaming the system, saying that they agreed that they sometimes changed diagnosis to get coverage, but "only if another diagnosis also correctly applied."

A likely hypothesis is that most or all participants would endorse such a qualifier for their "modifications." A further hypothesis is that more justifiable minimal modifications are the most common, along a continuum, with more blatant attempts to manipulate the system being less common.

Regardless of the motivations involved, it may be reassuring to note that practitioners will modify diagnosis or procedure codes more often for clients' protection, clients' reimbursement, or both, than for their own reimbursement. This percentage, approximately 33%, who reported that they sometimes changed codes for their own reimbursement is one of few statistics that was stable across groups, unaffected by gender, age and experience, practice setting, income level, or amount of managed care participation.

One interesting anecdote from the survey was a note from a psychologist owner of a group practice who declined to allow his providers to complete the survey. He felt that the survey could be dangerous and bad for the field. I have puzzled over this, believing that more information on the subject could only benefit the field. Perhaps he was concerned that the survey would reveal what most practitioners suspect: The system is perceived by practitioners as sometimes unfair to clients and providers, and ethically questionable behavior may be seen as a legitimate response.

However, the meaning of these findings is ambiguous because we often seem to lack a consensus on what is right or wrong in these times of change in professional practice (Lowman, 1994). The findings do suggest that practitioners experience themselves in transition, in conflict over questions of who is the client and what is fair and, hence, of the fundamental moral principles of justice and fidelity (Beauchamp & Childress, 1988; Pope & Vetter, 1992). Clearly, further work to define these issues, understand these conflicts, and explore possible resolutions is needed.

References

Ackley, D. (1997). *Breaking free of managed care*. New York: Guilford Press.

Alter, G. S. (1995, September). *Strategic challenges and opportunities for behavioral group practices*. Paper presented at the Behavioral Healthcare Tomorrow Conference, Dallas, TX.

American Psychological Association. (1992). Ethical principles of psychologists and code of conduct. *American Psychologist, 47,* 1597–1611.

American Psychological Association. (1996a). *Profile of all APA members, 1995*. (Research office report available from the American Psychological Association, 750 First Street, N.E., Washington, DC 20002)

American Psychological Association. (1996b). *1995 salaries in psychology*. (Research office report available from the American Psychological Association, 750 First Street, N.E., Washington, DC 20002)

Appelbaum, P. S. (1993). Legal liability and managed care. *American Psychologist, 48,* 251–257.

Austad, C. S., & Berman, W. H. (1991). Managed health care and the evolution of psychotherapy. In C. S. Austad & W. H. Berman (Eds.), *Psychotherapy in managed health care: The optimal use of time and resources* (pp. 3–18). Washington, DC: American Psychological Association.

Barnett, J. E. (1992). Ethical practice in a managed care environment. *The Independent Practitioner, 13*(4), 160–162.

Barton, W. E., & Barton, G. M. (1984). Definitions and concepts: Morals, ethics, values, attitudes and etiquette. In W. E. Barton & G. M. Barton (Eds.), *Ethics and law in mental health administration* (pp. 3–19). New York: International Universities Press.

Beauchamp, T., & Childress, W. (1988). *Principles of biomedical ethics* (3rd ed.). Baltimore, MD: Johns Hopkins University Press.

Bennett, B. E., Bryant, B. K., VandenBos, G. R., & Greenwood, A. (1990). *Professional liability and risk management*. Washington, DC: American Psychological Association.

Bersoff, D. N. (1995). *Ethical conflicts in psychology*. Washington, DC: American Psychological Association.

Broskowski, A. (1991). Current mental health care environments: Why managed care is necessary. *Professional Psychology: Research and Practice, 22*, 6–14.

Callahan, D. (1996, March). *Ethics, managed care and health care*. Paper presented at the Statewide Ethics Conference, Methodist Hospital, Indianapolis, IN.

Callahan, S. (1995). The role of emotion in ethical decision-making. In J. H. Howell & W. F. Sale (Eds.), *Life choices: A Hastings Center introduction to bioethics* (pp. 24–39). Washington, DC: Georgetown University Press.

Canter, M. B., Bennett, B. E., Jones, S. E., & Nagy, T. F. (1994). *Ethics for psychologists: A commentary on the APA ethics code*. Washington, DC: American Psychological Association.

Cantor, D. W. (1995). Maintaining our professional integrity in the era of managed care. *Psychotherapy Bulletin, 30*, 27–28.

Council on Ethical and Judicial Affairs of the American Medical Association. (1995). Ethical issues in managed care. *Journal of the American Medical Association, 273*, 330–335.

Crawshaw, R., Rogers, D. E., Pellegrino, E. D., Bulger, R. J., Lundberg, G. D., Bustow, L. R., Cassel, C. K., & Barondess, J. A. (1995). Patient–physician covenant. *Journal of the American Medical Association, 273*, 1553.

Cummings N. A. (1986). The dismantling of our health system: Strategies for the survival of psychological practice. *American Psychologist, 41*, 426–431.

Cummings, N. A. (1988). Emergence of the mental health complex: Adaptive and maladaptive responses. *Professional Psychology: Research and Practice, 19*, 308–315.

Cummings, N. A. (1995). Impact of managed care on employment and training: A primer for survival. *Professional Psychology: Research and Practice, 26*(1), 10–15.

Dubin, M. D. (1995). Grasping capitation. In G. Zieman (Ed.), *The complete capitation handbook* (pp. 29–35). Tiburon, CA: CentraLink/Jossey-Bass.

Elpers, J. R., & Abbott, B. K. (1992). Public policy, ethical issues, and mental health administration. *Administration and Policy in Mental Health, 19*, 437–447.

Fins, J. J. (1992). The hidden costs of market-based health care reform. *Hastings Center Report, 22*, 6.

Fox, R. E. (1995). The rape of psychotherapy. *Professional Psychology: Research and Practice, 26*, 147–155.

Freeman, M. A. (1995). Behavioral at-risk contracting in a changing healthcare environment. In G. Zieman (Ed.), *The complete capitation handbook*. Tiburon, CA: CentraLink/Jossey-Bass.

Geraty, R. D., Hendren, R. L., & Flaa, C. J. (1992). Ethical perspectives on managed care as it relates to child and adolescent psychiatry. *Journal of the American Academy of Child and Adolescent Psychiatry, 31*, 398–402.

Green, R. M. (1990). Medical joint-venturing: An ethical perspective. *Hastings Report, 20*, 22–26.

Haas, L. J., & Cummings, N. A. (1991). Managed outpatient mental health plans: Clinical, ethical, and practical guidelines for participation. *Professional Psychology: Research and Practice, 22*, 45–51.

Haas, L. J., & Malouf, J. L. (1989). *Keeping up the good work: A practitioner's guide to mental health ethics*. Sarasota, FL: Professional Resource Exchange.

Higuchi, S. A. (1994). Recent managed-care legislative and legal issues. In R. L. Lowman & R. J. Resnick (Eds.), *The mental health professional's guide to managed care* (pp. 83–119). Washington, DC: American Psychological Association.

In California, the state saves $7 for every $1 spent on substance abuse. (1994, October). *Managed Care Strategies,* p. 10.

Karon, B. P. (1995). Provision of psychotherapy under managed health care: A growing crisis and national nightmare. *Professional Psychology: Research and Practice, 26,* 5–9.

Kassirer, J. P. (1995). Managed care and the morality of the marketplace. *New England Journal of Medicine, 333,* 50–52.

Kovacs, A. (1996, March). *Creation and management of fee for service practice in the nineties.* Paper presented at the American Psychological Association Midwinter Convention, Scottsdale, AZ.

Langsley, D. G., & Kaplan, D. M. (1968). *The treatment of families in crisis.* New York: Grune & Stratton.

Lazarus, J. A. (1995, September). *Ethical challenges that result from benefit design and clinical parameters of managed care.* Paper presented at the Behavioral Healthcare Tomorrow Conference, Dallas, TX.

Lewin, T. (1996, May 22). Questions of privacy roil arena of psychotherapy. *The New York Times,* pp. A1, A8.

Lowman, R. L. (1994). Managed mental health care: Critical issues and next directions. In R. L. Lowman & R. J. Resnick (Eds.), *The mental health professional's guide to managed care.* Washington, DC: American Psychological Association.

Morreim, E. H. (1988). Cost containment: Challenging fidelity and justice. *Hastings Center Report, 18,* 20–25.

Morreim, E. H. (1991). Gaming the system. Dodging the rules, ruling the dodgers. *Archives of Internal Medicine, 151,* 443–447.

Murphy, M. J., & Phelps, R. (1997, March). *Managed care's impact on independent practice and professional ethics.* Paper presented at the American Psychological Association Midwinter Convention, St. Petersburg, FL.

Newman, R., & Bricklin, P. M. (1991). Parameters of managed mental health care: Legal, ethical, and professional guidelines. *Professional Psychology: Research and Practice, 22,* 26–35.

O'Rourke, K., Snider, B. W., Thomas, J. M., & Berland, D. I. (1992). Knowing and practicing ethics. *Journal of the American Academy of Child and Adolescent Psychiatry, 31,* 393–397.

Petrila, J. P. (1995, September). *Ethical challenges that result from legal and regulatory parameters of managed care.* Paper presented at the Behavioral Healthcare Tomorrow Conference, Dallas, TX.

Pope, K. S., & Vetter, V. A. (1992). Ethical dilemmas encountered by members of the American Psychological Association: A national survey. *American Psychologist, 47,* 397–411.

Rinella, V. (1986). Ethical issues and psychiatric cost-containment strategies. *International Journal of Law and Psychiatry, 9,* 125–136.

Rushing, B. (1996, March). *Leaders in state and local government panel.* Paper presented at the American Psychological Association State Leadership Conference, Washington, DC.

Savitz, S. A. (1995, September). Carrier-owned systems. In S. A. Savitz (Chair), *Behavioral healthcare industry overview.* Symposium conducted at the Behavioral Healthcare Tomorrow Conference, Dallas, TX.

Shore, K. (1995). Managed care: The subjugation of a profession. *Psychotherapy in Private Practice, 14*(2), 67–75.

Shore, K. (1996). *Managed cooperation: A medical/mental health care plan.* Commack, NY: National Coalition of Mental Health Professionals and Consumers.

Wyatt, R. C. (1995). Grappling with the ethical issues. In G. Zieman (Ed.), *The complete capitation handbook* (pp. 175–188). Tiburon, CA: CentraLink/Jossey-Bass.

Appendix A _____

Survey: Ethics, Values, and Attitudes Regarding Managed Care and Mental Health Services

1. Our society cannot afford services for all mental health needs, so some restrictions are inevitable. (strongly agree [SA], agree [A], neutral [N], disagree [D], strongly disagree [SD])
2. I would rather err on the side of too much treatment rather than too little.
3. Managed care organizations (MCOs) are parasites who profit from squeezing therapists and mental health clients for business interests.
4. I have modified/would modify a client's diagnosis or CPT (current procedural terminology) code to help the client get reimbursed. (never [N], sometimes [S], often [O])
5. I have modified/would modify a client's diagnosis or CPT code to protect client confidentiality, future employment, or future medical insurance.
6. I have modified/would modify a client's diagnosis or CPT code to ensure my reimbursement.
7. The basic ethical constraint of focusing on the client's best interests rather than the therapist's needs is compromised when therapists get a profit for reducing services (e.g., HMOs, MCOs, capitated contracts, and so forth). (SA, A, N, D, SD)
8. Therapists tend to provide longer term therapy because it's easier, more convenient, and more comfortable.
9. I have terminated clients before they wanted because they had received maximum benefits from treatment. (N, S, O)
10. Some copayment makes clients work harder and more efficiently in therapy. (SA, A, N, D, SD)
11. If you can solve a problem briefly, it is unethical to extend the treatment.
12. How long I see patients is affected by when their benefits run out.
13. I believe that the vast majority of MCOs keep clinical information confidential.
14. Client satisfaction is not an adequate measure of the value of therapy.
15. Utilization review has reduced unnecessary hospitalization and reorientation priorities to outpatient care.

16. Utilization review has forced me to organize my treatment plans more consistently.

17. Business customs of proprietary organizations (i.e., competitiveness, secretiveness, and marketing hype) are antithetical to the ethical standards of clinical mental health services (open sharing of information for the advance of science and health-care practice).

18. It is unethical to bill patients and insurance companies for an hour if you finish your work in a half-hour and chitchat for twenty minutes to fill up the time.

19. You have a case of an adolescent conduct disorder which you find is not covered by the insurance plan, because they believe that the diagnosis is untreatable. The father died, the mother is overwhelmed and poor. You know that you can help the family. You would: (check all that apply)

_____ a. Change diagnosis so treatment will be covered

_____ b. See pro bono

_____ c. Refer to public health services and/or support groups

_____ d. Other: specify if you can

20. I have given up advocating for additional benefits for a client who would have benefited from more treatment: (check all that apply)

_____ a. Too hard, gave up

_____ b. Didn't know how

_____ c. Didn't want the MCO to stop sending me referrals

_____ d. Client really didn't need more

_____ e. Other: specify if you can

Appendix B

Data Summary: Survey on Ethics, Values, and Attitudes Regarding Managed Care

Item no./abbreviated question	Respondents (%)				
	Strongly agree	Agree	Neu-tral	Dis-agree	Strongly disagree
1. Restrictions inevitable?	4.3	47.8	7.6	30.4	9.8
2. Rather err too much?	9.8	57.6	18.5	10.9	3.3
3. MCOs parasites?	18.5	37.0	27.2	14.1	3.3
	Never		Some-times		Often
4. Change diagnosis—client money?	9.8	30.4	44.6	14.1	1.1
5. Change diagnosis—protect client?	12.0	26.1	40.2	18.5	3.3
6. Change diagnosis—own money?	27.2	38.0	26.1	8.7	0
9. Max benefit—kick out?	17.4	25.0	41.3	15.2	1.1
	Strongly agree	Agree	Neu-tral	Dis-agree	Strongly disagree
7. Therapist profit equals conflict?	16.5	61.5	8.8	11.0	2.2
8. Long term comfortable.	3.3	22.8	10.9	50.0	13.0
10. Copay good.	23.6	67.4	3.4	4.5	1.1
11. Unethical to string it out.	37.5	47.7	5.7	4.5	4.5
12. Length depends on benefits.	3.4	30.7	6.8	40.9	18.2
13. MCOs confidential.	0	23.9	39.8	25.0	11.4
14. Satisfaction not adequate measure.	5.6	29.2	21.3	38.2	5.6
15. UR reduce hospital?	7.9	40.4	31.5	15.7	4.5
16. UR improve treatment plans?	1.1	51.1	17.0	26.1	4.5
17. Business ethics not psychological ethics.	14.6	40.4	25.8	16.9	2.2
18. Unethical to chitchat?	18.2	52.3	13.6	10.2	5.7

	Yes	No
19A. Adolescent—change diagnosis?	56.8	43.2
19B. Adolescent—pro bono?	55.7	44.3
19C. Adolescent—referrals?	70.5	29.5
20A. Give up advocating—too hard.	39.0	61.0
20B. Give up advocating—not know how.	14.6	85.4
20C. Give up advocating—referrals.	14.6	85.4
20D. Give up advocating—not needed.	18.3	81.7

Note. MCOs = managed care organizations; UR = utilization review.

2

Evolution of Practice and Values of Professional Psychology

Michael J. Murphy

The progressive political agenda that characterized government from the time of the Great Depression until the 1970s has shaped the American health-care system. The resulting system of health care was financed by government funding of programs and subsidized entitlements and by widespread coverage of health care by government, business, and industry through indemnity insurance. This health-care policy profoundly affected the emergence and shaped the practice of psychology as a mental health profession. Psychology's goals and values were consistent with the progressive agenda of the federal government, which influenced practice by funding programs and initiatives that nurtured the developing profession and in the process affected the definition of practice. As government's progressive policies were increasingly displaced by a more conservative orientation, the aims of psychology were less valued, and funding for programs decreased. The change in the agenda also affected health-care policy, and greater emphasis was placed on achieving cost reductions and controls through market pressures. As a consequence, psychology saw a decline in government support and was increasingly affected and shaped by the market forces. Managed care has brought about intensification of market pressures and changes in the psychologist–patient relationship and has altered the duties and obligations of the psychologist within that relationship.

In this chapter I examine the influence of American health-care policy and government funding and the effects of indemnity insurance on the professional practice of psychology, the values that guide that practice, and the duties and obligations in the psychologist–patient relationship. This discussion provides the foundation for considering how cost-containment strategies exercise influence on the nature and goals of treatment and change the relationship between patient and psychologist. The manner in which these changes have altered professional practice and continue to affect the values and ethics of psychologists is discussed, with particular emphasis on treatment decisions, confidentiality, conflict of interest, and professional duties. I also discuss changes in the role of informed consent and the obligations for psychologists to assist the empowerment of patients to exercise greater influence in health-care decisions. Finally, general strategies for psychologists to deal with the challenges to their practice, values, and ethical obligations are considered.

American Health Care

Government Policy

Examination of the evolution of American health-care policy and the system of payment through indemnity insurance provides a foundation for understanding the changes in the health-care system psychologists face at the present time. Throughout the history of the United States there has been a cyclic shift in political emphasis from a conservative view, in which government was seen as playing a relatively minor role in social welfare and in the regulation of private enterprise, to a progressive view, in which the role of the federal government was seen as supporting and nurturing the institutions that contribute to the general welfare (Schlesinger, 1986). In the 1930s and 1940s a progressive view of the role of the federal government emerged as a consequence of the Great Depression and World War II (Schlesinger, 1986). After the war, this vision of government was fueled by economic expansion, and progressive policies generally characterized the operation of the federal government until the economic reversals of the 1970s. Since that time there has been a growing ascendance of conservative concepts that now dominate current political dialogue. These economic and political forces have profoundly affected both health-care policy and professional psychology.

After World War II, health-care financing was shaped by the belief that the cost of improved health care would be funded by economic growth rather than by either the redistribution of government, business, and individual income or the rationing of health-care services (Fox, 1988). Policymakers further believed that health care was special and that the prevention and treatment of illness took precedence over many other social goals (Morreim, 1995). They reasoned that citizens had to have good health to participate in society and experience its benefits. This reasoning led to a strong commitment to governmental funding of biomedical research, training health-care professions, and the construction of hospitals and other facilities. It also led to the development of entitlement programs for older adults, disabled persons, and economically disadvantaged individuals.

Health-Care Coverage

The development and expansion of insurance for health-care coverage in business and industry after World War II paralleled government's health-care policies. Employers extended health insurance to employees, primarily through indemnity insurance, at a time when the cost of care was low. Health-care coverage was seen as mutually beneficial for employer and employee and thus became an expected part of employee and union con-tracts. The indemnity insurance plans had few mechanisms for controlling costs and left decisions regarding selection of diagnostic and treatment procedures to the providers. To further understand the effects of this sys-tem of coverage and the changes produced by managed care, it is necessary to examine the interests of the three principal participants in the health-care system: patient, health-care provider, and third-party payer.

The primary concern of the third-party payer is the cost of care. Im-mediately after World War II, the health-care system did not have exten-sive technological resources, and it was labor intensive and relatively low in cost. Therefore, cost containment was not a priority. Third-party payers exercised some control over cost through the use of deductibles and patient copayments, but the principal means of cost containment was control of access (Morreim, 1995). Thus, to gain access to reimbursement for services patients had to be covered, the provider had to be recognized, and the disorder had to be deemed medically necessary or covered by other pro-visions in the policy. Physicians have historically resisted any outside con-trol and the imposition of constraints or conditions on the funding of ser-vices (Havighurst, 1986). Thus, once access was granted, the payer exercised little regulation of the care provided.

Under indemnity insurance, the concerns of the provider are to give the best care possible without regard to cost factors and to maintain con-trol over decisions regarding that care (Morreim, 1995; Pellegrino & Tho-masma, 1988). Furthermore, indemnity insurance gives financial incen-tives to both individual and institutional providers for giving all care that might potentially benefit the patient. Under indemnity insurance the con-cern of the patient is naturally to gain access to the best available care for his or her difficulty. Thus, provider and patient concerns are consistent under indemnity insurance.

Consequences of the American Health-Care System

As a consequence of the federal government's policies and employers' health insurance packages, most Americans have come to expect access to all interventions offering the potential for benefit and payment by someone else for most of their care (Fox, 1988; Morreim, 1995).

In addition to shaping expectations, these policies led to a health-care system focusing on hospital services for acute care of disease and injury rather than one focusing on services that address prevention, functional impairment, quality of life, and rehabilitation (Kiesler, 1992). Both gov-ernment funding for research and construction of facilities and indemnity insurance coverage provided greater access to inpatient care and diagnos-tic and treatment procedures that were expensive and technologically so-phisticated. Furthermore, providers were encouraged to offer the maxi-mum amount of care that might be beneficial to the patient. The result was a tremendous increase in health-care costs that, in concert with other political and economic factors, led to the emergence of cost-containment strategies (Broskowski, 1994; Ginzberg, 1990).

Mental health services were tied to the health-care policy and financing system, but the nature of the problems, services, and delivery system kept it from the mainstream of health care. For the most part, these services remained labor intensive and did not produce the cost escalations associated with technology-based interventions. However, the cost of mental health care increased particularly in the areas of inpatient care of children and adolescents and with treatment of substance abuse (Mirin & Sedever, 1994).

Psychology as a Mental Health Profession

The same progressive ideology that shaped the American system of health care has affected the development of professional psychology. The goals, methods, and values of professional psychology were consistent with the federal government's progressive political orientation in the 1950s and 1960s. During this period government support assisted in the development of the professional practice. Psychologists increasingly moved into the health-care market and independent practice as they gained access to third-party reimbursement. Practice of psychology benefited from these trends, but it also had to accommodate to the system. Thus, psychologists became increasingly dependent on third-party payment systems. As a consequence, these practitioners became increasingly vulnerable to the effects of changes in the system. Understanding of the ethical issues psychologists confront as a result of these changes is aided by examining influences that shaped practice in both the past and the present.

Government Support of Professional Practice of Psychology

Historians of the profession document how psychology developed as a mental health profession with the support of government funding (e.g., Routh, 1994). The federal government advanced its progressive agenda by supporting the development of psychology through such initiatives as the Veterans Administration, training grants for doctoral programs, the community mental health centers program, and, more recently, inclusion in Medicare. State government support came from such sources as funding for education, employment in institutions for the mentally ill and in social programs, and inclusion in Medicaid. Governmental support allowed professional psychology to develop a core of knowledge, a foundation of techniques for assessment and intervention, models and institutions for professional training, a corps of providers, and a foundation of statutory recognition and regulation.

It was this initial funding that helped the profession develop during its early stages. Although reduction in psychology's federal funding began in the 1970s, because psychology was sufficiently well established as a mental health profession, it moved into the marketplace under the relative protection offered by systems of private and government-funded health-care coverage. This was further advanced by expansion of mental health coverage by insurance plans, mandated benefits, and legislation requiring the recognition of psychologists by insurance plans. The professional practice of psychology was able to sustain progress under third-party payment for professional services, and a substantial system of institutional and independent practice has grown from these roots.

The developments discussed earlier stress the overwhelming benefits arising from the identification of psychology as a mental health profession. To a great extent the benefits arose because of the special place health care holds in American society. Professional psychology's inclusion provided access to funding sources and levels of support that otherwise would not have been available (Fox, 1988; Kiesler, 1992). Government funding for training, research, facilities, programs, and services for health care has been more generously provided than for other social and educational programs, and fewer conditions and controls are imposed on this funding (Fox, 1988; Kiesler, 1992).

However, psychology's identification as a mental health profession, and its entry into the health-care market, have pervasively shaped the nature of professional practice in a manner that both foreshadowed and enabled managed care to exercise control over it. Furthermore, the practice of psychology has been shaped by and accommodated to a model unsuited for psychological care (Kiesler, 1992).

Impact of Health-Care Policy on Professional Psychology

Although psychology has benefited from inclusion as a mental health care profession, including gaining access to third-party payment and government support, this inclusion has limited practice and required troublesome accommodations. Various incentives have led psychologists to limit their practices to reimbursable mental health services. Health-care services beyond mental health and services outside of health care have languished with little effort directed at developing or marketing them. Psychologists were trained and organized their practices to work under the mental health care reimbursement system. As a consequence, psychologists have not been prepared or socialized to operate in the open market, and only recently have they moved into the larger health-care arena. As a result of this reliance on the mental health care system, professional psychologists have become vulnerable to changes in government support and health-care coverage.

Within health care, psychologists have made accommodations to a system that does not fit the services they provide. Thus, the values, goals, and methods of psychology are influenced by the medical model, despite a general recognition that this model is not appropriate for the types of problems encountered in mental health or for the psychological methods of intervention (Kiesler, 1992). These familiar arguments stress that the model underlying health care is oriented toward treatment of disease, rather than the promotion of health, and that it adopts a definition of pathology generally inappropriate for mental health. It is inappropriate because, in most instances, mental health problems are not adequately conceptualized as illnesses. Most disorders are reflective of functional impairment, problems in living, or subjective distress rather than disease entities with specific pathogenic antecedents and consequences that are the focus of treatment.

Mental health treatment is characterized by ambiguity about what constitutes pathology, diversity of treatment goals and orientations, and lack of specificity of the relationships between interventions and outcomes. In the past psychologists did not have to address and resolve issues associated with the multiplicity of perspectives. Under indemnity insurance payment systems psychologists were able to adopt the symptom-focused diagnostic systems but offer treatments consistent with the goals and objectives arising from their own orientation to treatment. In the process of making such accommodations, psychologists did not directly address the manner in which their interventions were incompatible with the medical model. Thus, they implicitly endorsed symptom-focused intervention as the goal of mental health interventions, and the goals and effects central to treatment approaches requiring longer term care were not recognized, studied, or valued. As discussed later in this chapter, managed care was able to foreclose the accommodations and advance cost containment by valuing only treatments that quickly treated symptoms.

As a mental health profession, psychology benefited from government policies and systems of health-care reimbursement and accommodated professional practice to them. Under managed care, the introduction of cost-sensitive policies and incentives made more explicit the manner in which practice is shaped. Managed care has also limited accommodations that can be made. In the remainder of the chapter I address the nature and impact of these changes and the professional and ethical issues that have resulted.

Impact of Managed Care on Professional Psychology

The forces that have led to the changes in health-care financing and delivery, collectively called *managed care*, have been widely discussed (e.g., Broskowski, 1994; Ginzberg, 1990; Lowman & Resnick, 1994; Reinhardt, 1989). The combined impact of rising health-care costs for both government and business is one explanation for why health care moved away from a system driven by providing care to a system increasingly driven by containing costs (Nickelson, 1995). While managed care is usually discussed as a single system, it is actually composed of a very diverse set of market interventions aimed at cost reduction. Specific interventions include combinations of strategies such as discounted rates of payment; increased use of deductibles and copayments; efforts to educate providers in the cost of their treatment decisions; prior approval; case management; use of gatekeepers; financial incentives, such as capitated arrangements; selective recruitment, retention, and referral to providers; development of competition among providers and disciplines; and direct controls, such as specifying a medication formulary and treatment protocols. These efforts are accompanied by structural changes in which there is movement toward organized and integrated systems of care, and providers share greater risk for the financial implications of the care they provide (Lowman & Resnick, 1994).

The diverse market interventions of managed care have had profound effects on psychologists, patients, and the psychologist–patient relationship. The strategies used to control costs result in patients and providers losing control (Munson, 1995). Providers lose control of crucial aspects of practice: fees, access to patients, confidential information, determination of goals of care, and selection of treatment methods. Patients lose control of the selection of who will provide their care and the range of care they may seek.

Issues of values and ethics arise as a consequence of the impact of managed care strategies on the relationship between the psychologist and patient. I now discuss how the effects of managed care are projected onto the patient–psychologist relationship, how this changes the nature of the relationship, and specific ways in which the values and roles of psychologists are affected.

Responsibilities of Psychologists in the Treatment Relationship

As stated earlier, under the indemnity system the psychologist–patient relationship was significantly shaped by the confluence of patients' interests in obtaining all care that would be of benefit and of providers' interests in rendering care. The system defined special responsibilities and associated obligations and duties owed by the professional to the patient. The professional has particular responsibilities and duties because of the special knowledge, skill, and power he or she holds in the relationship and because of the patient's vulnerability. The patient's vulnerability arises because of the difficult and threatening circumstances he or she faces and the power differential between the patient and the provider on whose skill, knowledge, and goodwill the patient must depend. This relationship places obligations and duties on the professional for a full commitment to the care of the patient and places the patient's interests above all other concerns, including the professional's self-interests. These responsibilities are defined and enforced by professional ethics and codes of conduct, state licensure and other provisions of law, and judicial proceedings for malpractice.

Under indemnity insurance, the convergence of provider and patient interests made it relatively easy for psychologists to place patients' interests first. However, under managed care the payer exercises influences that limit the ability of the psychologist to set aside all interests other than full commitment to the patients' needs. Thus, under managed care psychologists must take into consideration the limits of the coverage purchased by patient, the definitions of the goals and nature of treatment underlying that coverage, and the process of utilization review and case management associated with the system of care. The difficulties psychologists encounter in providing care are complicated because professionals and payers adhere to different codes of ethics and conduct. Thus, professionals have unique obligations and duties that go far beyond those of the contractual relationship that characterizes the typical business relationship that guides managed care companies (Brody, 1989). The differences in codes of conduct for psychologists and managed care companies have significant effects for the psychologist–patient relationship.

Managed Care and the Psychologist–Patient Relationship

Under indemnity insurance, psychologist and patient, within the context of the therapeutic relationship, determined the care that would best address a patient's needs. Under managed care, treatment is affected by the decisions patients make about the coverage they purchase well before they enter the therapeutic relationship. Cost controls that operate by limiting services and controlling service delivery are defined by the contract between the managed care company and the patient. Patients purchase health-care benefits with little anticipation that they will use them and are not confronted with the immediate implications for themselves and their families when making these health-care decisions (Morreim, 1995). It is only when they access services that the provider must explain the limits and conditions the patient faces under the plan they have purchased. As a consequence, the decisions made in business settings must be implemented in the clinical setting in the context of the relationship between patient and psychologist. Thus, the psychologist must attend to issues arising from the contractual relationship between patient and payer that is also reflected in the contract between the psychologist and the payer rather than an exclusive focus on quality care. The contractual relationships that patients and psychologists have with managed care companies reflect a fundamental change in the relationship between the patient and psychologist, and it is at the core of the ethical and values issues psychologists face.

The most widely used managed care strategies are utilization review and case management, and both are implemented in the clinical setting and directly affect the psychologist–patient relationship. The relationship is affected because the review and management strategies determine care, affect confidentiality, raise issues of conflict of interest between patient and psychologist, and affect the nature of psychologists' obligations and duties in the relationship. Each of these issues is addressed in turn.

Managed Care and the Nature of Psychological Treatment

While capitation and provider profiling are emerging cost-control strategies, managed care currently reduces costs primarily through discounted rates of reimbursement and systems of utilization review and case management. Utilization review and case management control costs through authorizing the setting in which the care is offered and the length of care regardless of setting (Austad & Hoyt, 1992). Managed care reviews tend to request specification of goals and objectives and evaluate interventions as to their appropriateness in achieving those goals. They then monitor the course of treatment according to how effective the therapist is in achieving the goals. In this system there remains considerable freedom for the psychologist in outpatient settings to assess the complex confluence of individual differences and the environmental stressors as they affect the direction, goals, and duration of treatment. However, treatments using more specifically defined procedures, and showing clear changes on targeted symptoms, are preferred, and most approaches to treatment have responded by developing shorter term and more focused therapies.

Many psychologists find that the most onerous aspect of this system is the time and inconvenience of the review procedures. Indeed, the transition to managed care interventions may not impose a marked change in the therapeutic interventions for many therapists. Research indicates that most psychologists adopt an eclectic or integrative stance that recognizes the diversity of goals that may be legitimately pursued, and they optimize their interventions on the basis of such factors as the patient's needs, wishes, capacity to change, and financial resources (Garfield, 1994). Still other psychologists adopt a position in which only clearly defined and empirically supported treatments are acceptable (Task Force on Promotion and Dissemination of Psychological Procedures, 1995). Behaviorally oriented and eclectic therapists clearly have an easier transition to managed care than those who are committed to longer term interventions. Issues of values, meaning, and quality of life central to many humanistic and psychodynamic approaches to psychological intervention have no place in managed care systems (Koren, 1995).

Psychologists who adopt longer term approaches to care see eclectic or targeted treatment approaches as inadequate and potentially detrimental to the patient. Briefer treatment is seen as insufficient because it does not allow patient and therapist to achieve goals that advocates of the longer term approaches see as central to treatment. The goals of longer term therapies generally include identifying and modifying those patterns that underlie and lead to the immediate problem. For example, psychoanalytic therapists believe that treatment must allow an analysis and working through of the neurotic elements of the patient's personality, and, in the absence of this, the disorder remains. These therapists find themselves and the profession facing ethical issues not seen by other psychologists.

Psychologists who are committed to long-term-care approaches will continually face pressures from utilization review and experience ethical dilemmas because they will be unable to secure approval for treatments they consider essential for their patients (C. C. Higuchi & Newman, 1994; Simon, 1994). While encountering ethical dilemmas, these psychologists will have difficulty advancing the notion that failure to provide longer term treatment falls below acceptable standards of care because of the widespread endorsement of shorter term interventions. They can execute their ethical obligations by obtaining informed consent. As a consequence, the process of informed consent must expand from a review of the treatment options and expected outcomes to include a review of the implications for treatment of the health-care coverage purchased by the patient and the review and authorization systems (Newman & Bricklin, 1991; Sabin, 1992).

One means by which proponents of longer term care may influence the current system is by making a convincing case that the emphasis managed care companies give to shorter term therapies reduces cost but sacrifices value. There is support for this argument. First, research findings suggest dose-related effects in which those who receive more treatment show greater gains than those who receive shorter treatment; those whose benefits were limited did worse than patients who did not have such limits (Herron, Eisenstadt, Javier, Primavera, & Schultz, 1994; Mone, 1994; Seligman, 1995). Second, there may be significant additional benefits associated with longer term treatments that are not assessed by research that focuses on symptom removal. It is important that research assess the potential benefits that purchasers may gain and the added value that would accrue from longer term care. However, it is not likely that demonstration of these benefits will influence managed care systems at the present time because managed care companies experience a rapid turnover of people covered under their plans and this rewards short-term cost savings over long-term savings. Such arguments will only work in a system that has greater stability than what currently exists.

At the present time, the role of longer term interventions may be outside managed care systems. Discounted rates in some payment systems have reduced fees to a point that patients can obtain access to care of their choice through self-pay with levels of confidentiality and privacy not afforded under managed care. This gives the opportunity for some psychologists to develop market niches that allow them autonomy to structure treatment and effectively compete on the basis of quality of care. It provides an opportunity for treatment approaches to clearly delineate valued outcomes that go beyond amelioration of symptoms. There is also indication that therapists are able to make accommodations to managed care systems by combining authorized benefits with systems of self-pay negotiated with the patient.

Psychologists who adopt eclectic approaches and employ a range of treatments also encounter problematic situations. The potential problems involved in making choices about the patient's mental health needs are illustrated in situations in which the psychologist sees patients with similar conditions who have different health-care coverage. Because plans offer a range of benefits, clinicians may see patients with different levels of coverage. Consider the circumstance in which a patient is covered by a traditional indemnity insurance program, and after the initial assessment session the psychologist believes that an objective personality test would yield valuable information for case conceptualization and treatment planning. The same psychologist may also have a patient who presents in a manner similar to the first but is covered by a managed care company that requires a justification for the testing and would likely deny the claim. Should the psychologist not administer the test to the managed care patient, would he or she be offering substandard care, or excessive services to the first? A system that values giving the highest level of care may give one answer, and a system that values economy and efficiency may give another. This simple illustration reveals how various systems of health-care payment can affect the care that patients receive, as well as the manner in which psychologists make decisions on behalf of their patients.

Within psychology there is a range of care that would be considered beneficial but not essential for treatment. The therapist has considerable latitude in determining what is beneficial and makes decisions based on the level of care that the patient has purchased. Although the therapist and patient can make decisions about maximizing benefits, there must be some minimum standard of care below which the treatment cannot fall, and the therapist has an obligation to ensure that the patient receives that level of care (Newman & Bricklin, 1991). The therapist also has an obligation to recognize that the patient has purchased and paid for a range of benefits and, while it is essential to provide informed consent, the provider has been contracted by the managed care company to provide that level of care (Hass & Cummings, 1991). Again it is essential that the care not fall below a minimum standard. This is a very different therapeutic duty than practicing under indemnity insurance in which the provider was only concerned with providing the best care to meet the patient's needs.

The therapist still has an obligation to inform the patient about the range of potential interventions and their benefits and limits as in the past. Managed care introduces new elements in which the psychologist must also inform the patient about the limits of coverage, follow procedures for utilization review, and advocate for the patient to ensure that the care meets the patient's needs and does not fall below an acceptable level (Newman & Bricklin, 1991). This last responsibility arises because psychologists encounter situations in which utilization review or session limits cause payment to be denied for care that the therapist believes is necessary for the patient's well-being. For example, patients who are potentially self-destructive or dangerous may be denied coverage for inpatient care. Or a patient who needs additional sessions to consolidate or stabilize gains may be denied additional sessions. In these circumstances psychologists remain responsible for the treatment of their patients but may find themselves unable to get approval for the services that they assess are needed (S. A. Higuchi, 1994; Newman & Bricklin, 1991).

Within managed behavioral health care there has not been any widespread effort to impose structured treatment guidelines that delineate specific procedures for outpatient care. However, such protocols are seen in medical settings. Such treatment guidelines would be highly problematic for professional psychologists. They would erode the capacity of the psychologist and patient to develop interventions that address the individual's needs and circumstances. They would bring psychologists into increasing conflict with utilization reviews that impose standard treatments that may be inappropriate for the situation and that impose a technical standard instead of professional judgment. Such a system would be difficult to develop, administer, and enforce. Nonetheless, professional psychology must address efforts to impose standardized protocols or manualized treatments and must seek to develop research-based guidelines that preserve the capacity of the psychologist to exercise professional judgment in developing the most appropriate treatment plans.

Impact of Managed Care on Patient Confidentiality

Under indemnity insurance it was necessary to provide the patient's diagnosis, but little information beyond this was required and patient confidentiality was generally not threatened. A significant by-product of managed care's efforts to contain costs is the loss of confidentiality. To provide meaningful utilization review decisions and to ensure accountability, the psychologist must disclose information to others, who in the process of collecting and storing that information may place the patient at risk for adverse decisions in a number of areas. Furthermore, the patient's knowledge of the possibility of disclosure affects the relationship by raising issues of trust that may constrain the free exchange of information that is essential to the treatment enterprise (Simon, 1994). Release of information with informed consent, guidelines requiring that payers safeguard information, and providers restricting disclosure to that which is necessary for case review do not overcome the erosion of trust that is the cornerstone of the effective relationship in treatment (C. C. Higuchi & Newman, 1994). Although psychologists have the same obligations and standards regarding confidentiality under managed care as in the past, concern is heightened because more information is disclosed and electronic means of storing, retrieving, and integrating information present greater threats of misuse. Furthermore, the professionalism of those conducting reviews is often unknown or suspect.

Psychologists find themselves in a difficult position. On the one hand they are motivated to edit or reduce the information released to the minimum necessary for case management. On the other hand, however, they may be motivated to present information in a way that emphasizes the seriousness of the condition in order to gain authorization for treatment. All such releases of information must be done within the context of informed consent, but they may have the effect of influencing what the patient feels free to report. Problems with confidentiality are to some extent reduced in systems that use provider profiling or capitation because there is a reduction in information released. However, these systems introduce new and difficult elements into the relationship.

Impact of Capitated Systems on the
Psychologist–Patient Relationship

Managed care strategies have included systems that place the provider at financial risk for treatment choices. Systems of capitated payment and case rates give providers a fixed reimbursement, and the psychologist then provides services that they assess as best addressing the patient's needs. The psychologist who practices with incentives to limit care confronts a set of circumstances radically different from those in the past. As previously discussed, the expectation that the psychologist should provide all services that will benefit the patient is replaced by a standard in which the psychologist gives care that effectively and efficiently meets the patient's needs. However, there is a level of care below which therapists cannot fall without failing to fulfill their obligations to their patients. Determination of this level of care is not straightforward because there is a very wide range of opinions about what constitutes a reasonable level of care for mental health problems. Practitioners providing services under incentives to limit care must fully inform and educate their patients about reimbursement arrangements. Psychologists who have financial incentives must also ensure that their performance is monitored with regard to treatment effects, outcomes, and patient satisfaction. Such evaluation must be done in a manner that is systematic and protects against bias (Morreim, 1995).

Impact on Professional Duties

All reimbursement systems may lead to difficulties around issues of recording of diagnosis and the coding of treatment procedures. In efforts to protect confidentiality, psychologists may take advantage of the overlap of symptoms between disorders and provide diagnostic codes that, while ensuring access to care, do not fully reflect the patient's condition. Thus, adjustment disorders will be diagnosed, rather than major depression. Anxiety or depression may be given as the primary diagnosis when borderline personality disorder may be more accurate. These are often efforts to protect the patient from potential adverse employment decisions and other harmful outcomes such as denial of life, disability, or health insurance coverage. While these diagnostic-coding practices may have been seen as a benign use of the least serious diagnosis under the indemnity insurance, they can present difficulties under a managed care system. Thus, a diagnosis of depression would lead to one anticipated length and level of care, and a diagnosis of borderline personality disorder would lead to quite another. Failure to code accurately a diagnosis jeopardizes the patient's access to care, and the clinician's credibility, and introduces errors into outcome assessment efforts.

Of greater concern are the changes in diagnosis that clinicians may undertake to gain access to payment for care for their patients. When a local company excluded claims for oppositional-defiant disorder, a psychiatric hospital showed a sudden increase in diagnoses of attention deficit disorder with hyperactivity. When inpatient services for this diagnosis were denied, there was an increase in diagnoses of agitated depression. These efforts to "game the system" are undertaken with the justification of assisting patients to secure benefits for which they have paid. However, such practices are clearly ethical violations and open the provider to a host of risks. Another practice involves selecting procedure codes in order to secure payment. Thus, psychotherapy may be submitted when couples are seen in marriage therapy. It becomes easier for the therapist to justify such coding practices because they are undertaken on the behalf of the patient, but in the long run, they undermine the credibility of the profession and the care provided and place the psychologist at risk.

Concluding Comments

In this chapter I have discussed economic and political factors that affect the nature of care given and that have dramatically shaped and reshaped the professional practice of psychology. American health-care policy and managed care strategies affect the therapeutic relationship and introduce new challenges to the obligation and duty owed by the psychologist to the patient. However, the essential elements of the ethical responsibilities arising from these duties and obligations are unaltered.

There are several aspects of the psychologist–patient relationship that require special attention under managed care systems. Patients must assume more assertive roles and exercise greater responsibility for decisions regarding their care. They must understand the risks and implications of decisions they make in selecting health-care coverage. Patients must also be more active and responsible in the therapeutic relationship in understanding the incentives under which the provider is working and advocate for care both with the provider and with the third-party payer. They must be able to understand and appeal inappropriate denials of coverage.

Psychologists have the obligation to assist the patient in assuming these roles. First, psychologists must ensure that patients have the necessary information to make treatment choices and balance their needs against the costs of care and the coverage they have purchased. Thus, informed consent involves not only discussing treatment alternatives and their consequences but also the nature of coverage and the process by which care is monitored. This implies a change in the patient–psychologist relationship in that the patient is less able to depend on the psychologist to determine and shape treatment and must assume greater responsibility and control.

Second, psychologists must act as the patients' advocate to assist them in obtaining the care needed. Psychologists' obligation to the patients' care is not suspended because of decisions regarding reimbursement but must be consistent with professional judgments and standards. Psychologists must assist in appeals of decisions and provide care until a reasonable alternative is found (e.g., by negotiating conditions for direct pay, pro bono services, and referral to other alternatives). Third, psychologists working under incentives to limit care need to disclose the nature of such arrangements and carefully review treatment plans and interventions to ensure appropriate care and unbiased assessment of outcomes.

There are indications that the more aggressive practices of cost containment are being limited because of changes in public opinion and the perception that profit is gained by a reduction of quality of care. Changes can be seen in legal and legislative initiatives directed at controlling managed care. While providers view managed care negatively, most psychologists seem to have accommodated to the system by making necessary changes in their practice patterns. However, in all likelihood, providers will continue to experience strong pressures to contain costs. Early indications are that the initial cost reductions have not produced a sustainable containment of the escalation of health-care costs. Psychologists must redouble efforts to protect patient and provider rights. Furthermore, practitioners must develop systems of care that reduce dependence on managed care reimbursement in order to place patients and psychologists back in control of services.

References

Austad, C. S., & Hoyt, M. F. (1992). The managed care movement and the future of psychotherapy: The future of psychotherapy [Special issue]. *Psychotherapy, 29,* 109–118.

Brody, H. (1989). The physician–patient relationship. In R. M. Vatch (Ed.), *Medical ethics* (pp. 65–91). Boston: Jones & Bartlett.

Broskowski, A. (1994). Current mental health care environments: Why managed care is necessary. In R. L. Lowman & R. J. Resnick (Eds.), *The mental health professional's guide to managed care* (pp. 1–18). Washington, DC: American Psychological Association.

Fox, D. M. (1988). The new discontinuity in health policy. In L. Berlowitz, D. Donoghue, & L. Menand (Eds.), *America in theory* (pp. 163–177). New York: Oxford University Press.

Garfield, S. L. (1994). Eclecticism and integration in psychotherapy: Developments and issues. *Clinical Psychology: Science and Practice, 1,* 123–137.

Ginzberg, E. (1990). High-tech medicine and rising health care costs. *Journal of the American Medical Association, 263,* 1820–1822.

Hass, L., & Cummings, N. A. (1991). Managed outpatient mental health plans: Clinical, ethical, and practical guidelines for participation. *Professional Psychology: Research and Practice, 22,* 45–51.

Havighurst, C. C. (1986). The changing locus of decision making in the health care sector. *Journal of Health Politics, Policy, and Law, 11,* 697–735.

Herron W. E., Eisenstadt, E. N., Javier, R. A., Primavera, L. H., & Schultz, C. D. (1994). Session effects, comparability, and managed care in the psychotherapies. *Psychotherapy, 31,* 279–285.

Higuchi, C. C., & Newman, R. (1994). Legal issues for psychotherapy in a managed care environment: Psychoanalysis and dynamic psychotherapy, the mental health provider and managed care [Special issue]. *Psychoanalysis and Psychotherapy, 11,* 138–153.

Higuchi, S. A. (1994). Recent managed care legislative and legal issues. In R. L. Lowman & R. J. Resnick (Eds.), *The mental health profession's guide to managed care* (pp. 83–118). Washington, DC: American Psychological Association.

Koren, B. P. (1995). Provision of psychotherapy under managed health care: A growing crisis and national nightmare. *Professional Psychology: Research and Practice, 26,* 5–9.

Kiesler, C. A. (1992). U.S. mental health policy: Doomed to fail. *American Psychologist, 47,* 1077–1082.

Lowman, R. L., & Resnick, R. J. (Eds.). (1994). *The mental health profession's guide to managed care.* Washington, DC: American Psychological Association.

Mirin, S. M., & Sedever, L. I. (1994). Mental health care: Current realities, future directions. *Psychiatric Quarterly, 65,* 161–175.

Mone, L. C. (1994). Managed care cost effectiveness: Fantasy or reality? *International Journal of Group Psychotherapy, 44,* 437–448.

Morreim, E. H. (1995). *Balancing act: The new medical ethics of medicine's new economics.* Washington, DC: Georgetown University Press.

Munson, C. E. (1995). Loss of control in the delivery of mental health services. *Clinical Supervisor, 13,* 1–6.

Newman, R., & Bricklin, P. M. (1991). Parameters of managed mental health care: Legal, ethical, and professional guidelines. *Professional Psychology: Research and Practice, 22,* 26–35.

Nickelson, D. W. (1995). The future of professional psychology in a changing health care marketplace: A conversation with Russ Newman. *Professional Psychology: Research and Practice, 26,* 366–370.

Pellegrino, E. D., & Thomasma, D. C. (1988). *For the patient's good: The restoration of beneficence in health care.* New York: Oxford University Press.

Reinhardt, U. E. (1989). Health care spending and American competitiveness. *Health Affairs, 8,* 5–21.

Routh, D. K. (1994). *Clinical psychology since 1917: Science, practice, and organization.* New York: Plenum Press.

Sabin, J. E. (1992). The therapeutic alliance in managed care mental health practice. *Journal of Psychotherapy: Practice and Research, 1,* 26–29.

Schlesinger, A. M. (1986). *The cycles of American history.* Boston: Houghton Mifflin.

Seligman, M. E. (1995). The effectiveness of psychotherapy: The Consumer Reports study. *American Psychologist, 50,* 965–974.

Simon, N. P. (1994). Ethics, psychodynamic treatment, and managed care. Psychoanalysis and dynamic therapy, the mental health provider and managed care [Special issue]. *Psychoanalysis and Psychotherapy, 11,* 119–128.

Task Force on Promotion and Dissemination of Psychological Procedures. (1995). Training in and dissemination of empirically-validated psychological procedures: Report and recommendations. *The Clinical Psychologist, 48*(1), 1–23.

3

Moral Issues in Managed Mental Health Care

Nicholas A. Cummings

In an early discussion of clinical, ethical, and practical guidelines for participation in managed care, Haas and Cummings (1991) identified three considerations: (a) The dilemmas presented by managed health-care systems are not unique but are present (albeit in a less stark form) in other financing arrangements; (b) there are particular questions psychologists should ask before associating themselves with particular plans, especially about types of limitations and possible effects on the patient–provider relationship; and (c) if the therapist has appropriate training, there are very few types of patients who could not be provided with at least some benefits in a managed care environment (Haas & Cummings, 1991, p. 45).

In the present discussions I will focus on the ethical and moral responsibilities of practitioners, not only in participating in managed care, but also in preparation for the rapidly evolving provider-owned networks that are emerging as attractive alternatives to the managed care companies (Cummings, 1995a). These practitioner-equity groups are in a position to contract directly with purchasers (large employers, insurers, purchasing alliances, and other payers), cutting out the so-called middleman. For this reason only, I look at one side of the equation, leaving discussion of the moral responsibilities of managed care companies to other chapters in this volume. Rather than letting managed care companies off the hook for the dilemmas they pose, the intent is to aid the practitioner who wishes to participate in managed care as an owner to prepare for that challenge.

In keeping with the intent of providing information that may be useful to the practitioner, case examples are utilized. However, these have met certain criteria: They are illustrative, instructive, and frequent. The selection of rare horror stories, and inflammatory behavior too common on both sides engaged in this passionate debate, do not meet the criteria of illustrative and instructive.

Moral Responsibility Versus Rules of Conduct

It is the purpose of this discussion to extend the definition of ethics beyond that of a code of conduct. This is imperative, as much of our ethics code was conceptualized before the emergence of managed care (Keith-Spiegel & Koocher, 1985). Strict adherence to the "letter of the law" has prompted one side to argue that participation in managed care is unethical (Wright, 1991), and the other to charge that the ethical code is obsolete, or at least shortsighted.

Originally ethics were defined as moral responsibility. The Greek classical era from which we derive our term *ethos* was not one of active professional societies that could impose sanctions. Rather, the appeal was to one's moral responsibility to make the profession the best it can be. It is an ideal. With the establishment of professional societies this moral imperative was codified and sanctions were adopted. Whereas moral responsibility is a vision of what the profession can ideally be, a code of ethics is the lowest common denominator of acceptable behavior. Conduct below that acceptable level is subject to sanctions. Because our current ethical code was engaged before there has evolved a professional consensus of conduct regarding the current era of health-care delivery, in this discussion I find it necessary to rely more on moral responsibility. In so doing it is recognized that a practitioner falling short of these standards of conduct is not necessarily guilty of anything, and is not in danger of applied sanctions.

The differences in approach, moral responsibility versus ethical code, can be illustrated by one issue that occupied the ethics committee for years (Pope, Shaver, & Levenson, 1980). The question was raised as to how long must therapy have been terminated before a dual relationship is permissible. A heated debate ensued as to whether it should be 1, 3, 5, or 10 years. This is a de juris approach (Stromberg et al., 1988), intended largely to protect the practitioner who wants to enter a nontherapeutic (romantic, business, etc.) relationship with the former patient. From the standpoint of moral responsibility, the focus is the patient and only the patient. The question is better asked in the following way: "How long after the termination of treatment does the patient remain vulnerable to the therapist because of a lingering transference?" For most patients this may be forever, rendering a set number of years irrelevant to the therapist's moral responsibility to the patient.

One of the greatest reasons for a misunderstanding between practitioners and managed care companies is the different source of responsibility each has. The managed care company is responsible to the buyer (i.e., the entity contracting the carve-out). It has a clear-cut contract with a health plan, insurer, purchasing alliance, or some other form of *intermediate consumer*. The therapist, on the other hand, has a therapeutic contract with the patient, defined as the *end consumer*. Intermediate consumers (buyers) clearly have different requirements from end consumers (patients), although in a well-designed system the two requirements would be interrelated. A managed care company must please the buyer by producing cost savings (efficiency), but if it also does not provide patient satisfaction and measurable treatment benefits (effectiveness), it cannot succeed. Similarly, the provider must be skilled in the latest efficient–effective treatment. Because the professions have too often in the past taken an unnecessarily hostile approach, the managed care industry has galloped ahead in becoming more and more business driven, rendering the equivalent of "employee" status on the practitioners. There are now mega-trends indicating that practitioner involvement will become a significant factor in the not too distant future.

The Emerging Megaprovider

In looking forward to the forthcoming era of the provider, and even the megaprovider, the practitioner must meet three challenges: (a) Providers must learn to control and predict their costs, (b) practitioners must over-come a number of inherently outmoded attitudes, and (c) new moral di-lemmas must be resolved in consensus.

The first of these has been discussed extensively (Cummings, 1995a), and the second is receiving considerable attention (Cummings, 1995b). These issues will not be readdressed here, and the reader who is unaware of the problems would do well to acquaint oneself with the literature. Our discussion focuses entirely on the moral responsibilities extant in the prac-titioner's becoming an equity participant in a group practice providing mental health and chemical dependency (i.e., behavioral health) services to a contracted population. It is secondarily applicable to a solo practi-tioner or a small group practice that becomes part of a managed care company's network of providers.

Training

Competence and training are so interrelated that a decision to separate them for discussion purposes is, at best, arbitrary. Yet recent findings in-dicate that to do so may be useful. The principle that psychologists should not practice beyond their competency, and the further principle that they must have adequate training and preparation for what they do, are taken for granted and seldom evoke much discussion. The exception has been the debate regarding possible prescription privileges and what might be the training for such psychologists (DeLeon, 1995; Denelsky, 1995; Rodg-ers, 1995). It is surprising, therefore, that two recent surveys (Kent, 1995; Levenson & Davidovitz, 1995) have revealed, when it comes to psycholo-gists' servicing managed care, that there is widespread disregard of the responsibility to acquire training adequate to practice.

Brief psychotherapy is not simply a truncated version of long-term therapy. It has its own parameters and requires additional training re-quirements, a position aptly demonstrated (Bennett, 1994; Budman & Gurman, 1988; Cummings, 1992). Belar (1989) not only emphasized the importance of brief therapy but also insisted on specific training in what has been termed *HMO therapy* as the most relevant to current managed care. Hoyt (1995) found that most therapists entering the job market today get their short-term therapy training on the job, often in an uneven and haphazard fashion. He called for comprehensive training and experience in brief therapy models. Friedman and Fanger (1991) pointed out that it is easier to teach brief therapy to students and novices because they do not have to unlearn previously ingrained assumptions about long-term therapy. The importance of "unlearning," or a change in attitudes, has been emphasized extensively by Friedman and Fanger and by Cummings (1995b).

There is a growing arsenal of efficient–effective psychotherapy (Bennett, 1994; Bloom, 1992) that is unknown to most practitioners, and even more surprising to those who educate and train graduate students. Balint (1957) first pointed out that effective brief therapy is the outcome of having been trained in brief therapy, a finding reiterated many years later by several authors (Bennett, 1994; Bloom, 1992; Budman & Gurman, 1983, 1988; Cummings, 1977). Levenson and Davidowitz (1995) conducted a national survey and found that although 65% of the respondents were working with managed care, less than 30% had any training in brief therapy, less than 50% had ever read a book on brief therapy, and a staggering 94% responded that they had been inadequately trained and needed to learn more about brief therapy.

In his survey of 233 psychology interns, Kent (1995) found that only 39% had received even one seminar on brief therapy in graduate school, and only 37% were receiving any internship supervision in brief psychotherapy. Yet by an overwhelming 95% these interns believed it was a valuable treatment, an equal 95% saw it as the most appropriate treatment in the real world, and 87% had already made up their minds to work in managed care after the completion of their internship. In the face of this career decision, the additional finding that only 15% had been formally taught anything about managed care is alarming.

When the nation's first carve-out system for managed behavioral health was established in 1985, the founders were so appalled by the disparity between training and the new practice expectations that they instituted at considerable expense a 130-hr, 2-week preservice intensive training with 4 hr per week of inservice training along with intensive supervision in brief therapy (Cummings, 1986; Cummings & Sayama, 1995). The finding that the level of training has improved only slightly in the past decade suggests that our profession may be teetering on the brink of moral irresponsibility.

Case Illustration 1

The difficulties encountered in the disparity between training and practice are illustrated by the psychologist who had practiced long-term therapy for over 10 years and had never had any training or experience in brief psychotherapy. She joined a managed care network because she had recently relocated with her husband to a new city and had difficulty reestablishing a solo practice. In the course of her affiliation with the managed care company she received over two-dozen referrals under the company's policy of six sessions per episode. The therapist essentially did with each patient what she had been doing for over 10 years: She used all six sessions taking an extensive history and administering a battery of psychological tests in preparation for the long-term therapy that would never take place. After the sixth session each patient was released without a definition of the problem, goal setting, and even the beginning of treatment. Most patients, though bewildered, did not complain. Three, however, complained bitterly to the payer who investigated the therapist and terminated her affiliation.

Case Illustration 2

With variations the foregoing is illustrative of a commonly encountered problem. No less frequent, but considerably more overtly troublesome, is the following example that is typical of the long-term therapist who is openly hostile to short-term therapy. The psychologist joined the network of a managed care company because his solo practice was sagging. His already hostile attitude toward short-term therapy was now augmented by his anger at the very managed care company with which he was affiliated, which he blamed for his declining practice. In the first session with each of the patients referred to him, he cautioned the patient to not expect much because he, the therapist, was being forced to conduct substandard treatment. This was often reiterated in each session. For example, at a certain point the therapist would declare that he should pursue a given issue with the patient, but that would lead to the need for more treatment, which would be disallowed under the terms of the substandard care. In the preceding example the therapist, though not competent to the task, was caring and sincere. Her patients, though dissatisfied, did not complain. In the latter example, the therapist's angry behavior evoked considerable complaints and he quickly came to the attention of the case manager. The managed care company sought the best possible solution to the problem, and even offered the psychologist training in brief therapy. He accepted but used all training sessions as a platform to berate anything less than long-term therapy. After all efforts at conciliation were exhausted, the therapist was terminated, after which he wrote a volatile letter to the American Psychological Association, complaining that the company was acting unethically toward patients.

In my own survey of case managers, I found that 60%–70% of all psychotherapists who initially join their networks would fall into one of these two illustrative situations, albeit their conduct is not as flagrant.

Competence

The therapist's moral responsibility to the patient can be conceptualized so that it completely cuts across the debate of long-term versus short-term psychotherapy. It begins with what has been termed the *Patient's Bill of*

Rights: "The patient is entitled to relief from pain, anxiety and depression in the shortest time possible and with the least intrusive intervention" (Cummings, 1988, p. 312).

It follows, then, that the therapist has an obligation to so hone his or her skills that this can be accomplished. It should be noted that efficient–effective psychotherapy does not mean "quick." It defies session limits, for some conditions require more therapy than others. The skilled therapist, imbued with the Patient's Bill of Rights, is effective and thereby also efficient. There is no therapeutic "drift" or unnecessarily protracted treatment.

In invoking the concept of the least restrictive alternative in the psychotherapy domain, the patient is encouraged to retain the major responsibility for what decisions are made in the therapeutic encounter:

> In making a therapeutic contract with the patient, we want to make clear that we are there to serve as a catalyst, but the patient is the one who will do the growing. This contract is stated: "I will never abandon you as long as you need me, and I will never ask you to do something until you are ready. In return for this I ask you to join me in a partnership to make me obsolete as soon as possible." (Cummings, 1988, pp. 312–313)

It follows, therefore, that when the patient is ready the therapist will encourage, gently prod, or generally empower the patient to take the next step. The vehicle throughout therapy is in the homework assignments, clinically tailored to the patient's needs and subsequent growth. It also follows that there is a treatment plan, shared with the patient, defining the problem, goals, and procedures. The treatment is solution focused, and there is an interruption of treatment but never termination. The patient is free at any time to return with other issues, thus constituting what has been termed "brief, intermittent psychotherapy throughout the life cycle" (Cummings & Sayama, 1995). Interestingly, every health-care profession functions within some variation of this model except for long-term psychotherapy.

Psychotherapy without a treatment plan and focused goals is like attempting to fly an aircraft without a flight plan and a compass. A persistent complaint of case managers is that only a small percentage of managed care network psychotherapists have even the slightest notion of how to go about developing one with a patient. Many unreasonable facsimiles are offered, often with such ethereal nongoals as self-actualization, increase in self-esteem, or institution of self-empowerment.

Case Illustration 3

A patient of about age 40 had been to four different psychotherapists in a 6-year period with a total of about 200 sessions. When his employer signed up with a managed care company, he decided to give his new mental health benefit a try. On the first session he had vague, nonspecific complaints.

His job was okay, but he was not as interested in it as he used to be. He had a good relationship for several years with a girlfriend, but he was no longer as enthusiastic about her as he used to be. He seemed to be describing a low-grade depression with a lack of zest, interest, or ambition. The managed care psychotherapist, in the interest of defining the problem and the goal, soon clearly discerned a classic "pot nonmotivation syndrome." Asking about his chemical use, he readily admitted extensive daily smoking of marijuana. This patient, a real estate broker, in spite of his outwardly "straight" appearance, made no effort to hide his habit. After an initial resistance, the patient decided to refrain from drug use, essentially in an effort to prove that the psychologist's diagnosis was in error. Within a few weeks his zest and enthusiasm returned, and he decided to give up marijuana forever. The current therapist, in a patient-approved exchange of information, asked the previous therapist how he could have missed a classic substance abuse syndrome. The reply was that several times he somewhat suspected that it might have been the case, but to probe into the subject would be "a violation of the unconditional positive regard for the patient."

One of the most frequently missed diagnoses is that of chemical dependency, in large part because the patient comes in with severe denial regarding the real problem, but also because many long-term psychodynamic therapists see addiction as only a secondary manifestation of a deeper conflict. However, there are all kinds of problems in which construction of a treatment plan will prevent lack of focus on the presenting problem.

Case Illustration 4

A somewhat obsessional man in his late 40s had been in treatment for 3 years "to save my marriage." No matter how helpful the therapist, the patient could not find a reason to stay with his wife. Yet he was eager to keep trying to solve his marital unhappiness, and in 3 years he never missed an appointment. He was eventually transferred to a new psychotherapist when his company changed to a managed care plan. His new therapist discovered while constructing a treatment plan on his first session that the patient had long ago decided to leave his wife, but his somewhat obsessional personality would not permit him to do so until he was certain "no stone was left unturned." The therapist discussed the matter with him and essentially gave him permission to implement his decision of 3 years ago. He returned for the second session, expressed complete relief, as well as gratitude for her not stretching his therapy out even more, and terminated.

Confidentiality: A Legitimate Concern With a Dark Side

Issues of confidentiality have generated more passionate discussion than any other topic in managed care (Barnett, 1995). Yet this issue is not new and dates back several decades to when psychotherapists first became eligible for third-party payment under indemnity insurance. Those who pay the bill have the right to determine if a certain procedure has indeed been performed and is within acceptable professional standards, whether this be an appendectomy or treatment of substance abuse. They also have the right to determine if the services delivered were within the scope contracted with the patient. The patient has conceded to this reasonable determination in accepting the health plan contract. The problem is that case managers have become more and more intrusive as their skepticism increases as to whether the psychotherapist is actually performing the services in the manner described.

Unfortunately, more than any other, the issue of confidentiality is used as a "red herring" by practitioners to conceal incompetence or breach of contract with the managed care companies. For cynical reasons the managed care companies are reluctant to give up unnecessarily intrusive procedures designed really to catch the therapist at his or her own game. The limits and necessities of information conveyance will eventually have to be resolved by a task-oriented, mutually conscientious joint effort between the professions and the managed care companies. In the meantime, as practitioners, it is our concern that often the issue of confidentiality is invoked to cover questionable practitioner conduct.

Case Illustration 5

A case manager noted repeated inconsistencies between what one practitioner claimed she did and the therapeutic outcome. A request was made for the therapist's treatment plan, which she steadfastly refused to turn over. A tug-of-war ensued, during which the psychologist wrote two inflammatory letters to the state psychological association. Eventually the practitioner admitted she had no treatment plans for any of the referrals she had accepted.

Case Illustration 6

In a similar situation the case manager kept discerning inconsistencies between what the psychologist stated he was doing in the treatment room and his universal requests for more sessions for all of his patients. He complied immediately when asked for his treatment plan but then balked at providing any information beyond that. After several weeks of acrimony, the information was provided. It became apparent that although the treatment plans were well formulated, they bore no resemblance to the actual treatment. The psychologist had been performing long-term psychoanalytically oriented psychotherapy, intending to keep on requesting extensions to the number of sessions approved in order to continue practicing this kind of therapy. Ignoring his own approved treatment plans was his way of continuing his life-long mode of practice, even if it meant being deceitful. When confronted he justified his behavior by insisting that long-term therapy was the only effective treatment, and he lied for the good of his patients.

Case Illustration 7

A practitioner steadfastly refused to turn over any information to the managed care company, whose provider profile of him indicated he was one of the most effective and otherwise conscientious practitioners. In subsequent discussions, the psychologist revealed that he greatly resented anyone looking over his shoulder and would rather resign from the network than comply. The managed care company, concluding he was one of its most effective–efficient providers, chose to exempt him from intrusion in return for his continued good work.

As surprising as this outcome may seem to most readers, this is a frequent arrangement that has been accorded with respect and appreciation to practitioners with proven effectiveness, and especially to groups of such practitioners. Case management is expensive and labor-intensive, and a well-run managed care company is delighted to forgo it when it is unnecessary.

Overdiagnosing

With indemnity insurance and in times past, providers characteristically underdiagnosed ostensibly for the protection of their patients. The most innocuous reimbursable diagnosis was overly used, whereas schizophrenia was seldom evoked as in many states the patient could suffer such consequences as loss of a driver's license or ineligibility for life insurance. In contrast, the era of managed care has seen the mushrooming of the use of severe diagnoses. Forced on many occasions to demonstrate concepts of "medical necessity" or "life threatening," practitioners' exaggeration of findings on evaluation has become widespread.

Case Illustration 8

A psychotherapist had a remarkable record of obtaining approval of treatment and for far more sessions than were characteristically granted by the managed care company. In a routine audit, it was discovered that in 100% of his evaluations, the therapist had reported severe suicidal risk. Discussions with the psychologist revealed that his only basis was the answer yes to the question that just about every human being would answer in the affirmative: "Have you ever in your life, for even one split second, thought of suicide?" Without any attempt to do an adequate suicidal risk evaluation, this psychologist proceeded to label each patient a severe suicidal threat.

There are many therapists who overly diagnose on a "specialty" basis. Managed care companies now maintain provider profiles, and such grossly unusual conduct is immediately identified as differing markedly from customary practice in a community.

Case Illustration 9

A practitioner in a small rural community on the border between a midwestern and southern state was treating four out of every five referrals for multiple personality disorder. He justified this as a consequence of the patient's living in an unsophisticated "backwoods" environment where dissociation was a way of life. Because psychotherapists were difficult to find in that part of the nation, the managed care company was unusually indulgent. Two years later, when this psychologist moved to a large and far more sophisticated metropolitan area, and four out of five referrals were still requiring treatment for multiple personality disorder, the managed care company realized this was the propensity of the psychologist, and not a characteristic of the patient population. Therapist profiles in the new community revealed that less than 1 in 40 patients were being treated for multiple personality disorder.

Accumulated national data by managed care companies on thousands of providers and hundreds of thousands of patients indicate that common areas of overdiagnosis, in addition to multiple personality disorder, are attention deficit disorder, which some practitioners have diagnosed in as high as 60% of boys in school, thus questioning that this is indeed a syndrome; posttraumatic stress syndrome for the most common of life's stresses; survival of incest; depression, which has been redefined to include just about any common mood alteration encountered in the normal course of living; and all manner of somatized response. These provider profiles reveal that psychotherapists, in general, do not overly diagnose. There seems to be a segment of practitioners who posses an uncanny ability to find in almost every patient the one psychological condition they most like to treat.

Case Illustration 10

Over a period of a year and a half it came to the attention of the managed care company that a clinic with which it had contracted was treating 100% of its referrals as survivors of incest. When the clinic director was questioned that surely at least 1 out of over 150 referrals must have not been incestuously molested, she became very angry and verbally attacked the case manager, accusing her of being insensitive and uncaring. The managed care company discontinued referring to this clinic, whereupon its director took the matter to the media, accusing the entire company of being uncaring and insensitive. Before the reader concludes that I have broken my promise not to present horror stories, it must be pointed out that with seemingly endless variation this example has been experienced by managed care companies, and with surprising redundancy.

Who Should Not Work in Managed Care?

Participation in managed care is voluntary. This does not mean that the choice is easy, for the only alternative to participation may be loss of practice. Yet the hard choice must be made, and if joining a managed care network is the decision, it cannot morally be done under a cloak of deceit. This does not mean giving up one's right to strive to change managed care—whether it be through the professional societies, the legislative process, or direct problem-solving negotiations with managed care itself. However, false reporting, inciting patients, and practicing beyond one's training and skills are all forms of morally irresponsible conduct once participation is established.

A Matter of Conscience

Managed care is diverse in its applications, but a simple definition is possible. Managed care can be defined as the partial subordination of clinical considerations to business principles in the interest of rendering health-care delivery economically viable. This is a tough-minded, no-nonsense definition. It acknowledges the reality that no system of health-care delivery existent in the world today, be it market oriented or socialistic, is without some inherent form of health-care rationing.

Practitioners who find strong philosophical disagreement with market-oriented solutions to health reform will not be happy in this system. This does not mean that those who work in managed care have to accept the obscenely high compensation some CEO's receive, the relegation of providers to almost "employee" status, or any other procedures that are clearly business abuses. However, those who inherently are opposed philosophically can only project their unhappiness on their patients and should seek other outlets for their skills.

A Matter of Belief

There are psychotherapists who steadfastly believe that only long-term therapy is effective and are inured to any evidence to the contrary. Such persons should never even attempt to work in managed care, for to do so would be a constant compromise with their cherished beliefs. Such a tug-of-war between practice in managed care and one's belief system can only result in unenthusiastic outcomes for the patient and demoralized unhappiness for the practitioner.

A Matter of Training

It is the professional responsibility of every psychotherapist who decides to work in managed care to obtain the requisite training. Offerings in time-sensitive psychotherapy abound, and one does not have to look beyond his or her weekly mail to find an appropriate training opportunity. This does not mean that the psychotherapist has to be a master brief therapist before joining a network, but some serious training after affiliating with a managed care company is in keeping with moral responsibility. Anyone unwilling to do these things should not work in managed care, as this would be deleterious to one's patients.

A Matter of Stamina

Brief psychotherapy practice is hard work. It is far easier to see eight patients four times a week in analytic practice than to experience the turnover with high volume that is typical of managed care practice. In addition, the therapist has to learn to carry a fairly large caseload of patients for whom he or she is responsible, but who need to be seen only occasionally.

A Matter of Therapist Personality

Effectiveness in short-term therapy is, in great part, a function of the patient as partner to one's own treatment. In this sense, the transference is minimized and self-reliance is accentuated. The patients most often conclude treatment with the conviction that they solved their own problem. It is long-term patients who express gratitude and shower the psychotherapist with gifts. With short-term therapy the practitioner is aware of the patient's satisfaction mostly from the friends and relatives who are referred back to the psychotherapist. For a therapist who needs the narcissistic supplies accorded by grateful, adoring patients, managed care practice is not for him or her.

Can the Skeptical Therapist Participate?

The therapist who is skeptical but willing to acquire the training and participate with an open mind is an excellent candidate. Often outmoded attitudes are most readily changed by behavior. Such a therapist could well experience the rewards and exhilaration that come from bringing to the patient relief from pain, anxiety, and depression in the shortest time possible, and with the least intrusive intervention. Many skeptical therapists who try it with an open mind become enthusiastic participants. A like number, however, only confirm the reason for their skepticism and appropriately should terminate the affiliation.

Summary and Conclusions

Limitations and reporting requirements by third-party payers have existed for three decades and have been accommodated by practitioners.

Managed care has escalated the degree of intrusion, and previously wide-spread underreporting practices devised to protect the patient's privacy no longer serve either the patient or the practitioner, who must demonstrate "medical necessity" to be eligible, respectively, for services and reimbursement. An ethical code that represents professional consensus achieved essentially before the health-care revolution often does not directly address the dilemmas confronting practitioners in the current era. In achieving a new consensus that will lead to updating this ethical code, the profession must address issues of moral responsibility that are broader than codification of minimum acceptable conduct and that do not carry sanction. In essence, the practitioner must ask what is the very best that the profession can be in the new health-care environment—an ideal that in every era has preceded codifications. Moral responsibility involves issues of adequate training and supervision, as well as the applicability of practitioners' core beliefs that may render him or her eligible or ineligible for participation. Ultimately, moral responsibility is the concern for the patient, not protection of the profession. In this discussion I have looked at the fact that many, if not most, of the practitioners who currently participate in managed care are not qualified either by training or by attitude to do so.

Participation in managed care is voluntary. Unfortunately, a decision to not participate may result in loss of practice. For some so philosophically opposed to the evidence of effective time-sensitive therapy, this may morally be the only alternative. For others, with more of an open mind, participation must be preceded by preparation. Finally, managed care companies vary tremendously from flagrant disregard of important clinical consideration to surprising sensitivity and willingness to dialogue with the profession. The characteristics in managed care companies, for which the practitioner must be aware, have been delineated previously and the psychotherapist would do well to review these (Cummings, 1991; Haas & Cummings, 1991).

References

Balint, M. (1957). *The doctor, his patient and the illness*. New York: International Universities Press.

Barnett, J. E. (1995). The managed care dilemma. *Psychotherapy, 20*(2), 54–57.

Belar, C. D. (1989). Opportunities for psychologists in health maintenance organizations: Implications for graduate education and training. *Professional Psychology: Research and Practice, 20*, 390–394.

Bennett, M. J. (1994). Can competing psychotherapists be managed? *Managed Care Quarterly, 2*, 29–35.

Bloom, B. L. (1992). *Planned short-term psychotherapy: A clinical handbook*. Boston: Allyn & Bacon.

Budman, S. H., & Gurman, A. S. (1983). *Principles of brief therapy*. New York: Guilford Press.

Budman, S. H., & Gurman, A. S. (1988). *Theory and practice of brief therapy*. New York: Guilford Press.

Cummings, N., & Sayama, M. (1995). *Focused psychotherapy: A casebook of brief, intermittent psychotherapy throughout the life cycle*. New York: Brunner/Mazel.

Cummings, N. A. (1977). Prolonged or "ideal" versus short-term "realistic" psychotherapy. *Professional Psychology, 8*, 491–501.

Cummings, N. A. (1986). The dismantling of our health system: Strategies for the survival of psychological practice. *American Psychologist, 41*, 426–431.

Cummings, N. A. (1988). Emergence of the mental health complex: Adaptive and maladaptive responses. *Professional Psychology: Research and Practice, 19*, 308–315.

Cummings, N. A. (1991). Ten ways to spot mismanaged mental health. *Psychotherapy in Private Practice, 9*(3), 79–83.

Cummings, N. A. (1992). The future of psychotherapy: Society's charge to professional psychology. *Independent Practitioner, 12*(3), 126–130.

Cummings, N. A. (1995a). Behavioral health after managed care: The next golden opportunity for professional psychology. *Register Report, 20*(3), 1, 30–33.

Cummings, N. A. (1995b). Impact of managed care on employment and training: A primer for survival. *Professional Psychology: Research and Practice, 26*(1), 10–15.

DeLeon, P. (1995). Perscription privileges: Entirely new battle grounds. *Psychotherapy, 20*(2), 8–13.

Denelsky, G. (1995). Prescription privileges: Fundamental change for psychology. *National Psychologist*, July/August, 18–19.

Friedman, S., & Fanger, M. T. (1991). *Expanding therapeutic possibilities: Getting results in brief therapy*. Lexington, MA: Lexington Books.

Haas, L. J., & Cummings, N. A. (1991). Managed outpatient mental health plans: Clinical, ethical and practical guidelines for participation. *Professional Psychology: Research and Practice, 22*, 45–51.

Hoyt, M. F. (1995). *Brief therapy and managed care: Readings for contemporary practice*. San Francisco: Jossey-Bass.

Keith-Spiegel, P., & Koocher, G. P. (1985). *Ethics in psychology: Professional standards and cases*. New York: Random House.

Kent, A. J. (1995, August). *Survey of interns' knowledge of brief therapy and managed care*. Paper presented at the 103rd Annual Convention of the American Psychological Association, New York.

Levenson, H., & Davidovitz, D. (1995, August). *National survey of mental health professionals on brief therapy*. Paper presented at the 103rd Annual Convention of the American Psychological Association, New York.

Pope, K. S., Shaver, L. R., & Levenson, H. (1980). Sexual behavior between clinical supervisors and trainees: Implications for professional standards. *Professional Psychology, 11*, 157–162.

Rodgers, D. A. (1995). Prescription privilege primer. *National Psychologist*, July/August, 16–17.

Stromberg, C. D., Haggerty, D. J., Leibenluft, R. F., McMillan, M. H., Mishkin, B., Rubin, B. L., & Trilling, H. R. (1988). *The psychologist's legal handbook*. Washington, DC: Council for the National Register of Health Service Providers in Psychology.

Wright, R. H. (1991, Spring). Toward a national plan. *Advance Plan, 1*, 14–16.

4

Managed Care and Managed Competition: A Question of Morality

Karen Shore

Many clinicians feel profoundly demoralized by managed care. Erich Fromm (1955) wrote that people do not like to think that society as a whole may be lacking in sanity, so they point to mental health problems of a few "unadjusted" individuals to avoid thinking that the culture may be "out of synch with the needs of man." Who among those who support managed care would want us to think that the demoralization of clinicians today is high because the corporate–industrial model of health care is "insane"? Instead, the industry and its supporters point to the "inability" of some clinicians to adapt, when, I suggest, the reality is that the current corporate culture in health care is insane and is out of synch with the human needs of both patients and clinicians.

Though some clinicians have adapted to managed care, why do so many abhor it? Why have so many "opted out" of managed care, despite the possible loss of one's livelihood, a beloved profession, and meaningful work? Why do so many feel that managed care tramples their ethics, morals, and values? And, how do we decide whose ethics, morals, and values the nation should be using to guide its mental health care policy? At present, it is being guided haphazardly by the "bottom-line" morality of managed care. In this chapter I take a closer look at the immorality of managed care and the chilling application of business ethics and values to health care. Although this chapter primarily addresses managed mental health care, most of my comments and conceptualizations can be applied to all managed health care.

The Immorality of Managed Care and Managed Competition

Morality has to do with how we treat other people. Ethics, the philosophy of morality, provides guideposts for "doing the right thing." Most moral systems adhere to some version of the "Golden Rule": We must treat others as we want to be treated and refrain from doing to others what we would find hurtful ourselves (Solomon, 1993). I judge the morality of managed care by how it treats human beings, both patients and clinicians. By that standard, managed care organizations are immoral.

Humanists (e.g., Fromm, 1955) speak of "rational" and "irrational" authority, the former being based on true superior knowledge. Currently, managed care companies assume that their knowledge of patients' needs within therapeutic relationships is superior to that of therapists and patients in regard to that most delicate art of healing of the human spirit. Managed care companies, run by businessmen and businesswomen, often for profit, can only pretend to have this type of superior knowledge.

In fact, they exercise irrational authority through their basic assumption that neither patients nor clinicians can be trusted to make cost-effective decisions. Therefore—a business rationale concludes—patients' and therapists' behavior must be controlled. Managed care's control over patients, clinicians, and the process of decision making is damaging to both patients and clinicians. At best, managed care is paternalistic; at worst, it is dictatorial and uninformed about, or unconcerned with, the true nature of healing. Managed care companies' irrational exercise of power is immoral (a) by its removal of personal power and the instillation of fear, (b) by its fostering of unhealthy dependency, (c) by its retraumatization of patients, (d) by its preying on the vulnerable, and (e) by its putting the need for money over the needs of people. I analyze each action in turn. All of these characteristics of managed care impede the healing of our patients and undermine the ethical standards of our profession.

Removal of Personal Power and the Instillation of Fear

First and foremost, managed care is immoral because it makes people powerless. Managed care's cost-containment mechanisms require that consumers lose three critical, basic rights: the right to privacy, the right to choice, and the right to make one's own treatment decisions. The ethicists Garrett, Baillie, and Garrett (1993) stated that attacks on the consumer's freedom of choice and other unnecessary restrictions are "attacks on human dignity and thus are prima facie, presumptively, evil" (p. 5).

Clinicians also lose power to managed care, which creates a system in which clinicians become dependent upon managed care companies for referrals and income. Further, because managed care companies control the flow of money, and because few patients are able to pay for adequate care without their insurance, many clinicians fear speaking out against managed care or advocating too strongly for their patients. The consequence of challenging managed care can be the loss of one's livelihood and of a beloved profession.

Under managed care, consumers will never again have the right to choice, privacy, or decision-making power, certainly not without financial penalty, and clinicians will never again work for themselves or be able to consistently put their patients first without fear of the managed care companies' retaliation. These consequences for both patients and clinicians, which undermine and restrict the rightful exercise of a human being's free will, are immoral.

Fostering of Unhealthy Dependency

Patients often form a dependency on their therapist. This is a natural occurrence, especially for those who were unable, as children, to form a stable, healthy, and appropriate dependency on relatively healthy parents and who, as adults, either cannot trust others or become overly dependent, even on people who are unhealthy for them. Typically, therapists consider the patient's dependency on the therapist to be temporary—a developmental step that can be useful in establishing the patient's trust in the therapist and in the ability of the patient to do the work of therapy. For many patients, this temporary dependency on the therapist is not only useful, but may very well be necessary in helping them gain sufficient emotional maturity to handle their own life reasonably well and end treatment without negative results.

I have spent this time reviewing what many experienced clinicians will readily recognize as a normal part of the therapeutic alliance to illustrate the difference between healthy dependency and the type of unhealthy dependency that managed care companies create.

Some managed care companies have been known to warn their therapists against "fostering" a dependency. For example, Vista Health Plans of San Diego, California, in a newsletter for their network clinicians dated August 1995, circulated a brief article by Michael Walker, PhD, titled "Therapist Dependent No More," which provided "tips" on facilitating a client's transition from support in the therapeutic relationship to getting support from other sources. Tip 1 said, "Set up the expectation from the very beginning that therapy is temporary support." Tip 2 stated, "Clients who have been in long term therapy in the past are socialized to expect therapy must be long term to be effective. Be compassionate, and gently steer them toward the short term model." Tip 5 stated, "Have clear, specific, measurable and relatively small treatment goals." Tips 4 and 5 assured therapists that clients can learn to solve one problem and generalize "the *process* of problem solving" to other problems in the clients' life. Through their lack of understanding of, or their lack of concern for, the therapeutic process (i.e., their irrational authority), some managed care companies strive to train their therapists to stave off dependency from the first session, as if the dependency were harmful to patients and created by therapists in order to keep patients in treatment as long as possible.

Ironically, perhaps hypocritically, while railing against dependency and working to prevent the patient's natural and potentially healing temporary dependency upon the therapist, managed care companies force both patients and clinicians into a state of "permanent dependency" through their restricted lists of approved clinicians, their control over the form of therapy, their almost total control over the flow of money, and their power to define "medical necessity." This control over the patient's treatment and the economic dependency of clinicians on the companies are permanent as long as managed care exists. As Jean Baker Miller (1986) said, relationships of temporary inequality and dependency represent the context of human development; those of permanent inequality and dependency represent the condition of oppression. Some may counter that both patients and clinicians can cancel health plan contracts at any time. However, because all managed care plans operate under similar models, there is little hope for patients or therapists to gain independence or a sense of control over treatment under managed care.

Retraumatization Through Loss of Privacy

Because of the utilization review process required by many managed care companies, patients must give up their privacy in order to use their benefits. This experience, for a good number of patients, recreates the infringements on their privacy and control that may have created their mental health problems in the first place.

Privacy is considered one of the cornerstones of a democratic society, and it has always been considered a cornerstone of effective psychotherapy. In fact, the privacy required for psychotherapeutic healing was even acknowledged and protected recently by the United States Supreme Court in the *Jaffee v. Redmond* (1996) decision. In a 7–2 decision, the Supreme Court stated, "Because effective psychotherapy depends upon an atmosphere of confidence and trust . . . the mere possibility of disclosure of confidential communications may impede development of the relationship necessary for successful treatment" (p. 1924).

Before managed care, the clinician only needed to report a patient's diagnosis to the insurance company. Now, details of the patient's problems must be phoned or written and sent to the managed care companies. The threat of a breach in confidentiality of records is very real, given self-insured plans and centralized data banks, and should be of concern for both patients and therapists.

We as clinicians must also differentiate between confidentiality of records and the more abstract sense of personal privacy. Certainly, some managed care companies may have good processes in place for safeguarding the information of individual patients from nonprivileged persons. However, maintaining a person's sense of privacy—that is, when and to whom they disclose information—is quite different from providing assurances of confidentiality of records.

Good mental health requires that people have the ability to draw a circle around themselves and protect themselves from unwanted intrusions into the most personal and private places of their minds and bodies. Many of the patients we see in treatment have suffered violations of their personal privacy. How can a patient learn to trust a therapist when we as therapists betray their personal privacy ourselves by phoning or writing reports about their lives to the managed care companies or insurer? Even if an insurer keeps patient records confidential, the utilization review process has already forced a violation of the patient's personal privacy. Some patients have reported feeling extreme humiliation from the intrusiveness of the utilization review process. To emphasize how traumatic this may be for patients, imagine if all gynecological and proctologic examinations and procedures had to be videotaped, and then the tapes had to be sent to the insurer as a utilization review check on physician diagnosis and treatment technique. Would proponents of managed care utilization reviews insist that this utilization review procedure is fine and that men and women who do not submit to the videotaping must forego their insurance? Many mental health patients feel as exposed and humiliated by disclosure of their emotional problems as most of us would if our physical examinations were photographed and preserved on videotape.

Many therapists consider the managed care system unethical because of this required intrusion, which is necessary if patients are to use their managed care benefits (and for many patients, therapy is affordable only through their health benefits). Although it may be tempting for supporters of managed care to simply state that if the patient does not want to submit to utilization review, then he or she should simply not use his or her benefits, the ramifications of such a choice can be debilitating—both emotionally and financially. I think that managed care's creation of a process that forces patients to weigh their need for healing against their healthy desire for privacy and financial stability is immoral. The very process of having to choose between these basic human needs may retraumatize patients at a time when they already feel exposed and vulnerable.

Preying on the Vulnerable

Which brings us to another point of managed care: Managed care hurts people most when they are vulnerable and, perhaps most insidiously, *because* they are vulnerable. Subscribers are told they will get all "necessary" treatment, but they are not told that "medical necessity" is based on the managed care company's own changeable and, at times, arbitrary standards. People never really know until they are ill whether their care will be covered (leading me to think that all managed care companies should be named *MaybeCare*). Some patients are forced to fight for treatment when they should be focusing on getting well.

What of the special vulnerability of mental health consumers? As reported by psychiatrist Lawrence Sack (1996), an insurance executive once told a group of psychiatrists: "We will cut your patients' benefits the most because your patients will complain far less effectively than other patient groups, and we can get away with it." Mental health patients, often too humiliated, depressed, anxious, or disorganized to fight for treatment or to protest publicly, are managed care's perfect victims. To knowingly limit or withhold treatment according to an assessment of a patient populations' perceived weakness is the epitome of unethical behavior.

Putting Money First

Managed care is also immoral because it is exploitative. When Ron Fox, past president of the American Psychological Association (APA), suggested to a managed care executive that a government plan might some day end managed care's windfall, the executive replied (paraphrased by Dr. Fox): "The goose has laid another golden egg that the government may take away before too long, so we intend to get our share while we can" (R. Fox, personal communication, 1992).

Despite managed care's rhetoric about the economic logic of prevention, profitability can only be achieved by skimping on care in the short run. Indeed, because a significant percentage of subscribers leave their plans each year (e.g., approximately 23% of HMO enrollees left their plan in 1996 ["America's Top HMOs," 1997]), it is easy to apprehend from a business perspective that spending on prevention now will only benefit some other insurer later. Lawsuits and fines for violating regulations are considered by some managed care companies as business risks, which are factored into profit equations. The very structure of managed care, in which treatment is considered "medical loss" (see Anders, 1996, p. 62)— that is, a "financial loss"—to the insurer, and the insurer decides whether and what treatment is necessary, is a system that encourages and indeed requires undertreatment. There is a very serious conflict of interest when insurers make treatment decisions and then get to keep whatever money is not spent on treatment. Although the fee-for-service (FFS) system did provide some incentives for overtreatment, the incentive for undertreatment in systems like managed care—which control patients, clinicians, and treatment—is far more dangerous for patients than incentives for overtreatment in a system that allows patients the freedom to make treatment decisions with their chosen clinicians.

The Ethics of Business and Industry

I am not condemning all business as immoral and unethical. However, the ethics of business, in which the activity of commerce and the accumulation of money are primary, can and often do lead to decisions, procedures, language, values, and goals that are at odds with professional therapeutic ethics, in which the patient is primary. Economist Milton Friedman (1988) said that to believe that corporate officials have a "social responsibility" beyond the interests of stockholders shows a "fundamental misconception of the character and nature of a free economy" (p. 349). The only social responsibility of business, he said, is to use its resources to increase profits, as long as competition is open and free, without deception or fraud. To expect managed care companies to include social responsibility toward quality of care or patients as part of their inherent business concerns would be folly.

Albert Carr (1988), an ethicist who has written on business ethics, compares the ethics of business to that of poker, equating deception by executives with poker's "bluff." Carr stated, "By conscious mis-statements, concealment of pertinent facts, or exaggeration—in short, by bluffing— they [executives] seek to persuade others to agree with them" (p. 69). He said that if executives feel obligated to tell the whole truth all of the time—that is, refuse to bluff sometimes, ignoring lawful opportunities— they will be at a great disadvantage in business. Carr (1988) also wrote:

> Cunning deception and concealment of one's strength and intentions, not kindness and openheartedness, are vital in poker. No one thinks any the worse of poker on that account. And no one should think any the worse of the game of business because its standards of right and wrong differ from the prevailing traditions of morality in our society. (p. 70)

According to Carr (1988), if the law allows one to "make a killing," he or she would "be a fool not to take advantage of it. . . . There's no obligation on him to stop and consider who is going to get hurt" (p. 70).

Carr (1988) noted that a business will change its practices if the laws change or if public opinion becomes "clamorous." Otherwise, he said, "as long as a company stays within the law, it has the legal right to shape its strategy without reference to anything but its profits" (p. 71). I now provide three examples of business concepts which, when applied in a purely material, product-oriented business might certainly be ethically unobjectionable but, when applied to human beings become ethical violations.

Acceptable Losses

Those operating from a business model will likely make very different decisions than those operating from a professional model as they try to solve ethical dilemmas. Fromm (1964) wrote that industrialization leads us to treat people as numbers. We become interested in people as objects, in their common properties, in the statistical rules of mass behavior, not in living individuals (Fromm, 1964, p. 57). Fromm (1964) also wrote that "in giant centers of production . . . men are administered as if they were things" (p. 57). Steve Salerno (1994), criticizing managed care practices, wrote in *The Wall Street Journal* that managed care saw no need for routine mammograms for women under age 50. The few women under 50 whose cancers could be found by such tests become "acceptable losses" in a system designed for broad-based cost containment. Salerno pointed toward the American Cancer Society's Walter Lawrence, who indicated that the problem is a culture in which every decision is assessed in terms of statistics, probabilities, and dollars (p. A16). Certainly, if these were, say, aging cars, this method of assessment would not present an ethical problem; but consider the human corollary of when a 45-year-old mother of three dies from breast cancer because her insurer did not provide for yearly mammograms. There is no "equation" in human costs that can account for the pain and suffering due to this decision.

Avoidance of High Cost

In a product-oriented business, it is perfectly understandable for a business to try to avoid high costs. Julian Simon (1995), the professor of business administration who suggested that airlines resolve overbookings through incentives that would make it worth an overbooked passenger's while to give up his or her seat, wrote of his concern that Medicare HMOs might avoid high-cost patients. Simon's business experience brings him to a solution for health care that I find chilling. Simon (1995) wrote that "the only way to keep HMO's from rejecting the high-cost 'lemons' is the true market method of making the lemons worthwhile by auctioning them off to the lowest-bidding supplier" (p. A14). An AIDs patient, for example, would be described at auction. The lowest bidding insurer would get the patient and the bidded amount from the government. "Every insuree," he said, would get covered "because there is some price at which every insuree would be profitable for some company" (p. A14). Simon believed this system would work well for both Medicare and Medicaid, for the auction scheme "works on the principle that at some price even the rottenest fruit is worth picking" (p. A14). However, as with the example indicated above, to equate, say, an overripe tomato with a son dying of AIDS is an ethical grotesquerie. So, although Simon's logic seems sound from an economic standpoint, his language and idea reflect an industrialist's lack of understanding of the human consequences of these decisions.

"Gag Clauses"

As another example, consider the different perspectives of therapist and business ethics on the issue of provider contract gag clauses, technically called *nondisparagement* clauses, which prohibit clinicians from saying anything negative about the managed care companies to anyone, even prohibiting them from discussing treatment options with patients for which the managed care companies do not wish to pay. *The San Francisco Chronicle* (Russell, 1996) quoted Beau Carter, the Executive Director of the Integrated Health Care Association, in a defense of gag clauses: "It is not inappropriate for someone in a contractual relationship to say I don't want you bad-mouthing the contractor to a patient" (p. A17). From a practical, business-oriented point of view, this makes perfect sense. However, from a humanistic, caring, and patient-centered point of view, this is dangerous, cruel, and oppressive. Policies based on Carter's rationalization mean that clinicians may not be able to follow their professional or their personal ethics and morality.

Luckily, public clamor has forced regulators to end extremely dangerous medical practices like "drive through deliveries," and there is a growing clamor to outlaw managed care companies' gag clauses. Unfortunately, we cannot rely on public clamor to legislate proper and sufficient mental health care.

The Ethics of Business, Competition, and Industrialization Versus The Ethics of Mental Health Professionals

As can be seen from the few examples indicated previously, I question the morality of applying the values and principles of business, corporate competition, and industrialization to mental health care. As we have seen, there are a number of effects of what Fromm (1955) would identify as the type of industrialization that reduces a person to "an abstraction, whose essence can be expressed in a figure" (p. 108). It seems to me and many others that the industrialization of health care is hurtful to the spirit and well-being of many patients and clinicians.

The industrialization of health care brings to mind Erich Fromm's (1941/1969) description of the transition from medieval artisan craftsmanship to twentieth-century industrial capitalism. According to Fromm, the personal concern and accountability that constituted the ethical practice of the artisan, who worked directly for an individual customer, was eventually lost to huge, impersonal organizations. Eventually, monopolies developed that exploited customers and workers, and governments were unable to effectively regulate them. The owners were too distant from workers and consumers to be concerned with either as real people. Economic expediency settled all financial decisions (Fromm, 1941/1969). A competitive character structure developed and a corporate attitude of bureaucratization, abstractification, and quantification (Fromm, 1955) led to relationships of manipulation and instrumentality (Fromm, 1941/1969). As I see it, the industrialization of health care reflects the same changes.

Patients and clinicians have become commodities to be bought and sold, which denies them dignity as individuals. Profits are valued over human welfare, and the product has to do with moving people along an assembly line of care as quickly as possible, without regard to their individuality or their human needs and feelings, as if they were bottles moving along a conveyor belt. Patients and clinicians are seen as "interchangeable parts," to be put together or torn apart on the basis of the financial needs of the managed care company. Given that competition and executives with a "competitive character" drive managed mental health care, is it any wonder that connection, patience, and subjectivity are demeaned and devalued?

We cannot be naive. Rousseau and Hume believed that compassion and "fellow-feeling" are the "basis of all morality and the emotional glue that holds society and, ultimately, all humanity together," but that these sentiments could be destroyed by the "corruption" of a competitive society (Solomon, 1993, p. 133). These sentiments and ideals are what the mental health care profession has traditionally been about. Introducing the values of capitalism, competition, and industrialization into the therapeutic relationship has already caused great changes and threatens to produce even worse ones if the usual practice of mental health care is allowed to follow the industrialized path. Although there are certainly others, I outline below three critical therapeutic areas that I believe are being corrupted by the industrialization and corporatization of mental health care and the valuing of competition. These elements are our quality of care, the empathy we have for our patients, and the integrity of our language.

Quality of Care

Managed care threatens to destroy the quality of care and the excellence of the professions. Managed care, coupled with an employer-based system of insurance and strong competition, brings a search by the employer for the cheapest plan and a search by the insurer for the least possible treatment provided by the "cheapest labor" possible. Employers are often more concerned with cost than quality (Lau, 1995). Only 20% of managed care companies studied by Foster-Higgins rated quality improvement as one of the factors most important to their commercial success (Meier, 1994). Also troubling, a Rand Corporation/UCLA study found that only 23% of 100 capitated physician-owned managed care companies ranked "quality of care" as their most important concern ("Physician-Led MCOs," 1996).

The industry has created a topsy-turvy world in which the most compliant, naive, narrowly focused, and cheapest clinician is considered the "best." The more training one gets, the more useless one becomes in a system that values "cheap labor." In psychotherapy, having a doctorate is now a liability. Some hospitals and health plans are even replacing master's level therapists with bachelor's level "associate counselors" (P. Gumpert, personal communication, 1996; Sleek, 1995). Managed care increasingly has shown that it does not wish to use clinicians who do comprehensive psychotherapy. One therapist, who wished to remain anonymous, wrote in a letter to the National Coalition of Mental Health Professionals and Consumers that an HMO said it would no longer refer patients to him because he was "doing too good a job," that he was curing patients instead of ameliorating the crisis, and because only "crisis" was covered under their plan, they considered him "inept." This absurd definition of quality, if allowed to continue, can only undermine the profession's legitimate standards of quality.

Even some of our professional associations' leaders show signs of having been overwhelmed by the all-encompassing presence of managed care. Tim Schnabel (1995) attended a conference on managed care sponsored by the Georgia Association for Marriage and Family Therapy (GAMFT) and described the meeting in an article he wrote for the Georgia association's newsletter. He described a panel, which included representatives of a few managed care companies in the area, chaired by a past president of GAMFT. After listening to the managed care company's representatives, a family therapist asked, "How am I supposed to cure a highly dysfunctional family of five with a schizophrenic mother in 10 to 20 sessions?" Schnabel reported that the GAMFT past president gave a "swift and firm" response: "Get that word [cure] out of your vocabulary. You will not be *curing* anybody anymore. You will be *managing* schizophrenia, *managing* dysfunction or *managing* depression [italics mine]." It can become impossible to give our patients the treatment we know will heal them when others control what constitutes "quality of care."

The Loss of Empathy

I have seen how the industrialization in health care destroys empathy, personal caring, and the dignity of individuals. Managed care companies and the business ethics they bring to mental health care abstractify and objectify both patients and clinicians, destroying the spirit of those who value connection, caring, compassion, the uniqueness of each individual, and respect for human dignity. It dehumanizes what should remain a human service. The result is massive demoralization, depression, and despair felt by large numbers of clinicians and consumers alike.

Many clinicians who must now "market themselves" to managed care companies feel forced into an alien and unwanted "marketing orientation" (Fromm, 1955), in which the sense of self stems not from being a "loving and thinking individual, but from a socio-economic role" (Fromm, 1955, p. 129).

Being forced into a market-driven environment has been devastating for many caring clinicians. How can we tolerate the abstractification, bureaucratization, objectification, and quantification of human beings when our nature tends toward relatedness and caring for individuals? The corporate culture and the mind-set it creates add a new, calculated profit–loss business ethic into our relationships with our clients, which have left many of us depressed and demoralized, threatening to change our relationship with our patients and interfering with our natural desire to be empathetic.

The fierce competition in health care contributes to the loss of empathy. Erich Fromm (1941/1969) wrote that "the relationship between competitors has to be based on mutual human indifference" (p. 139). Otherwise, he said, competitors would be "paralyzed in the fulfillment of the economic tasks" (p. 139), which are "to fight each other and not to refrain from the actual economic destruction of each other if necessary" (p. 139). We have all seen in the business world how competition can lead to greed, cheating, lying, cutting corners, the desire to "win," and a lack of concern for others. This business ethic threatens to destroy the creation of an empathic relationship with our patients. Within a managed care environment, extreme pressure is placed on therapists to shift their primary focus from quality of care and people to concerns over money. Corporate competition is leading capitation rates to be based on the ideal premium, not on the costs of proper care. It has created a "survival" mentality in which too many clinicians may be willing to do things they would not have done before in order to survive.

The Insidious Changes to Language

Those familiar with George Orwell's *1984* (1949/1981) will understand the importance that language has in creating a new morality. In this novel, The Party controlled society, in part, by creating the language "Newspeak," which had the effect of narrowing the range of human thought, which in turn lessens the likelihood of rebellion.

In today's managed care environment, we see the same insidious "relabeling" of functions and human relationships. Necessity of care in mental health is determined by "impairments in functioning" and treatment is called *behavioral health care*. These terms' ultimate effect reduces the reality of the suffering of patients by avoiding an awareness of the patient's internal emotional pain, life circumstances, and history. We are to provide intermittent "episodes" of treatment that focus on the obvious problem or crisis at hand, lest we see the whole person in the context of his or her whole life and understand how much really needs to be done.

Today, we begin to forget that "covered lives" are people. Managed care prefers to conceptualize "populations" rather than individuals. When we have personal one-on-one relationships with patients, it is not acceptable to lose even one needlessly. However, if one considers thousands or millions of "enrollees" whom one never sees up close, it apparently does not seem so bad to "lose a few" in order to cut costs.

As for therapists, we have been given the name *provider*. This term strips clinicians of professional identity, negates the concept of having specialized training, and implies a sense of interchangeability. At best, it is a sterile, industrial word that does not imply a human or professional quality, as do the perfectly good words *professional*, *clinician*, and *practitioner*, which we have used for at least a century. The industry's preference for the word *provider* is a manifestation of the industry's lack of human relatedness and its lack of concern with individuality and identity.

The fact that the word *provider* is now so ubiquitous is indicative of the power of the industry—of its ability to take control over our thinking and our language, as well as our work. As some African Americans have changed their last names to African names because they considered their American surnames to be their "slave name," given to them by their oppressors, so I refuse to use the word *provider* in that it was imposed upon us by people who seek to take control over us and force compliance through coercion and intimidation. I will not use the word *provider* because I will not allow the industry to oppress me.[1]

Managed care companies' industrialized language also helps to mask its destructive nature, and we should be careful of the all-too-easy adoption of this language, for it has large consequences for how we conceptualize our patients, ourselves, and our profession.

The Free-Market Fallacy

However, for those outside our profession, these losses noted earlier might not seem sufficient to give up what they would consider to be the ultimate benefits of free-market economies. Here, I must digress a bit to challenge the labeling of the current system of managed care as a free market. Certainly, we have all witnessed the follies and destruction of controlled economies as wide-ranging as North Korea and Russia. Indeed, I freely admit to and support the benefits of largely free-market economies.

---

[1]Although control over clinicians by managed care does not involve the ownership of workers, nor the physical and emotional abuse experienced by American slaves, the analogy holds to the extent that clinicians have been "renamed" against their will and many feel forced to work for managed care—a controlling, powerful industry they do not respect and from which they desire freedom and independence.

However, I question the logic of calling managed care and managed competition the "free-market solution" for two reasons. First, a free market depends on the ability of those who actually use goods and services to decide upon their necessity and value. Under managed care and managed competition, the users of health care are still the patients, but they are no longer the "buyers" of services. Nor are clinicians any longer the "sellers." Under managed care and managed competition, the insurers sell a "product," called a *health plan*, to employers, who are now the buyers of services. The free-market fallacy of managed care is that neither patients nor clinicians—the ones who literally use and provide care—have direct access to a market—which is the essence of a free marketplace.

Second, a free market depends upon the law of supply and demand. However, the mental health care industry currently controls supply by deciding how much of what treatments shall be available and who shall provide them. It also controls demand by deciding who needs how much of what treatment. To call the current system of managed care a "free market" is not only misleading, it is absurd.

Whose Ethics, Morals, and Values Should We Use, Anyway?

I now return to the central question of which ethical system should underlie mental health care. Kassirer (1995) wrote that "whether health care should be subjected to the values of the marketplace is a fundamental question facing us today" (p. 50). After all, the primary purpose of a business is to make money, whereas the purpose of a professional practice is, first and foremost, to take care of people.

Professional ethics traditionally put the patient's needs first. When independent, caring clinicians feel conflicted between the patient's needs and their own, their personal and professional morality makes them struggle to put the patient first. In a democratic system, patients able to contract directly with independent clinicians can easily replace a clinician they do not trust. The economic power of managed care companies, though, forces patients to use clinicians with whom they may not feel comfortable. Furthermore, the clinicians they may be forced to use may themselves be forced into abiding by the managed care companies' value system and treatment outlines, with which they do not agree. Given the consequences of a business ethic, we must ask the question, Whose values, morality, and ethics should our nation use as the foundation for its health-care system?

In philosophy, there are three main systems of morals and ethics. *Consequentialism* judges acts by their effects. *Utilitarianism*, "the greatest good for the greatest number," is one such theory and is associated with John Stuart Mill and Jeremy Bentham. In the second main system, *deontological ethics*, acts are judged by analyzing formal properties of the action, such as duty, justice, and reason, but not by the act's consequences. Immanuel Kant, a deontologist, is often considered to be responsible for a focus on morality in ethics, but his ethical decision making is technical, relying on reason and duty to the exclusion of compassion and other emotions. Kant dismisses emotion as insignificant in ethical decision making (Solomon, 1993). The third school of moral and ethical thinking, known as *virtue ethics*, is associated with Plato, Aristotle, Hume, Rousseau, Fromm, and several feminist theorists. Virtue ethics reintroduces emotion and personal relationship into ethical and moral decision making (Solomon, 1993).

Garrett et al. (1993), virtue ethicists, suggested that right and wrong be judged by how our acts affect the "development of the individual person living in a community and a society" (p. 5). Morality is not based upon adherence to the right principles, but upon sympathy, compassion, and concern for the freedom and dignity of individuals in society. What makes us moral is, first, our personal concern for those closest to us and, second, our concern for people we have never met and for humanity in general (Solomon, 1993).

Many feminist authors (see Gilligan, 1982; Noddings, 1984) have also added another element to the debate on which type of ethics should predominate. These authors emphasize that the discussion of ethics has historically been dominated by men presenting a male ethic of rational principles as if it were the whole of ethics (Solomon, 1993). Carol Gilligan (1982) critiqued Lawrence Kohlberg for basing his description of moral development on interviews with men and generalizing the results to "people." Kohlberg's (see Kohlberg & Kramer, 1969) work led to the conclusion that girls and women get "stuck" at what he considered a midlevel "Stage 3" because their moral decisions are based on being a "good person" and on a concern with the hurt their decisions would cause others, rather than on reason and principle.

Gilligan (1982) argued that women's moral development is simply different than that of men. Other feminists would argue that an ethic based on caring, relationship, and compassion is superior to ethics that value reason and principle over emotions like compassion and caring. I believe most male and female psychotherapists, and many men and women in other health-care fields, would deem it important to value the emotions at least as much as reason and principle, if not more so, when making moral and ethical decisions.

An Ethic of Caring

So, in this morass of a debate over the ethics of business and its effect on mental health care, which set of ethics should we use? Nel Noddings (1984) offered a feminist "Ethic of Caring." The heart of this ethic is relatedness, our "human affective response," our caring, and our commitment to sustain caring.

Noddings (1984) stated that the ethics of principle and moral reasoning is framed in the "language of the father," the "detached one" (p. 2). The "mother's voice" in ethics would focus on human caring and the memory of caring and being cared for, which, Noddings argued, forms the foundation of ethical response. This mother's voice and an ethic of caring can, of course, spring from both men and women.

Ethical caring arises out of natural caring—that is, that relation in which we respond as "one-caring" out of love or natural inclination. Natural caring is the human condition that we perceive as "good," Noddings (1984) said, "toward which we long and strive, and it is our longing for caring—to be in that special relation—that provides the motivation for us to be moral. We want to be *moral* in order to remain in the caring relation and to enhance the ideal of ourselves as one-caring" (p. 5). Rooted in relation, joy is seen as the basic human affect. Joy results from seeing our caring being received and fulfilled in the other. Joy enhances our commitment to the ethical ideal and sustains us as one-caring. Also, hopefully, the feeling of being cared for renews in the other his or her own commitment to act similarly toward others (Noddings, 1984).

Those who favor logic and principle approach moral and ethical questions through detachment from the actual people involved—that is, through an abstracting process. Those who value caring over reason, said Noddings (1984), approach moral questions by concretizing situations. As an example, caring is easy when we know and like those needing help. However, when they are strangers to us, we want to see their faces, look into their eyes, and understand the whole situation if possible, rather than resort to logic and abstraction. Under a system of ethics based on caring, if direct contact is not possible, we try to bring the people close by imagining them as real, concrete people, trying to apprehend their reality and feelings. We try to feel what we would decide if the person in need were us instead of them; if it were our child, our mate, our sister, our father, instead of theirs. We become "engrossed" with them and relate to them through a vision of our most ethical self, which involves our own best memories and visions of caring and being cared for. We feel a commitment to being caring and to sustain our caring attitude. We care about our ethical self and feel good about ourselves if we live up to our ethical ideal (Noddings, 1984).

An ethic of caring does not mean an abandonment of reason or objectivity, however. These are necessary and critical tools for human thought. Noddings (1984) warned, though, that we must keep our objective thinking tied to relationship, lest we "climb into clouds of abstraction." She stated, "If I do not turn away from abstractions, I lose the one cared-for. Indeed, I lose myself as one-caring, for I now care about a problem instead of a person" (p. 36).

The Results of the Abstracting Ethics of Business

This brings us to the central core of the problems with communications between therapists and managed care companies. Whereas most therapists rely on an ethics based on relationships and caring, business relies on logic and abstractions. To provide an illustration, when therapists in California questioned a managed care executive about the impact of managed care on their patients as individuals, the executive replied, "Managed care does not deal with individuals. It deals with populations" (R. Clifford, personal communication, February 1996). How can we hope to win arguments about our patients when we must appeal to people whose natural tendencies are to distance and abstractify individuals?

A father told me it took his two young boys quite some time to trust their therapist. Then his insurance at work was changed to managed care, and the managed care company refused to allow the therapist into the network, despite the father's persistent protests. Finally, the father, a streetwise man, called the management office, two or three states away, saying he was going to drive there and bring poster-size pictures of his children so they could "see" who they were hurting. The managed care company responded by promptly moving the father's account to an office 1,500 miles further away. He called again, saying he had a friend who owned his own plane and that he was now going to fly to this new office, this time bringing his children. The managed care company then allowed the therapist into the network. This father was trying to make his children concrete human beings to an organization that was too distant and lacking in relatedness and compassion to care about his sons as real people. However, what happens to those who are less assertive than this father? What happens to those who are too depressed, anxious, frightened, defeated, or impaired to advocate as did this man?

If we allow ourselves to begin thinking about building a health-care system based on an ethic of caring, we might well ask "How do we judge right and wrong under an ethic of caring?" I believe that to want to avoid needless pain and to treat others as we would ourselves or our loved ones is the ethic upon which we should build our mental health care system, indeed, our entire health-care system. Those in positions of caretaking and authority should be people who live by the morals and ethics of caring. Managed care businesses do not.

Can Business Ethics Ever Correlate With Mental Health Care Needs?

Nel Noddings (1984) said that organizations tend to diminish the ethical ideal. Noddings argued that institutions themselves cannot be moral—only individuals can be moral and ethical because only individuals can care, can bring distant people close, and can imagine their pain. Noddings warned that institutions too easily fall into abstract problem solving, shifting from the person to the "problem." Institutional decision makers may lack the necessary degree of physical and emotional closeness to and engrossment in the patient that an individual clinician would have. They may focus on satisfying formulated requirements for caretaking, abstractifying, and categorizing people and exercising strategies upon groups of them.

Does this not describe managed care? Industrialized mental health care has developed a simplistic, superficial, and overly objective treatment model that fits arbitrary statistical norms but that does not fit the needs of many real people, for it neglects the needs of the individual's heart, mind, and soul, which inevitably affects what we call "mental health." Real people seeking mental health care depend on something industrialist organizations cannot enter into their equations: feelings, thoughts, hopes, fears, wishes, memories, unconscious processes, dreams, and emotional needs.

The people who come to therapy are *not* the "worried well." They are people in pain, and their pain leads to real problems in our communities, like anger, hatred, troubled parents, troubled marriages, troubled children, problems in school and at work, vandalism, crime, divorce, abused children, and so forth. Real psychotherapy, especially the more intensive and comprehensive forms of therapy that attend to the whole human being, must be crafted by highly trained artisans, grounded in a variety of sciences, who appreciate each individual's uniqueness and see the need for each of our citizens to be as emotionally and physically healthy as possible.

Health "care" is the purview of the professions. Do not confuse this with health "services," which is managed care's product, performed by providers, many of whom feel forced into a corporate efficiency that—because of its business ethics—has little or no incentive to be concerned with human life, individuality, or dignity and that has little structural capacity to show empathy, caring, or patience. Real, live human beings, both patients and clinicians, are being hurt in spirit, mind, and body. The values and ethics of business and industry are inimical to quality health care, to caring for the individual, and to human dignity. Industrialists and business people are not the right people to be running health care.

To understand how the ethics of managed care can oppose, to the extreme, the ethics and values of individuals within our profession, I offer as an example a feminist, Laura Brown. In 1994, Brown stated that in managed care, nonfeminist values and theories constantly intrude into the therapist–client relationship. She stated that feminist therapy involves liberation from oppression, a growth in relationship, and an empowerment of both client and therapist. "How will it be possible," Brown (1994) asked, "to be ethical and feminist in a service delivery context in which decisions are made by neither therapist nor client, but by an anonymous, corporate third party interested in profits and the bottom line?" (p. 226).

I answer, "It is not possible." One cannot practice feminist or any therapy that values a patient's free will and a safe, private, trusting therapeutic relationship and also be a part of managed care.

Rejecting the Ethics, Morals, and Values of Managed Care and Managed Competition

How easily people accept the idea that "managed care is here to stay." This phrase is propaganda used to intimidate us into acceptance of managed care. Nothing is necessarily "here to stay." Once thought indestructible institutions in their day, the Holy Roman Empire fell, slavery in the United States ended, Hitler was defeated, and Communism has waned.

Could it really be that managed care is more powerful than those forces? The truth is that managed care is here now. It will only be here to stay if we all become helpless and refuse to think, create, and act.

So many psychologists and other clinicians believe they must "adapt," even if they deplore managed care. Even many leaders in our professional associations have recommended that we adapt and see managed care as an opportunity. Yet, a large number of us have experienced managed care as dehumanizing, oppressive, demoralizing, demeaning, immoral, and destructive. Who are we if we adapt to something we believe is wrong and hurtful?

We Can Reject Managed Care's Adoption of Paternalism Due To Scarce Resources

Garrett et al. (1993), commenting on health-care ethics, observed that as resources become scarce, societies may downgrade the dignity of the sick, elderly, poor, and powerless. Without compassion, they say, we might help others as if we were dealing with blocks of wood to be moved around. Arrogance might lead us to paternalism and domineering behavior, even as we pretend to help others. A strong paternalism involves the usurpation—the coercive seizure—of a competent patient's right to make decisions, and those who justify that paternalism in health care, they write, act as if there were only one correct decision in every case.

We Can Reject the Adoption of Managed Care's "Ethos of Selfishness"

In addition to this sense of paternalism, we must also avoid what Michael Lerner (1995), psychologist and publisher of *Tikkun Magazine*, calls our society's "Ethos of Selfishness," in which the goal of work is to maximize money and power. Lerner sees managed care, with its seven-digit executive incomes and its bottom-line focus, as part of this ethos. I have talked with colleagues who reported having patients who committed suicide after their treatment was withheld by managed care companies. Patients' mental health needs are not being met as well as therapists, unfettered by arbitrary time limitations, could meet them. Because it's cheaper to provide medication than talk therapy, mental health patients are increasingly being pushed onto medication while psychotherapy is being abbreviated (Berner, 1995; Pollock, 1995) and are being denied the care they truly need. Under the limits and values of managed mental health care, we will not be able to solve our society's problems with homelessness, crime, violence, substance abuse, teen pregnancy, child abuse, or the problem of troubled adults forming troubled relationships and raising another generation of troubled children.

Under the competitive, industrial model, the "fittest" therapists may be those who either see people in a more detached and mechanical way or who can, without guilt, exploit and undertreat patients and ignore their needs for privacy. The clinicians who survive may be those who manifest what Fromm (1947) called a "marketing orientation." For clinicians with this orientation, personal success will depend not on their relationships with patients and the quality of their work but on the salability of their packaging. To survive in the "new marketplace," therapists are told they must become fierce competitors, though this may be contrary to the nature of those who place relationship and caring as their highest value.

How odd and absurd that the qualities that make us excellent therapists will now make us unsuccessful, yet those qualities that would make us thrive in this environment are qualities that can be hurtful to our patients and to ourselves.

We Can Reject Managed Care's Destruction of the Joy and Purpose of Our Work

Consumers of health care value relatedness with their clinicians, and vice versa. Managed care, though, demands broken relationships and brief encounters. Managed care has interfered with the joy many of us clinicians have found in our work. We want the joy of relatedness, the joy of the giving and caring, and the joy of seeing our caring received. We want the joy of seeing people's lives change because we made them feel listened to, understood, and cared about, and because we helped them listen to and care about themselves until they were able to understand and do what was necessary to change their lives. Most of us do not want to go into program development, or to become entrepreneurs, or to relate to a "population," or to undertreat patients and move on quickly to the next case. We want connection. We want to be engrossed with one person or one family at a time. We cannot rid ourselves of these very human desires—nor should we.

We Can Reject Managed Care's Breaking of Relatedness With Patients

The leadership in Huxley's (1932/1969) *Brave New World* tried to create a perfectly efficient, bureaucratized, and industrialized society. They tried to break the need for connection. People did not have parents. They were conceived in dishes, "incubated," and the embryos were "decanted" in bottles until they were "hatched," after developing according to particular predetermined standards. Relationships were to be brief and people were only to use each other, lest they form attachments. People were made to feel ashamed of their longings for connection and meaningful relationship. The desire for connection and the pain of its loss, as well as feelings of discontent or rebellion, were dulled by a societywide dependency on the drug "soma." Those who refused soma, who wanted to feel their human feelings and strive toward connectedness and self-determination, were banished to remote islands.

Managed care wants us to ignore feelings, memories, and emotions

and medicate them instead of heal them. They want us to break our relatedness to patients and to serve the managed care company instead.
Indeed, Michael Jeffrey of the former American PsychManagement (now
Value Behavioral Health), told therapists ("Psychotherapy Finances' Managed," 1993) "We are looking for providers who see their role as preserving
the benefit plan" (p. 1).

Let me state clearly, I will not serve benefit plans instead of people,
and our professions should protect their students from having to be
"trained for the marketplace." We should resist being ruled by people who
do not understand that to weaken our sense of relatedness with our patients and the joy of helping compromises both us as therapists and our
patients, and even, I would submit, undermines the health of society as a
whole. We do not have to accept this industrial lack of relatedness as the
norm.

The corporate industrial model threatens to remove meaning from our
work. We must resist becoming cogs in someone else's wheel, a wheel that
turns too quickly for us to provide proper care and consideration for our
patients. We cannot close our eyes to their pain, nor will we ignore our
own demoralization. We can reject this model of industrialization.

The Wrongful Exercise of Power:
The Totalitarian Nature of Managed Care

I have thus far looked at managed care in a way that focuses on individual
patients, individual therapists, and the relation between the two. I now
broaden my focus to look at managed care within the broader context of
the form and use of power. In my opinion, managed care is a system of
corporate dictatorship. Any dictatorship is immoral, but it is especially so
in a democratic society. I now compare the characteristics of managed care
to economic and moral systems that developed within totalitarian regimes
by focusing on the strikingly similar strategies by which both systems
have gained, and have remained, in power.

Although various totalitarian regimes have been established in the
twentieth century—each with its own unique characteristics, depending
on the country and the time of history—there are certain characteristics
that have been common to all. Here I discuss some of these common qualities and some disturbing parallels I have found in the way in which managed care has grown and is developing.

In the past, when I have compared the power strategies of the managed care industry to those of totalitarian regimes, the reactions have run
the gamut from people who ardently agree to people who angrily tell me
that I am trivializing people like Hitler and the horrors of the Holocaust
and other dictatorships. Because of my personal experiences as a woman
and a Jew, I have studied issues of power. Being a psychoanalyst, too, I
focus on characterological qualities that underlie behavior, wondering
what makes someone a person who can feel fine about controlling others
and even hurting people while doing so. Authoritarian behavior and char-

acter can be seen in individuals within families, in the workplace, in education, in government, in bureaucracies, in all forms of institutional politics, and so forth. We need to know whether or not we are seeing it in managed care organizations and in those who lead them, for the power of managed care executives and companies plays a very big role in health care today. We need to know whether we can make managed care a fair, pro-patient system or whether we must create a different system in order to protect patients and professional training and practice. Certainly, managed care has not brought the death and destruction wrought by political dictators. However, most Americans no longer have control over decisions that seriously affect their medical and mental health and in all too many cases, their lives.

I have discussed these comparisons at length elsewhere (Shore, 1995a, 1995b, 1995c, 1995d), and those who are interested in a more complete discussion of this analogy than I am able to provide in this space should refer to those documents. In the following I provide a summary of eight similarities between the strategies of totalitarian regimes and the strategies of managed care companies.

Economic Chaos and Control

First, totalitarian regimes arise from economic and political chaos when a charismatic leader or group claims to have the solution to the nation's problem. Certainly, the chaos we have seen as a result of rising health costs has given managed care the economic window of opportunity to come into power and control that one seventh of our economy that represents health-care spending.

Ways of Gaining Power

Second, like totalitarian forces, managed care companies have gained power through a variety of means: some legal, some using undue influence, scapegoating, and propaganda. Just to take *propaganda* as an example, managed care's promises involve "high quality at low cost." Their literature to beneficiaries and employers promises that patients will receive all "medically necessary" treatment, and their advertisements make us believe we will enter a world in which we will be fully cared for by the company. The reality, though, may be quite different. Many managed mental health plans will not cover treatment for "chronic or ongoing" mental health problems. For example, a letter in my files from an HMO in central New York State to participating mental health clinicians reads, in regard to outpatient benefits: "Our goal is to treat the acute phase of the illness, not the ongoing chronic or supportive phase" (letter dated March 1994). A similar letter in my files from a plan in California states the following: "One thing all benefit plans have in common is: Coverage is restricted to conditions subject to improvement through short term therapy" (letter dated April 13, 1994, from Individual Practice Associations, San Bruno,

CA, to "Dear Mental Health Provider"). Managed care scapegoats clinicians by painting them as greedy, psychodynamic therapy by calling it wasteful, and psychotherapy patients by calling them the "worried well" or invoking the "Woody Allen image."

Bureaucracies

Third, both systems are characterized by vast, controlling, and hierarchical bureaucracies. Those patients and clinicians who have worked with a managed care company know first hand the labyrinthine rules, regulations, and paperwork needed to conform to the managed care system. There are rules for obtaining permission to begin treatment and rules for permission to continue treatment after the approved number of sessions has been used. When treatment is denied, there are often two or three levels of appeals to go through to try to obtain permission to continue treatment. Some clinicians now have "provider manuals" from as many as 20 managed care companies, each describing their own treatment guidelines and bureaucratic procedures.

Ideology of Conquest

Fourth, both managed care companies and totalitarian regimes have a central value of an ideology of conquest. Such ideologies consider it a natural right of stronger entities to conquer weaker ones. In this health-care marketplace of mergers and acquisitions, it is natural that large, strong corporations will take over clinicians' practices and smaller corporations. Furthermore, some managed care companies also manifest expansionist goals. For example, United HealthCare Corporation of Minneapolis was reported to be joining with two South African companies to bring South Africa its first managed care plan ("South Africa to Be Offered," 1995). By becoming worldwide entities, managed care's expansion abroad brings the possibility of the industry having unfathomable sums of money and unimaginable influence in both national and international politics.

Suppression of Opposition

Fifth, both totalitarianism and managed care systems promulgate a specific ideology while attempting to suppress opposition. Often, statements are made that the system's ideology is what is best for those who are subjected to it. For instance, the managed care industry lobbies against all alternatives to managed care. It also claims that short-term, problem-solving therapy is "best." For instance, *Business Insurance Magazine* (Schachner, 1994) quoted my statement that managed care treatment is not the same as psychotherapy. In response to my statement, Alan Savitz, former medical director of Human Affairs International (HAI), responded by saying that my "accusation that managed care is not equivalent to psychotherapy may be true, but it's in the best interest of patients" (Schachner, 1994, p. 36).

There are several techniques that managed care companies have used to suppress opposition. For example, clinicians who do not believe that the brief therapies are the best may be driven from the insurance market or intimidated into silent compliance.

Use of methodologically questionable studies. Efficacy studies are often misused by managed care to declare the brief therapies are "best" for particular diagnoses. However, a recent review (I. J. Miller, 1996) found that much of the research favoring time-limited therapy did not actually measure what it was said to measure. Other studies were found to be duplicate publications rather than original studies. Still other studies misreported their results in the direction opposite to the actual results. Correctly classified, the actual research showed that clinically determined treatment is superior to time-limited therapy. The good results for brief therapy obtained by meta-analyses of therapy seemed to be best explained by the fact that the studies measured variables that change easily and studied patients with less severe problems than patients researched in long-term therapy studies. Furthermore, Miller found that reviews of research indicate that increasing the length of therapy generally increases the benefit of treatment.

In addition, a *Consumer Reports* study ("Mental Health: Does Therapy Help," 1995) provided the most recent validation of long-term therapy's effectiveness. This led the study's consultant, Martin Seligman (1995), to question efficacy studies themselves as appropriate determinants of psychotherapy outcomes. To fail to discuss the limits of research is unethical. To profit by using such questionable methodologies to justify the systematic denial of needed therapy is immoral.

Use of intimidation. Knowing they cannot naturally have the loyalty of clinicians who feel forced to work for them, managed care companies suppress opposition through fear, economic threats, and sometimes even in contracts with gag clauses. (Fortunately, such gag clause restrictions in some areas are now being outlawed.)

We must be very sensitive, indeed, to the ways in which the power strategies of managed care can disempower, oppress, and injure innocent people and how managed care has the power to put clinicians out of work if they do not comply with managed care philosophies, guidelines, and mandates or if they speak out in opposition.

Economic intimidation and control over workers was a strategy of many of the totalitarian regimes. According to William Shirer (1959/1981), Hitler's propaganda minister, Joseph Goebbels, set out to subjugate the arts and the professions. "Those who were even lukewarm" about Nazism were usually "excluded from practicing their profession or art and thus deprived of a livelihood" (p. 242). This strategy is also used by the managed care industry to control clinicians' behaviors and decisions, and those who do not comply may be excluded from insurance reimbursement and possibly from practicing their profession altogether.[2]

Alan Savitz, the former medical director of HAI, told an audience of therapists: "If you want to make a living, decide now and change your approach" ("Psychotherapy Finances' Managed," 1993, p. 2). Paying lip service to managed care's short-term philosophy will not be enough, he warned, "If you are faking it, it will come out soon" ("Psychotherapy Finances' Managed," 1993, p. 2). The statement is chilling and brings forth images of the "telescreen" used by the totalitarian regime in George Orwell's *1984* (1949/1981) that allowed the Party to see into people's private homes and see and hear all that the person did and said. Statements or actions against the Party would lead to the person being "vaporized." Many clinicians have told me they were dismissed from panels shortly after they argued with or challenged a managed care company. In areas where patients must rely heavily on managed care, therapists who are not "managed care friendly" may be unable to practice; that is, they may find themselves professionally "vaporized."

Even some patients are afraid to protest lest their insurer retaliate and withdraw authorization for previously approved sessions or deny other needed treatments. One patient told me her managed care company threatened to deny all future psychotherapy benefits if she complained further. When New York State's Assembly held hearings on managed care in January 1994, several clinicians told me that they, their patients, or both were too afraid of retaliation to testify.

Control of Professional Education

Sixth, another characteristic of totalitarian regimes is their desire to control education in order to control current thinking and to quell future questioning of the system. Nick Cummings (1991) warned that the third generation of therapists who came after managed care began will be trained in managed care techniques. Graduate schools are already replacing training in psychodynamic therapy with a focus on brief techniques in order to "prepare students for the marketplace." Tufts Medical School and the Tufts Associated Health Plan created the Tufts Managed Care Institute ("Medical School and Health Plan," 1995) to teach physicians and medical students how to practice in a managed care environment. In another example, an advertisement in *The New York Times* (March 10, 1996) sought applicants for a psychiatric postresidency fellowship that would prepare psychiatrists for leadership roles in mental health care policy and decision

---

[2]By drawing this comparison, I do not mean to imply that the harm and destruction caused by managed care is at all comparable to the horror brought by the Nazis. As a Jew of Eastern European descent, I would not minimize the horror of the Holocaust. However, given my ancestry and having been born and raised just after World War II, when American Jews were freshly reeling from the impact of the Holocaust, I have always been keenly aware of the dangers of political power strategies that can allow one group of people to disempower, oppress, and even kill others. I am comparing the power tactics, not the depth and breadth of destruction.

making in a managed mental health care setting. The fellowship was sponsored by the New Jersey Medical School "in collaboration with" Green Spring Health Services Managed Behavioral Healthcare. Peter Kramer (1995) worried that soon training will fall into the hands of inexperienced clinicians "who have no memory of what it is to be beholden to patients first" (p. 18).

A new report from a committee of the APA (Spruill, Kohout, & Gehlmann, 1997) recommends that graduate programs in clinical and counseling psychology prepare students for the realities of the marketplace of managed care by adding courses on the application of business and economic principles to mental health populations. Students would be taught about using limited resources, ensuring proficiency in brief therapy, understanding risk-based health-care delivery service, marketing to managed care companies and employers, and information technology.

Managed care's influence over clinician education is, on the surface, to make managed care operate more efficiently, but it is also, I believe, to ensure that new trainees know no other system and nothing other than short-term therapies, thus eliminating opposition. It is not inconceivable that within 5 years, unless we turn the tide, we will see managed care companies buying or building their own medical and graduate schools, giving them even greater control over the training of future professionals.

Disregard for Human Dignity

Seventh, totalitarian regimes have always been characterized by their pervasive disregard for human dignity. Historically, totalitarian regimes have gained wealth and power, leaving their subjects miserable and the society's institutions destroyed. With a similar lack of concern for human needs, managed care companies' demands and incentives to deny, delay, or minimize treatment have caused unnecessary suicides, pain, and stress. Harvard University and McLean Hospital showed a dramatic rise in rehospitalizations of psychiatric patients because of reduced length of stay (Talan, 1995). It is not difficult to find stories in the media of unnecessary suffering and death due to the delay or denial of medical care by managed care companies.

Meanwhile, managed care companies pile up billions of dollars in wealth for the corporations (Anders, 1994) and millions for their executives (Freudenheim, 1995). The sale of U.S. Healthcare to Aetna brought U.S. Healthcare's Chairman, Leonard Abramson, and his family approximately $967,000,000 in cash ("U.S. Healthcare Chief," 1996). This money could have provided over 33,000,000 psychotherapy sessions, if only U.S. Healthcare would have spent merely $30 on each session and allowed the patient and clinician to negotiate the copayment.

Some may argue that to implement managed care's cost-cutting strategies may merely be considered irresponsible, but not unethical or immoral. However, to implement them knowing that people will remain in pain and that money that could have helped them is going to corporate profit and executive wealth is cruel and immoral.

Even if we achieve some meaningful legislation, the people who run managed care are people who *can,* seemingly without guilt, require "drive-through" deliveries and mastectomies; who *can* implement gag clauses and eliminate clinicians who are not managed care friendly; who *can* refuse to cover the emergency room expenses of a person with severe chest pain who did not get approval to go to the emergency room first; and who *can* decide that a young child who witnessed the horrifying death of her father and is still mute and suicidal at the 10th psychotherapy session can have no more therapy (letter in files of the National Coalition of Mental Health Professionals and Consumers, 1994). I assert that it is in their character to do such things. These are not the people to whom our health care should be entrusted.

Merger of Government and Industry

Finally, the last characteristic of totalitarianism I discuss is the typical merger of government and industry to carry out the regime's policy. For example, to help achieve his political goals, Mussolini established 22 state-controlled "corporations," one in each major trade or industry, that dictated wages and working conditions (Smith, 1982). Although the fascists sought to make a tool of industry, we now have an industry seeking to make a tool of government. In the fall of 1996, the managed care industry, ostensibly working alongside professional and consumer groups, convinced Congress to pass a mental health parity law, saying that parity will not be as expensive as previously thought because we now have managed care. The old estimated costs of parity were based on the fee-for-service model. The new estimated costs of parity were based on all mental health care being managed. The parity laws are expected to result in an increased use of managed care for mental health care, and the managed care companies jumped on the parity bandwagon knowing this.

However, managed care parity is not true parity, for parity means that mental health patients, like medical patients, must be given treatment that helps them get well or that will achieve their highest possible functioning. We have already seen how managed care companies define mental health treatment as "crisis" management and that its philosophy of treatment often neglects underlying, ongoing, and chronic conditions. Managed care parity is only the illusion of parity.

Looking at these eight comparisons, it seems that managed care's fit with the characteristics of totalitarianism is quite good. However, unlike totalitarian regimes, where the regime was so powerful as to squash most forms of rebellion, we—in a democratic society—have options, to which I now turn.

Facing Managed Care: Opt Out, Regulate It, or Replace It?

Given this larger system, what is the individual to do? There have been a number of different ways in which individual therapists have chosen to deal with the reality of managed care. One option has been to opt out entirely. Take as one example Helga Bolgar. Speaking on a panel at the APA Convention in Washington, DC in 1992, Bolgar (1992) said, "I left Vienna 50 years ago—the day Hitler walked into Austria—and I haven't been associated with any form of control since—and managed care smacks of control." Her example is strong and powerful. It may be more reassuring to know that there are many younger, less established clinicians who are also refusing to deal with managed care. Some are finding that they can survive well economically by building up a self-pay practice. Others are "diversifying." Others would rather accept a lesser income but retain their integrity. Still others find that they must leave the field and find other work in order to maintain their integrity. Although these clinicians are leaving the work they love, they cannot bring themselves to hurt their patients, to allow themselves to be used and exploited by the industry, or to contribute to a system that they consider unethical and immoral.

Laura Brown (1994), however, fears that by opting out of the system, we may create a loss of access for those who only have managed care with which to pay for therapy. This is an extremely important consideration. Although opting out may be a good and ethically necessary solution in the short term for many, it obviously can only be a temporary and incomplete solution.

Another branch of thought maintains that the solution to managed care is to regulate it better. However, merely regulating managed care still leaves insurers and employers in charge of health care. To limit our goals to regulating managed care reminds me of the adults we treat who were abused by their parents and are still, as adults, trying to make their abusive parents treat them as they want and should be treated. We know that survivors of abuse will not flourish until they realize that they cannot control their abusive parents' behavior and that they must leave their parents' home, literally and figuratively, and build their own nonabusive home. We should follow our own advice: The best way to end the abuses of managed care is to build something better. We must replace managed care with a more pro-patient system.

The Basis for a New Health-Care System

In 1995, Michael Lerner, speaking to an audience of mental health clinicians, said that if we want a culture based on caring and meaning, we will have to envision it and begin building it ourselves. It is my belief that most citizens of this country, and most clinicians, want a mental health care system based on a morality of relationship, an ethic of caring, and the values of cooperation and responsible freedom.

We must realize that no amount of regulation will make managed care a fair, ethical, or moral system, for, as stated earlier, managed care requires that consumers lose the rights to privacy, choice, and decision making, and it requires that clinicians' economic survival depends on satisfying the managed care company rather than the patient. As these are the cost-containment mechanisms of managed care, we will forever be trying to regulate this industry to protect consumers and quality, and the industry will forever fight regulation that would impede its cost-containment methods and lower its profits. This is an irresolvable problem that demands that we find an alternative (Shore, 1995a). It does not matter that managed care is the dominant force. It is an immoral force and we must reject it, fight against it, and build something better.

I encourage all clinicians who know that managed care is harmful to follow the feminist attitude of working toward subverting oppression (see Brown, 1994). Lerner (1995), in his address to clinicians, observed that the power of the women's movement was that they refused to be helpless against a huge culture. He urged that we do the same in health care. Lerner asked, Who decided that the criterion of efficiency is the bottom line of a corporation and not the physical and mental health of people? He offered as an alternative "a new bottom line of people" that would judge efficiency and productivity by the degree to which legislation and organizations produce ethical, spiritual, and sensitive people who can sustain relationships and who are loving and caring.

We must move out of depression, fear, denial, and resignation and mobilize our anger into power and constructive action. We must build a new, nonabusive system in concert with the medical–surgical community, for a good mental health plan cannot exist in the midst of a health-care system that is destructive to caring, compassion, privacy, and freedom.

The goal of a health-care system should be to ensure that we have a physically and mentally healthy nation. The plans and structures we devise to achieve that goal will be successful or unsuccessful, depending on the values upon which they are based. We have already seen that this value cannot be one of competition. The value of competition leads to a desire to "win" and to greed, cutting corners, and callousness. Instead, I believe that our health-care system should be based on four main values:

1. We as a society need a system based on the value of cooperation, not competition. The value of cooperation seeks solutions that enhance and are fair to all parties involved.
2. We need a system based on responsible freedom, not on paternalistic or authoritarian control.
3. We need a system based on an ethic of caring, not on the ethics of business.
4. We need a system that values health-care workers for their training and knowledge, not one that values health-care workers who are the cheapest labor possible.

On the basis of this set of values, I have devised a set of ideas called *managed cooperation* (Shore, 1996). I do not think it will be "the answer," but I think it provides food for thought. It addresses some of the problems that led to managed care, and it values people and their need for dignity and responsible freedom.

In the FFS system, the consumer paid little out-of-pocket and had little incentive to be cost-conscious. Managed care does not change the incentives nor make consumers cost-conscious. In fact, its minimal or absent copayments separate consumers even more from the financial consequences of their treatment. Managed care removes all responsibility from the patient and, instead, institutes external authorities to make decisions for them. It also establishes financial incentives and threats that influence professional decision making.

To preserve the consumer's freedoms of choice, privacy, and decision making, yet contain costs, incentives must be built into a health plan that lead patients to ask two basic questions of the clinician: (a) "Why is what you are recommending really necessary?" and (b) "Why are you charging what you are charging?" I assure you that if consumers do not routinely ask these questions, someone else will be hired to do it for them.

Consumer freedom can only be protected by incentives that make the consumer cost- and utilization-conscious. To accomplish this, yet be sure all people can afford needed treatment, the managed cooperation plan (Shore, 1996) suggests a fixed-dollar insurer reimbursement for each procedure, with fees, and thus, copayments, set by each individual clinician or clinic or negotiated by the patient and clinician on the basis of the patient's ability to pay. (Note that this is not reimbursement and copayment based on a percentage of the fee as in traditional fee-for-service plans.) Sliding scale deductibles and sliding scale premiums (with government aid for those with very limited incomes) are also possibilities.

To be sure no one is taken advantage of, I envision the creation of Regional Boards—made up of consumers, insurers, and practitioners—that would recommend insurance reimbursement levels for each procedure. Insurers would then set reimbursements for each procedure at somewhat below the level of an appropriate fee. The Regional Boards would also inform citizens as to what the reasonable fee ranges in their area would be, based on training and experience, although they would not set fees. Clinicians could provide current and prospective patients with their fee schedule upon request so that patients could "comparison shop."

There are a number of consequences with a fixed-dollar insurer reimbursement and a copayment set by each clinician or negotiated by clinicians and their patients: (a) The insurer's liability is limited; (b) patients and clinicians become more cost-conscious, yet treatment is affordable to all, as many clinicians are very willing to reduce their fees for patients who need it; (c) patients retain the three basic rights (choice, decision making, and privacy); and (d) practitioners are encouraged, though not forced, to work on a sliding scale and to set reasonable fees. The clinicians are also guaranteed at least a minimum payment for each procedure (the fixed-dollar reimbursement) and can set their fees according to their training, talent, and reputation. They will also have to compete, but in a truly free market, along with other clinicians according to their fees and personal qualifications.

The Regional Boards, insurers, and the professions could make medical and mental health information easily accessible to beneficiaries. An educated public will increase quality and will help reduce waste without denying freedom. In psychotherapy, pamphlets could describe the various forms of psychotherapy and the training undertaken by the many different professionals in the field. Literature could also inform patients what to do if they feel their therapy is not working well.

Last, the managed cooperation plan advocates a phaseout of employer involvement in health care (Shore, 1995d, 1995e, 1996) in order to return control of health care to the consumer of care. The growth of managed care is due, in part, to the fact that people have come to rely on employers to provide health insurance. Premium money is really the employees' money, but as long as it seems as if it is the employers' money, employers will intrude, directly or through managed care companies, into insurance and treatment decisions. Employers should return premium money to the employees in the form of income so that individuals can buy and own their own policies. Premiums should be 100% tax deductible for individuals, just as they are for employers. Group rates could be had through purchasing cooperatives.

A full-service mental health alternative to managed care that is compatible with managed cooperation is the American Mental Health Alliance (AMHA) in Massachusetts (617-536-7171). This plan is in synch with the ideals, ethics, and values of the National Coalition of Mental Health Professionals and Consumers, a politically active, grassroots, interdisciplinary organization I cofounded that is working to expose, regulate, and replace managed care. We believe that the AMHA idea can contain costs while preserving connection, privacy, dignity, and self-determination. As of this writing (January 1997), the AMHA is building chapters in 20 states.

The AMHA is an open network, interdisciplinary worker cooperative that assumes that the best work is done by empowered clinicians and patients. It relies on a collaborative professional relationship between the clinician and the plan, rather than on one of oversight and micromanagement. Costs are contained by minimizing administration costs and offering consultation with experts for clinicians with complicated cases. Any surplus funds are reinvested in treatment. AMHA hopes to establish contracts with employees in which fees will be determined by a fixed per-session reimbursement, with the copayment negotiated by each patient–therapist pair to reduce unnecessary visits while making treatment affordable to all. Hospitals involved allow the outpatient therapist to continue to work with the patient through the hospitalization. It is too soon as of this writing to know whether the AMHA model will succeed, but it is a worthy pursuit.

Another alternative is Medical Savings Accounts (MSAs). MSAs involve a high-deductible catastrophic policy paired with a tax-exempt MSA for medical expenses below the deductible. Because the money in the MSA is felt to belong to the consumer, and whatever money is not used by the end of the year can be saved tax free by the consumer for future needs, the consumer is more likely to discuss the necessity of treatment and fees with the clinician.

Critics of MSAs charge that MSAs are best for the healthy and wealthy. However, if designed with all of our citizens in mind, those with lower incomes and high medical expenses would be covered as well as they would be in a good indemnity plan. To make MSAs suitable for the poor, we would have to use government funds to contribute to premiums and MSAs for them. The argument that MSAs will deplete the risk pool has been aimed exclusively toward MSAs, yet managed care has already depleted the risk pool. Further, in MSAs, the catastrophic indemnity portion relies on a large risk pool. Remember that the MSA is merely a benefit design. I believe it could fit into single-payer plans and health-care cooperatives and would not be limited to private insurance markets. It is even possible, I think, to use MSAs to "save" the Medicare system by allowing baby boomers to save money tax free for later medical expenses. Because most baby boomers will be healthy until after age 65, many could save tens of thousands of dollars. This money would be used before turning to public Medicare funds. However, if not regulated, MSAs could create the same problems with "cherry picking" the healthy and denial of reimbursement in the indemnity portion as do managed care plans and other current forms of insurance.

Some favor a single-payer plan in which state or federal taxes are used to create a government-run health plan. In actuality, we already have two forms of single-payer plans in our Medicare and Medicaid systems. On the positive side, only a single-payer plan can include all of our citizens in the same risk pool and eliminate competing plans that might otherwise cherry-pick the healthy. Also, the use of a single government payer is probably the easiest, though not the only, way of guaranteeing coverage regardless of health or employment status. As with private payer plans, though, the benefit design is crucial, for any government plan could decide to use government employees or private managed care companies to manage the benefits, just as Medicare and Medicaid are now doing. If our nation devised a managed single-payer plan that did not allow care to be provided outside the system, it could become illegal for a patient to pay for treatment that is denied by a case manager or to contract privately for mental health or any other care for which the patient wanted complete privacy. Also, because making changes in a government plan requires lobbying and legislation, it could be very difficult to make any needed changes in a single-payer plan.

Whichever way the new system of mental health care (and overall health care) is to evolve, there are a number of basic ingredients that must be included for any system to work.

- The benefit design is crucial, whether there is a single-payer or a private system. We need to create benefit designs that use cost-containment mechanisms that preserve consumer choice, privacy, and decision making, that prevent fraud and abuse, and that make consumers cost- and utilization-conscious but that do not prevent, deny, or delay proper treatment. We must consider health care both a right and a responsibility, and we must find ways to subsidize health care and health insurance for those who truly cannot afford it.

- We need to allow experimentation with a variety of benefit designs (FFS, MSAs, managed cooperation, AMHA, and other designs yet to be devised) in single-payer plans, private insurance plans, and in health-care consumer cooperatives in order to ascertain which plans are best for the medical and mental health of all our citizens—rich and poor, healthy and sick.
- We must also challenge our professional associations to rewrite their codes of ethics to address situations created by managed care. So far, our professional organizations have seemed to prefer telling us how to make an opportunity of managed care and how to work within it rather than to declare it unethical and replace it with a better plan.[3] My concern is that managed care will force the professions to rewrite their ethics codes so that we can fit into this system, when what we need is to hold firm to our standards and demand that any health-care system not violate them. At this writing, a new committee has been established within the APA Practice Directorate to look at and address the new ethical dilemmas brought by managed care. If this committee finds few violations, then we must assume that our Ethics Code is inadequate for the era of managed care and it must be rewritten to deal with the new dilemmas. The New Jersey Board of Medical Examiners was to hold hearings to consider regulations that could make it unethical for physicians to sign managed care contracts with gag clauses or with financial incentives to withhold necessary care or limit referrals to specialists or emergency rooms. In the first effort of its kind, this Board hopes that if such practices are ruled unethical, insurance companies will no longer be able to require physicians to sign such contracts (Scott, 1996).
- We must let America know that we cannot industrialize psychotherapy or any health-care service without sacrificing compassion; the primacy of patients' need over costs; the freedom of patients to make their own decisions with their chosen clinicians; the value of human relationships, including the patient–clinician relationship; and the ability to obtain care close to home, family, and friends. We cannot have a system that causes patients to mistrust their clinicians' motives or to wonder whether they have been given all pertinent information. Nor can we have a system that makes clinicians mistrust themselves or that discourages or impedes advanced training.
- We also need to be honest that quality mental health care will cost more than what some people might like, and we need to be up front

---

[3]If you believe managed care is immoral and unethical, you must demand that your professional associations declare it as such. I further encourage you to join the National Coalition of Mental Health Professionals and Consumers (516-424-5232 or toll free 1-888-SAY-NO-MC). Being independent of professional organizations, the Coalition can speak out strongly and unambivalently about the need to replace managed care with a more pro-patient system.

in defending a quality health-care system that may require more economically costly routes than what we now have with managed care. Joan Callahan (1988), writing about ethics in professional life, stated that "finding the most economic solution to a problem may not be to find a morally permissible solution to that problem" (p. 12). "Sometimes," she said, "important moral considerations like fairness or the respect for individual rights to self-determination require that we take the more economically costly routes" (Callahan, 1988, p. 12). If the public demands high quality and freedom of choice, privacy, and decision-making power at managed care prices, we may have to tell the public that this is not possible. We may need to rethink our values and priorities, for our citizenry is the only source of funding we have.

- Last, we should not consider ourselves solely as clinicians trying to survive economically in the era of managed care. Each of us, and all of our loved ones, are consumers of health care. The loss of choice, quality care, and highly trained clinicians, along with the deprofessionalization of services, the loss of privacy, the loss of the consumer's decision-making power, and the weakening of our research and teaching facilities will affect us all in some way.

Our system must prize the physical and mental health of all our citizens. Graduate and professional schools must not "prepare students for the marketplace" but for work with real people with real, complex problems. All who believe managed care is destructive to body, mind, and soul must do whatever they can to work toward the creation of alternatives to managed care and managed competition.

Conclusion

In my opening paragraph, I wrote of Erich Fromm's (1955) assertion that people do not like to think that society as a whole is insane, so they often declare those who protest the status quo to be "unadjusted" individuals and try to marginalize them, rather than thinking that the culture is "out of synch with the needs of man." At this point, I conclude by stating that there is nothing wrong with you if you cannot or will not "adapt" to managed care. It is the corporate, industrial culture in managed care that, as Fromm would say, is insane and out of synch with the needs of man.

Managed care is the reality of the current marketplace. Just because managed care is now the most common mode of health insurance and health-care delivery does not mean that it is morally acceptable, for nothing can change the fact that it is wrong to invade the privacy of vulnerable people. It is wrong to deny them choices and impede their abilities to make treatment decisions for themselves and their loved ones. It is wrong to make treatment decisions based on the financial needs of managed care companies, just as it is wrong for insurers to hold a metaphoric economic guillotine over the heads of clinicians to intimidate them into submission and to silence their opposition. It is wrong to increase wealth by with-holding treatment and information from patients, and it is wrong to weaken our professions, our research, and our teaching hospitals. By doing these things, our people and our health-care system will be damaged for decades.

We must decide that people are our most precious resource. There is enough money to take excellent care of everyone—we just need to reprior-itize and make people more important than anything else. We can build a system with a "bottom line of people" (Lerner, 1995). We can have both solo practices as well as integrated systems of delivery. We can have cost-containment mechanisms that do not use the force, control, and invasion of privacy imposed by managed care. We can change the incentives in insurance so that patients become cost- and utilization-conscious and, through their financial responsibility for their decisions, maintain their freedom. We can eliminate employer involvement in health care so that citizens can take back control over their own health care. We can build a new medical and mental health care system based on an ethic of caring, a morality of relationship, and the values of cooperation and responsible freedom.

We as clinicians and as citizens must begin building that system now, for what is at risk is our entire health-care system, and along with it, the medical and mental health of our people and our nation. Managed care is not necessarily "here to stay." It is certainly not the last idea that will ever come along. Managed care can be replaced by a more ethical, moral, and pro-patient system if we work for it and if we fight for it.

References

America's top HMOs: State-by-state rankings. (1997, October 13). *U.S. News and World Report*, 69–78.

Anders, G. (1994, December 21). HMOs pile up billions in cash, try to decide what to do with it. *The Wall Street Journal*, pp. A1, A5.

Anders, G. (1996). *Health against wealth*. Boston: Houghton Mifflin.

Berner, R. (1995, April 8/9). HMOs push Prozac therapy. *The Patriot Ledger*, pp. 1, 18.

Bolgar, H. (1992, August). *Short term therapy: Treatment or deception?* Bertram Karon (Chair), panel discussion at the 100th Annual Convention of the American Psychological Association, Washington, DC.

Brown, L. S. (1994). *Subversive dialogues: Theory in feminist therapy*. New York: Basic Books.

Callahan, J. (Ed.). (1988). *Ethical issues in professional life*. New York: Oxford University Press.

Carr, A. Z. (1988). Is business bluffing ethical? In J. Callahan (Ed.), *Ethical issues in professional life* (pp. 69–72). New York: Oxford University Press.

Cummings, N. A. (1991, Spring). Out of the cottage. *Association for the Advancement of Psychology, 1–2*, 14.

Freudenheim, M. (1995, April 11). Penny-pinching H.M.O.'s showed their generosity in executive paychecks. *The New York Times*, pp. D1, D4.

Friedman, M. (1988). The social responsibility of business. In J. Callahan (Ed.), *Ethical issues in professional life* (pp. 349–350). New York: Oxford University Press.

Fromm, E. (1947). *Man for himself: An inquiry into the psychology of ethics*. New York: Fawcett World Library.

Fromm, E. (1955). *The sane society*. New York: Ballantine Books/Fawcett Premier.

Fromm, E. (1964). *The heart of man*. New York: Harper & Row.

Fromm, E. (1969). *Escape from freedom*. New York: Avon Books. (Original work published 1941)

Garrett, T. M., Baillie, H. W., & Garrett, R. M. (1993). *Health care ethics: Principles and problems* (2nd ed.). Englewood Cliffs, NJ: Prentice Hall.

Gillespie, N. C. (1988). The business of ethics. In J. Callahan (Ed.), *Ethical isues in professional life* (pp. 72–96). New York: Oxford University Press.

Gilligan, C. (1982). *In a different voice: Psychological theory and women's development*. Cambridge, MA: Harvard University Press.

Greene, J. (1995, September 22). Doctors get a bonus if patients go home. *Orange County Register*.

Huxley, A. (1969). *Brave new world*. New York: Perennial Library, Harper & Row. (Original work published 1932)

Jaffee v. Redmond, 135. L. Ed. 2d 337, 340, 116 S. Ct. 1923 (1996).

Kassirer, J. P. (1995). Managed care and the morality of the marketplace. *New England Journal of Medicine, 333*(1), 50–52.

Kohlberg, L., & Kramer, R. (1969). Continuities and discontinuities in child and adult moral development. *Human Development, 12*, 93–120.

Kramer, P. (1995, Spring). Caps for sale. *Association for the Advancement of Psychology, 6*, 17–18.

Lau, G. (1995, July 31). Employers place an HMO cost above quality. *Investor's Daily*.

Lerner, M. (1995, March). *The assault on psychotherapy*. Speech presented at the Family Therapy Network Symposium, Washington, DC.

Medical school and health plan announce creation of managed care institute in Boston. (1995, August 30). *BNA's Managed Care Reporter, 1*(9), 218–219.

Meier, B. (1994, March 31). Health plans promise choice but decisions may be hard. *The New York Times*, pp. A1, B8.

Mental health: Does therapy help? (1995, November). *Consumer Reports*, 734–739.

Miller, I. J. (1996). Time-limited brief therapy has gone too far: The result is invisible rationing. *Professional Psychology: Research and Practice, 27*, 567–577.

Miller, J. B. (1986). *Toward a new psychology of women* (2nd ed.). Boston: Beacon Press.

Noddings, N. (1984). *Caring: A feminine approach to ethics and moral education*. Berkeley: University of California Press.

Orwell, G. (1981). *1984* (Rev. ed.). New York: Penguin Books. (Original work published 1949)

Physician-led MCOs acting like insurance companies. (1996, February). *Behavioral Healthcare Tomorrow*, p. 12.

Psychotherapy Finances' managed care conference. (1993, July). *Psychotherapy Finances, 19*(7, Issue 231), 1–2.

Pollock, E. J. (1995, December 1), Managed care's focus on psychiatric drugs alarms many doctors. *The Wall Street Journal*, pp. A1, A11.

Russell, S. (1996, January 18). Proposition 103: Author to take on HMOs. *San Francisco Chronicle*, p. A17.

Sack, L. (1996, August). What will managed care do to the profession of psychiatry? *Psychiatric Times*, 41, 42.

Salerno, S. (1994, January 18). High price of managed care. *The Wall Street Journal*, p. A16.

Schachner, M. (1994, January 10). Mental health group practices on rise. *Business Insurance, 3*, 36.

Schnabel, T. (1995, November/December). My clear choice about being a managed health care provider—No way! *Georgia Association for Marriage & Family Newsletter*.

Scott, G. (1996, February 1). State board drafting new rules for regulation of HMO doctors. *The Star-Ledger*, pp. 1, 13.

Seligman, M. E. P. (1995). The effectiveness of psychotherapy: The Consumer Reports Study. *American Psychologist, 50*, 965–974.

Shirer, W. L. (1981). *The rise and fall of the Third Reich*. New York: Touchstone. (Original work published 1959)

Shore, K. (1995a, November 4). *The immorality of managed competition and managed care.* Paper presented at Preserving Psychotherapy Conference, Atlanta, GA. National Coalition of Mental Health Professionals and Consumers, Commack, NY.

Shore, K. (1995b). Managed care: The convergence of industrialization and totalitarianism. *Psychologist–Psychoanalyst, 15*(4), 15–19.

Shore, K. (1995c). Managed care: The subjugation of a profession. *Psychotherapy in Private Practice,* 14(2), 67–75.

Shore, K. (1995d, November 5). *Moving America beyond managed care and managed competition.* Paper presented at the Preserving Psychotherapy Conference, Atlanta, GA. National Coalition of Mental Health Professionals and Consumers, Commack, NY.

Shore, K. (1995e). Why we need to move America beyond managed care and managed competition. *Psychologist–Psychoanalyst, 15*(3), 12–15.

Shore, K. (1996). *Managed cooperation: A medical/mental health care plan.* National Coalition of Mental Health Professionals and Consumers, Commack, NY.

Simon, J. (1995, September 22). A modest proposal for Medicare reformers. *The Wall Street Journal,* p. A14.

Slater, D. (1995, September 29). Activist nurses take aim at "corporatized health care." *Express.*

Sleek, S. (1995, March). A varied practice is the key to security. *APA Monitor,* p. 28.

Smith, D. M. (1982). *Mussolini.* New York: Vintage Books.

Solomon, R. C. (1993). *Ethics: A short introduction.* Dubuque, IA: Brown & Benchmark.

South Africa to be offered first managed-care. (1995, September 14). *The Wall Street Journal.*

Spruill, J., Kohout, J., & Gehlmann, S. (1997). *Final Report of the American Psychological Association Working Group on the Implications of Changes in the Health Care Delivery System for the Education, Training, and Continuing Professional Education of Psychologists.* Washington, DC: American Psychological Association.

Talan, J. (1995, May 24). Study: Managed-care squeezes hospital stay. *Newsday,* p. A19.

U.S. healthcare chief will get $1 billion. (1996, June 15). *The New York Times,* p. 32.

5

Toward a Social Ethic of Mental Health Care: Long-Term Therapy, Short-Term Therapy, and Managed Health Care

Carol Shaw Austad and Thomas C. Morgan

Edward J.

Edward J. worked as a midlevel executive in the insurance industry for 15 years. Although he suffered from bouts of depression all of his adult life, medication and individual therapy enabled him to cope. His favorable response to the new antidepressants, the serotonin reuptake inhibitors, made him symptom free most of the time. Despite his struggles with a mood disorder, he prided himself on being an excellent breadwinner for his family. Two years ago, his company downsized and laid him and 550 other employees off. Edward J. not only lost his job, but his health insurance as well. Through COBRA (the Consolidated Omnibus Reconciliation Act; Dacso & Dacso, 1995), he was able to maintain his coverage by paying his own monthly premiums. After 12 months, his financial situation worsened. He lost his house and could not afford COBRA payments. He became immobilized with severe depression. He was unable to pay out of pocket for his psychiatric bill— nearly $250 for medications, $200 for monthly therapy sessions, and another $120 for his psychiatric-medication consultation. He went without any treatment for several months.

Last April, Edward committed suicide. The note he left stated that his wife and children could live well from what they collected from his life insurance and that his family was better off without him.

Alice B.

Alice B., a single parent, toiled as a cleaning lady at a local hospital for 30 years. Her life revolved around her schizophrenic son, whose first psychotic episode occurred at the age of 16.

Alice, relentlessly determined to help her child, sought the best care. Mental health professionals insisted that he needed long-term, thrice weekly sessions. Her employer's indemnity health insurance covered only 50% of psychotherapy charges up to a $2,000 yearly limit. She took on a second job. When her son turned 21, he could no longer be included on Alice's policy. She took on a third job cleaning in private houses. More than half of her meager income was spent on psychotherapy for her son.

Despite hundreds of hours of therapy and thousands of hard earned dollars, the promise of long-term therapy was unfulfilled. All treatment ended in disappointment. Her son was not restored to normalcy.

Alice began to worry about her own retirement. She realized she could not continue to pay for her son's failed treatment. Not one of the doctors who had received thousands of her dollars would treat her son pro bono. He wound up in the public system, where he stood in line to receive minimal care. She felt she had been "taken." Embittered and cynical, she asked, "How many Caribbean vacations have I paid for while my son languishes in the state mental institute?"

Michael H.

Michael H. is a chemical engineer. After 4 years of weekly psychotherapy, he gained insight into the roots of his interpersonal conflicts. He has become a better husband and father. He was appreciative of the fact that his employer-provided insurance benefit covered 80% of the cost of therapy with no yearly limit.

As Michael entered a crucial phase of therapy in which he had started to understand his core conflicts, his employer switched insurance to Mic-Co. This managed mental health care company would agree only to pay for sessions with a Mic-Co therapist who informed him that further psychotherapy was not medically necessary. Enraged, Michael appealed the decision but received approval for only six sessions. His complaints to the insurance commissioner gave him only an additional five sessions.

Michael decided to accept his previous therapist's offer to lower his fees by 20%. After paying out of pocket for several months, therapy put a crunch on his budget. He decided his first priority was to ensure his children's college education. He terminated treatment, feeling angry and frustrated.

Edward, Alice, and Michael's stories illustrate the deplorable conditions that exist in our mental health care system today—Americans are uninsured, underinsured, and deprived of care.

Although many blame managed care for this state of affairs (Austad, 1996b), we believe the most important single cause of a failed mental health-care system is a lack of a well-articulated social ethic to guide Americans in distributing health care—and psychotherapy—in a fair and equitable manner.

In this chapter, we examine five issues that play a role in this want of a social ethic in our mental health care system.

Issue 1: Tolerating the deficiencies in the general health-care system and the "scapegoating" of managed care.
Issue 2: Emphasizing the importance of the individual ethic while neglecting the advancement of a social ethic.
Issue 3: Letting a bias for long-term psychotherapy rather than scientific and objective thinking dominate psychotherapy.
Issue 4: Failing to examine how profit influences clinical care in and out of managed care, thus confusing guild interest with public interest.
Issue 5: Failing to establish whether psychotherapy is a business or a health-care entitlement.

Tolerating Deficiencies in Health and Mental Health Care Systems

Appalling health-care conditions exist today in our country. Repeatedly, our own citizens are deeply hurt.

- Over 40 million Americans have no health insurance and go without needed care. Millions more are underinsured (Friedman, 1991; Himmelstein & Woolhandler, 1995).
- People have been ruined financially in order to pay for medical care (Castro, 1994; Navarro, 1992).
- People are held hostage to their insurance plans, unable to change jobs for fear of losing their health insurance (Castro, 1994; Himmelstein & Woolhandler, 1995).
- Individuals have been disqualified from insurance and thus denied treatment because of "preexisting conditions" (Austad, 1996a, 1996b; Spencer, Frank, & McGuire, 1996).
- Political leaders are divided on whether health care is a right or privilege and on whether our health entitlement programs should continue (Kissick, 1994).
- Mental health care has been a second-class citizen and has often not been reimbursed at the same rate as medical treatments. Constant lobbying for legislative changes for parity for mental health continues and is finally beginning to pay off (Sleek, 1996).
- The needs of ethnic minorities are not considered in any systematic way, thus resulting in additional barriers to access and treatment (Abe-Kim & Takeuchi, 1996).
- Many of our chronically mentally ill citizens are homeless and being "cared for" within the criminal justice system (Bogdanich, 1991).

We, as citizens and health professionals, permitted social injustices to grow like unplucked wild saplings into mighty oaks in our health and mental health care systems. Why?

The Paradox of American Health Care

What Americans are told about their health care places them in a schizo-phrenogenic or double bind (Haley, 1976). On one hand, they constantly hear that the American health-care system is the best in the world and that the quality of health care in other countries pales in comparison (Scheidemandel, 1994). Yet, how can any system with so many uninsured, financially pressed citizens who live in a state of anxiety, which is generated by the uncertainty that accompanies a lack of universal coverage, be superior?

True, our exquisitely sophisticated medical technology is second to none. Our magnificent science and equipment is the most advanced in the world (Castro, 1994). However, how does having the best CAT (comput-erized axial tomography) scan in each of six hospitals in one city or the owning of a superb, but unnecessary, MRI (magnetic resonance imaging) help if one single autistic child in need of early intervention goes without needed care because his or her family lacks insurance or the money to obtain it?

Europeans and Canadians are often taken aback at the complexity and confusion of our health system. They ask how we can endure the insecurities it generates (Navarro, 1992). For example, their initial en-counter with our system is often a culture shock. A British exchange stu-dent of the first author arrived at a local emergency room to seek treat-ment for a fever, rash, chills, and nausea. Surprised and indignant at the care he received at the hands of what he described as the "money-minded" American health-care workers, he queried me with "Why do you Ameri-cans think that the British system is so unworthy? At home, I go to a hospital and I receive treatment. Here, I am questioned to death about my ability to pay before I even get help. By the time I filled out the pa-perwork demanded of me, I felt worse than when I started!"

Many Europeans take health coverage for granted. They find it incon-ceivable and incomprehensible that citizens of an advanced nation could suffer financial ruination as a result of health costs or that in a time of crisis, a sick person must worry about affording appropriate care—whether it be for a physical or mental condition (Katz, Hoffer, & Manning, 1996).

Recently South Africa's constitution made health care a right, giving the United States the dubious honor of being the only industrialized coun-try in the world in which its citizens are not entitled to medical care (Na-varro, 1992). While living in Canada for 5 years, I found my own personal health-care experiences to be close to ideal. A recent article in the *Amer-ican Journal of Public Health* confirms my subjective impressions (Katz et al., 1996). The common perception that Canada saves money by deliv-ering fewer medical services is untrue. Overall, northeastern Canadians averaged 19% more visits than their American counterparts. Yet, despite the reality of the physical and emotional suffering caused by our lack of universal coverage, many continue to believe what amounts to propa-ganda—that we have the best medical care in the world. As a result, we rebuff the idea that a government-sponsored national health system can resolve our problems. Could a nationalized health-care system be any more deleterious to our mental health than what we have now? How have we, as health-care professionals and as citizens, condoned these appalling conditions? Have we turned our backs on the sick and the vulnerable? Who is responsible for this state of affairs?

Managed Care: The Paper Tiger

Although many mental health professionals cry out that managed care is the culprit causing the demise of high-quality mental health care and even the ruination of long-term psychotherapy (Karon, 1995; Pipal, 1995; Welch, 1994), these assumptions are simply wrong in our opinion (Austad, 1996b). By blaming managed care, we are like pedestrians who throw rocks at the car that ran over their feet while ignoring the driver of the auto. We fail to recognize the deeper causes of this vast predicament.

Many mental health professionals have reified managed care and have lumped all forms of it together as if all managed care companies were manifestations of a single consciousness, condemning it, and holding it responsible for the present failings of the health system (Fox, 1995; Gibson & Weissberg, 1994). Such generalizations mean we fail to discriminate the good from the bad forms of managed care (Morris, 1994). Each case must be judged on its own merits. Many forms of managed care exist that range from a prepaid comprehensive integrated system, such as a nonprofit staff-model HMO, to the simple administrative shells that process claims and execute second opinion and utilization reviews (Spencer et al., 1996; Stein, 1994). Furthermore, managed care is evolving daily, so that in order to make accurate judgments about value, ethics, and usefulness, we need to understand the characteristics and quality of each type (Cummings, Pallak, & Cummings, 1996; Richardson & Austad, 1994).

Managed care is but one symptom of a sick health-care system (Austad, 1996a). Complex political, legal, social, and professional issues underlie the birth and ascent of the variegated forms of managed care (Dacso & Dacso, 1995). The question that begs to be answered is what particular conditions in our society have nurtured such a sudden, successful takeover of our health system by managed care?

We need to realize that warring against managed care is like fighting a paper tiger. The metamorphosis of American health care into a for-profit managed care system represents the ultimate triumph of the values of profit over those of humanitarianism. Much like confronting the car that ran over the pedestrian's foot, scuffling with managed care distracts providers and other citizens from dealing with the more substantive problem of deciding whether health care should be a profit-making endeavor. To resolve the predicament at a deeper level means we must converse and communicate with the car's driver about the law he or she violated. Just as no driver is above the law, no managed care firm is above the law. If the laws were changed, the driver—and managed care companies as drivers—would have to conform or pay the consequences.

Who is driving our runaway health-care vehicle? Who should establish a social ethic to guide policies about how health care ought to be distributed? Not managed care, but who? Before we decide, let us look at how psychotherapy fits into the general health-care scheme.

Rugged Individualism and a Missing Social Ethic

Psychotherapy is now entrenched in our health-care system. Participation in therapy no longer carries the negative stigma it once did. In some circles, it is even stylish—a status symbol and a highly valued exercise in which the therapist serves as a guide to enhance personal growth (Morris, 1994). Psychotherapy provides legitimate treatment for a multitude of problems identified by the *Diagnostic and Statistical Manual of Mental Disorders* (4th ed.; American Psychiatric Association, 1994) and is at least a partly reimbursable medically necessary procedure (Berman, 1992; Bloom, 1992, 1997).

As psychotherapy has gained in acceptance, it has gained in popularity and use. Mental health providers, proliferating at an exponential rate, render treatment to many more people for many more problems than ever before (Dawes, 1994). Thousands of therapists give millions of people millions of sessions each year (Austad, 1996b). Psychotherapy is now a health resource with medical, social, and economic value. In 1987 Americans made 79.5 million outpatient psychotherapy visits (Olfson & Pincus, 1994). Yet this increase in prevalence has not been followed by consideration of its cumulative effect on the health-care system and society. What is the impact of all of these sessions of therapy on society? Psychotherapy must be conceptualized from an epidemiological or public health perspective by clinicians as well as businesspersons. For example, we often read about how an increase in cesarean sections or heart transplants affects the overall health-care system (Castro, 1994).

Our American culture holds "rugged individualism" in high esteem. Our laws and mores center on protecting the rights of the individual. Each mental health profession has a code of ethics to govern professional behavior (P. S. Appelbaum, 1993; Haas, 1994). Although each of these standards endorses the general precept that members of this profession ought to promote the social good, we continue to perceive psychotherapy as a private, individual exercise and allow it to be ruled by the values of individualism (Bartlett, 1994). It is the individual ethic that is carefully articulated in detail (Harris, 1995; Kerns, 1993; R. Newman, 1994). The amount of attention provided to a social ethic dims and pales in comparison.

The tenets of long-term therapy are more consistent with the canons of an individual ethic than with those of a social ethic. Long-term therapists work to maximize the gain of the individual patient and do not necessarily directly address the needs of the collective. Maximizing the amount of time and number of sessions for each patient, their credo is to do everything possible for each person (Austad, 1996b; Hoyt, 1994).

Why have mental health professionals emphasized the individual ethic and neglected the development of the social ethic? When we spend our time attending to the needs of one suffering individual, the intensity and immediacy of the therapy dyad allow us to put large-scale social issues on the back burner. We can overlook the suffering of those who are weak, sick, and in need of but without psychotherapy when they are not in our immediate view. By helping our individual patient, we satisfy our altruistic urges and distract ourselves from more global problems. We think that if we take care of the needs of our own patients, then other therapists will likewise take care of their patients. Yet, in reality, those who have no therapists at all to advocate for them go without. Values that emphasize the importance of the individual and not the collective have made it easy to place high appreciation for long-term intensive psychotherapy above other forms of treatment (Webb, Rothschild, & Monroe, 1994).

The Domination of Long-Term Bias

Historically, the field of psychotherapy has been permeated with a core belief that long-term therapy is the "gold standard" and that shorter forms of therapy are less worthy "copper alloys" (Koss & Shiang, 1994). Thus, the values of long-term therapy are that the best care is the most care and that good therapy is long therapy. Long-term therapists want to do everything possible to improve a patient's character, which Hoyt (1994) referred to as *therapeutic perfectionism*.

Until recently, very few have questioned the veracity of these convictions. We call this *long-term bias*—or a belief in the superiority of long-term over short-term psychotherapy in the absence of sound definitive empirical proof (Austad, 1996a, 1996b). In embracing such values, mental health professionals have curiously tolerated a gap between practice and research.

It has been traditional for researchers and clinicians to banter. Clinicians complain that researchers act like ivory tower academicians in that their concerns for methodological soundness are so rigid that their resulting studies are irrelevant to the conduct of real therapy (Bergin & Garfield, 1994; Shapiro, 1996). Researchers charge that clinicians base practice on clinical lore and fail to integrate empirical findings and values into their practices and techniques (Bergin & Garfield, 1994; Wilson, 1996).

It is true that within psychotherapy research today, we have established only one incontrovertible fact—psychotherapy is helpful most of the time (Lambert & Bergin, 1994). All other findings are associated with some degree of controversy. For example, the debate rages about whether psychotherapy has specific effects. The "equal outcomes phenomenon" holds that psychotherapy techniques do not have specific effects and that one type of therapy is not more effective than another form of therapy (Barlow,

1996; Bergin & Garfield, 1994). However, a growing number of researchers are reinterpreting the literature, insisting that some interventions, particularly some forms of short-term treatments, are better than other forms of therapy for specific disorders (Barlow, 1996; Olsen, 1995; Quick, 1993; Shapiro, 1996). One important fact is that the clinical community has not been able to produce compelling evidence that long-term therapy is more effective than short-term therapy (Bloom, 1997). Although patient satisfaction results indicate that patients report greater satisfaction with longer therapy in some recent studies (Seligman, 1995), patient satisfaction is not a measure of effectiveness and there are still no definitive controlled studies that show the fact without dispute. As a matter of fact, Lambert and Bergin (1994) commented that the use of "long-term therapy cannot be easily justified on the basis of research" and that the lack of empirical evidence leaves us wondering about how necessary long-term therapy is for the majority of patients.

Furthermore, the psychotherapeutic community has ignored information about how patients actually use psychotherapy (Fonagy & Target, 1996; Phillips, 1985). Computers make information about aggregate psychotherapy encounters more readily available. We now know that up to one half of people who initiate mental health treatment do not return after one session. By the 5th or 6th session, less than 70% of those who began therapy remain; after 26 sessions, only 10–15% of patients continue. The national average or mean number of sessions is 5–6 (Bloom, 1997; Phillips, 1985; Taube, Goldman, Burns, & Kessler, 1988).

While obviously the majority of people receive short-term psychotherapy, much of our knowledge about psychotherapy has been derived from long-term patients. Cohen and Cohen (1984) called this *the clinician's illusion*, explaining why there is such disparity between the beliefs of long-term therapists and the reality of epidemiological data. Because long-term therapists work primarily with long-term patients, these therapists attribute the characteristics and course of treatment of patients who are currently ill or in treatment to all patients. Clinicians erroneously conclude that the long-term patients he or she treats represent all psychotherapy patients. Generalization from a sample as small as that of long-term patients may lead to an inaccurate picture of the population of all psychotherapy participants.

Why have we tolerated this gap between epidemiological information and practice? Why has the belief in the superiority of long-term therapy over short-term therapy gained such a strong toehold on psychotherapy practice? Why has it reached nearly mythical proportions?

The Profit Motive: In and Out of Managed Care

Could the existence of long-term bias be partly the result of a motive to protect personal and economic interests? We are in no way saying that clinicians have consciously put their own interests above patient welfare, but it is human nature to be subtly affected by self-interest and to be unaware of our own motivations. We cannot dismiss the notion that financial incentives influence clinical thinking and decision making. A growing body of research clearly demonstrates that payment does shape clinical behavior (Austad, 1996b; Austad & Sherman, 1992; Davis & Austad, 1997; Nash et al., 1993). For example, one study of physicians in a medical health center in the Northeast showed that the same doctors practicing in the same setting serving the same patients changed their practice patterns as a function of the payment system. Doctors augmented their revenues by increasing the number of tests and X-rays ordered (Hemenway, Killen, Cashman, Parks, & Bicksnell, 1990). Patrick, Padgett, Burns, Schlesinger, and Cohen (1993) analyzed insurance payment patterns for 1978 and 1983 and showed definitively that mental health providers adjust clinical treatment in a way to maximize dollar gain. England and Cole (1993) pointed out that the use of psychiatric services is sensitive to the amount of available dollars and that the profit motive plays a role in utilization and decision making in medical and mental health treatment. Until this recent economic upheaval, when payers put pressure on practitioners, we went without clinical guidelines. Is it a coincidence that we are now in a race to implement guidelines, standards, and outcome research (Clemens, 1995; Newman & Tejeda, 1996)? Is it a coincidence that there is a strong move afoot to protect long-term therapy for all (Bowers & Knapp, 1993; Sands, 1994)? Long-term therapy is the most profitable and prestigious form of therapy (S. Appelbaum, 1992). A dream career for many neophyte therapists is to acquire a "Madison Avenue" psychoanalytic practice comprising 8–10 analysands who faithfully attend sessions five times a week at the rate of $150 per session or more. Such is a good life, of helping others while enjoying high levels of prestige, status, intellectual challenge, autonomy, and a six-figure income. Few therapists reach this pinnacle, but many aspire to it.

In this scenario, the interests of the therapist and the individual patient are compatible. The long-term therapist enjoys a contemplative life in a long-term practice, and the long-term patient maximizes his or her quality of life. In the ideal world, these would be the ideal conditions for the practice of psychotherapy. A problem arises when we consider the collective good in a world of limited resources. While the long-term therapists and patients enjoy the luxury of a less harried life in a long-term practice, the interests of a few individuals are served, while the interests of many are neglected. That means there are many in need who go without.

Protection of the interest of the long-term patient and the long-term therapists has been a mission of many professional organizations or guilds (Rodriguez, 1994; Simon, 1994; Stechler, 1994). In the evolution of modern-day psychotherapy, is it not time for our professional organizations to temper the guiding light of the individual ethic with a social ethic? Is it not time to put patient interests above guild interests? Are not patients more important than profits—everyone's profits whether it be providers in cottage industries or corporate health-care executives? Does it make sense for professional organizations to protect those who have a basic benefit package—even if it is with a managed care plan—while doing less for those who have no benefits at all (viz., the quiet needy who have minimal social power and even less money than the insured)? We must fight for the rights of those who have no health care at all (Sabin, 1994a, 1994b). For example, although deinstitutionalization was intended to be a noble plan to free chronic mental patients from a life of unjustified restraint and needless confinement, elements of it have backfired (Bloom, 1992, 1997). We now must deal with a huge homeless population. We allowed the social programs that helped deinstitutionalized patients to survive in the community to be slashed, dismantled, and dissolved. As mental health professionals watched deinstitutionalization proceed in the absence of appropriate support systems, they did not pursue reform with the same enthusiasm with which they now aspire to control managed care.

Is It Business or Health Care—Or Both

The relationship between profit and mental health care is seldom talked about openly (Austad, 1996b). Psychotherapy practices are a mixture of business and health care so that private psychotherapists today exist in a world of definitional uncertainty and ambiguity. It is important to determine if psychotherapy is a business or a health entitlement in order to determine by which rules it should be governed. If it is a health-care venture, it should be governed by the rules of professionalism. If it is a business, then professionals do not need to be protected from competition (Goldsmith, 1984).

If psychotherapy is first and foremost a health-care resource, then professionals render it. Because professionals are not business people, they are exempted from the rules of conducting business. They can charge ordinary and customary fees and do not have to compete like businesses do. In exchange for this exemption from the duress of running a business, the profession is self-regulated and is trusted by the public to have ethics above reproach. American society awards doctors, and doctors of the mind, the special status of health professionals in exchange for our noble dedication to serving the sick (Starr, 1982). This means we are expected to abide by a patient-centered ethos by giving our absolute loyalty to our patients, keeping their confidences, and placing their welfare above all else. We are also expected to police our own profession and to monitor, identify, and correct any unethical behaviors on the part of our colleagues. Thus, by virtue of the status of "doctor" or helper, health professionals are awarded special status and are protected from the usual rules of competition in business because helping the sick is seen as a profession and not a business (Rodwin, 1993).

Today, however, much money passes hands in the name of psychotherapy. In 1987, Americans paid $4.2 billion dollars for 79.5 million psychotherapy visits. More than 80% of these visits were to mental health professionals for the treatment of mental health conditions (Olfson & Pincus, 1994). In short, psychotherapy is a business—and a booming one at that. The reality is that psychotherapy is a billion-dollar industry affecting our national health-care costs.

Given the fact that mental health care was a cottage industry and is quickly undergoing an "industrial revolution," we must ask, are we, as therapists, business owners or health-care professionals? Do we treat patients or consumers? When we say that therapists are in the "business of helping," it sounds like an oxymoron. In our American health-care system, we as therapists are constantly in a situation whereby patient welfare is pitted against provider income—whether it be in private practice or managed care. In private practice, more is better—but what if the patient does not need more? Also, in many managed care settings where less is better, what occurs if the patient needs more? There are ethical dilemmas present in both fee-for-service and managed care settings (Berman, 1992).

So how should health care, and psychotherapy, be provided? Should the rules and ethics of business govern it? Or should it be regulated as a public health resource delivered by professionals and not by businesspeople? We must decide.

The Solution: Toward a Social Ethic

So we are positioned at the verge of a new era. We must take a stand. It is the authors' position that professionals should promote a social ethic to govern the overall practice of psychotherapy. Psychotherapy should be an essential health-care resource, and it should be fairly and equitably distributed. To do so, we need to object to the deficiencies in our general health-care system and stop scapegoating managed care as the major problem. We must promote the public health and find a way to distribute psychotherapy in a fair and equitable manner. To do so, the following steps are essential.

Step 1: Decision. Is health care, and therefore psychotherapy, a right or a privilege for Americans? If psychotherapy is a right, then we must find a way to distribute it fairly so that those who need it have it. If it is a privilege, and an economic entity, then the rules of the marketplace prevail and those who can pay for it get the most and the best. As psychologists and health professionals, it is our obligation to commit to a moral position on health and mental health care. All citizens should be entitled to necessary health care, including psychotherapy. They, like the citizens of all other industrialized countries, need the security and certainty afforded by a comprehensive, universal health benefit. Until we do this "right thing," our mental health care system will remain in its present state of confusion.

Step 2: If psychotherapy is established as an entitlement, how do we distribute it fairly? Table 1 illustrates a plausible guiding schema. It describes and identifies the basic combinations of needing, wanting, and receiving psychotherapy and identifies eight basic groups according to their need for therapy, their desire for it, and whether they actually receive it (Austad, 1996b).

Thus, it is possible to distribute psychotherapy more fairly to those who need it if we classify patients according to the care they want, need, and receive and also give a name to the groups that they represent. The two overtreated groups identified in Table 1 are the "worried well" and the *involuntary, iatrogenic*. The worried well are people who receive unnecessary discretionary care simply because they want psychotherapy. An example of the worried well is someone who uses therapy to improve their already excellent personal skills. Involuntary patients receive treatment that they do not want or need and as a result may suffer iatrogenic effects. An example is a man whose wife forces him to attend therapy sessions. After some indoctrination, he see himself negatively, as an identified patient who requires psychological help (when it is his wife who has the problem). Both of these groups use an inordinate share of the psychotherapy resources and, thus, can deprive those who need these benefits. Psychotherapy treatment would be better invested in both the *unaware* and *aware*—deprived groups that need psychotherapy but cannot obtain it because of financial constraints (e.g., chronic schizophrenic patients). Those who want none, need none, and get none are not problematic, whereas an ideal distribution can be found in the want much, need much, and receive much groups.

This framework can help us to systematically look at "want" and "need" in relationship to the use of psychotherapy and whether a person or group of people receives a fair share of psychotherapy—the health-care resource. In a world of limited resources, problems arise when one person or group uses a disproportionate amount of psychotherapy and does not pay for it. This may cause harm to others because the depletion of the resource means they are deprived of either wanted or needed treatment.

There will always be people who need, but cannot afford, long-term psychotherapeutic contact. When a person or group is unable to pay for necessary psychotherapy, should not a compassionate society support these unprotected citizens? If we are to have a good health-care system, it will be one in which receipt of care will be based on true need, not ability

Table 1. Potential Combinations of Wanting, Needing, and Receiving Psychotherapy

Want	Need	Get	Category
Much	Much	Much	Optimal condition
Much	None	Much	"Worried well"
Much	Much	None	Aware, needy, deprived
Much	None	None	Not needy, frustrated
None	None	None	Optimal condition
None	None	Much	Involuntary, iatrogenic
None	Much	None	Unaware, needy, deprived
None	Much	Much	Involuntary, needy

Note. Reprinted with permission from Carol Shaw Austad, *Is Long-Term Psychotherapy Unethical? Toward a Social Ethic in an Era of Managed Care* (p. 201). Copyright 1996 by Jossey-Bass, Inc., Publishers.

to pay. In such situations we can use these guidelines to recommend ways to distribute mental health resources fairly—such as asking overtreated groups to share with undertreated groups. For example, if the "worried well" who are receiving discretionary care are being treated at the expense of the "aware, needy, and deprived," resources might be conserved by having the worried well use only necessary care or increase the pool of resources by paying for their own discretionary care. The involuntary, those who do not want or need but get psychotherapy (e.g., forced by family or the courts), might willingly surrender some resources to the more needy.

Step 3: Distinguish medically necessary versus discretionary psychotherapy. Much like the plastic surgeons discriminate between essential reconstructive surgery from merely cosmetic surgery, mental health professionals ought to arrive at some criteria to distinguish medically necessary from discretionary psychotherapy. A simple rule would be similar to the following: Necessary care should be an entitlement and funded by whatever source is the payer, whereas discretionary psychotherapy ought to be self-funded. The discrimination between what therapy is necessary versus what therapy is discretionary would form the basis for deciding what psychotherapy should be entitlement versus self-funded in an insurance or a national health services program. Once psychotherapy is divided into categories according to the earlier indicated standards, then we can set up rules by which it is governed.

Step 4: Empiricism and temporal eclecticism. Psychotherapy time and treatment guidelines should be guided by empirical data. For example, therapists should not insist that a patient needs 500 sessions of psychotherapy in the absence of temporal standards and empirically based guidelines for treatment. Claims that are made in regard to time for therapy need to have an empirical base in order to justify the treatment, as well as to give the clinician some guidelines as to how he or she is doing. The creation of a public database on utilization and outcome would help us to refine and understand these categories and accumulate meaningful information about the topic.

Step 5: Health care should be nonprofit. Taking care of patients and managing the resources of the system so as to serve as many as well as possible should be our top priority. Profits should be realized as savings to be turned back to patients (or national health care) in the form of lowered premiums. More people could have more benefits. Moving from for-profit to not-for-profit health care means a major change in expectations for providers and payers about how they should be paid for their work. Salary ranges could be fixed and regulated.

Step 6: Ethical decision making about resource allocation should include all stakeholders, including patient and payer participation. A number of medical ethicists have proposed that patient groups should participate in ethical decision making—perhaps as minicommunity mental health councils—that would meet with professionals and, together, help to decide on resource allocation, such as how to justly distribute benefits, ration services, and use any savings. Such arrangements would increase the likelihood that justice is done. Patients can be very sensitive to a social ethic. If they think everyone is acting out of compassion and not out of self-interest, they can be a strong asset. The provider's role in ethical decision making should be clarified. Can a psychotherapist keep an individual ethic in mind and still work for the greater social good? If the system is fueled by not-for-profit motives, then the answer is yes.

Step 7: Develop and use socially relevant models of psychotherapy. Before recommending open-ended psychotherapy approaches, we should make sure that they would truly benefit the patient. A way to increase the likelihood that those who need psychotherapy will receive it is to support the development and use of models of psychotherapy that deliver cost-effective, necessary care and that do the most good for the most people (Zimet, 1989). High-quality long-term care does not necessarily mean traditional long-term therapy whereby the patient meets weekly or more with the ambitious goals of restructuring the patient's character. If there is not enough psychotherapy for everyone who wants it, we must at least ensure that all of those who need it receive it. Important for the future of psychotherapy is Nicholas Cummings's model of psychotherapy, *Brief intermittent psychotherapy throughout the life cycle* (Cummings & Sayana, 1995). It is a prototype for modern psychotherapy, an umbrella under which other models of psychotherapy can be organized and integrated. In this model, psychotherapy is a series of intermittent encounters designed to help a patient accommodate to life's inevitable reoccurring crises and situations. When sufficient help is obtained, the patient stops seeing the therapist for regular sessions and returns only when necessary. The role of the therapist is similar to that of the family doctor. Therapy can continue over a long period of time.

Step 8: Social action. Instead of spending resources fighting managed care, it would be far more effective to see more mental health professionals form coalitions and support causes similar to the Physicians for a National Health Program—a group of physicians that is working toward the goal of covering all Americans under a single comprehensive public insurance program that has no copayments, no deductibles, and a free choice of provider. Groups such as this have come forward with program proposals complete with budgets that make sense and that appear to be workable (Clemens, 1995; Elpers & Abbott, 1992; Hartmann, 1992).

Conclusion

The source of the dysfunctional mental health, and health-care, system is not managed care alone. When we, as professionals, place our energy into fighting managed care, we deflect our resources from where they ought to be. The millions who are uninsured, underinsured, or inappropriately insured can be helped only if we adhere to a social ethic for all of health care and distribute psychotherapy and other health-care resources on the basis of need and medical necessity. We must change our present mental health and health-care system. Dreadful circumstances such as those faced by Edward, Alice, and Michael should not be tolerated.

References

Abe-Kim, J., & Takeuchi, D. T. (1996). Cultural competence and quality of care. *Clinical Psychology, 3*(4), 273–295.

American Psychiatric Association. (1994). *Diagnostic and statistical manual of mental disorders* (4th ed.). Washington, DC: Author.

Appelbaum, P. S. (1993). Legal liability and managed care. *American Psychologist, 48*(3), 251–257.

Appelbaum, S. (1992). Evils in private practice. *Bulletin of the Meninger Clinic, 56*(2), 141–149.

Austad, C. S. (1996a). Can psychotherapy be conducted effectively in managed care settings? In A. Lazarus (Ed.), *Controversies in managed mental health care* (pp. 229–249). Washington, DC: American Psychiatric Press.

Austad, C. S. (1996b). *Is long-term psychotherapy unethical? Toward a social ethic in an era of managed care.* San Francisco: Jossey-Bass.

Austad, C. S., & Sherman, W. O. (1992). The psychotherapist and managed care: How will practice be affected? *Psychotherapy in Private Practice, 11*(2), 1–9.

Barlow, D. H. (1996). The effectiveness of psychotherapy: Science and policy. *Clinical Psychology, 3*(3), 236–240.

Bartlett, J. (1994). Practice guidelines. In R. K. Schreter, S. S. Sharfstein, & C. A. Schreter (Eds.), *Allies and adversaries: The impact of managed care on mental health service* (pp. 153–168). Washington, DC: American Psychiatric Press.

Bergin, A., & Garfield, S. (1994). Overview, trends, and future issues. In A. E. Bergin & S. L. Garfield (Eds.), *Handbook of psychotherapy and behavior change* (pp. 821–830). New York: Wiley.

Berman, W. H. (1992). The practice of psychotherapy in managed health care. *Psychotherapy in Private Practice, 11*(2), 39–45.

Bloom, B. (1992). *Planned short-term therapy.* Boston: Allyn & Bacon.

Bloom, B. (1997). *Planned short-term therapy* (2nd ed.). Boston: Allyn & Bacon.

Bogdanich, W. (1991). *The great white lie.* New York: Simon & Schuster.

Bowers, T., & Knapp, S. (1993). Reimbursement issues for psychologists in independent practice. *Psychotherapy in Private Practice, 12*(3), 73–87.

Castro, J. (1994). *The American way of health.* Boston: Little, Brown.

Clemens, N. (1995). Position statement on medical psychotherapy. *American Journal of Psychiatry, 152*(11), 1700.

Cohen, P., & Cohen, J. (1984). The clinician's illusion. *Archives of General Psychiatry, 41*, 1178–1182.

Cummings, N., Pallak, M., & Cummings, J. (1996). *Surviving the demise of solo practice.* Madison, CT: Psychosocial Press.

Cummings, N., & Sayana, M. (1995). *Focused psychotherapy: A casebook of brief intermittent psychotherapy.* New York: Brunner/Mazel.

Dacso, S. T., & Dacso, C. C. (1995). *Managed care answer book.* New York: Aspen Publishers.

Davis, S., & Austad, C. S. (1997). *Ethical decision making amongst managed care psychotherapists.* Unpublished master's thesis, Central Connecticut State University.

Dawes, R. (1994). *House of cards.* New York: Free Press.

Dorken, H. (1994). Managed care intervenes where state regulation fails. In S. A. Shueman, W. G. Troy, & S. L. Mayhugh (Eds.), *Managed behavioral health care: An industry perspective* (pp. 113–126). Springfield, IL: Charles C. Thomas.

Elpers, J. R., & Abbott, B. K. (1992). Public policy, ethical issues, and mental health administration. *Administration & Policy in Mental Health, 19*(6), 437–447.

England, M. J., & Cole, R. (1993). Discussion of use of inpatient services by a national population: Do benefits make a difference? *Journal of the American Academy of Child and Adolescent Psychiatry, 32*(1), 153–154.

Fonagy, P., & Target, M. (1996). Should we allow psychotherapy research to determine clinical practice? *Clinical Psychology, 3*(3), 245–250.

Fox, R. (1995). The rape of psychotherapy: *Professional Psychology: Research and Practice 26*(2), 147–155.

Friedman, E. (1991). The uninsured. *Journal of the American Medical Association, 265*(19), 2401–2405.

Gibson, R. W., & Weissberg, J. H. (1994). Reflections on managed care, health reform, and the survival of dynamic psychotherapy. Psychoanalysis and dynamic psychotherapy, the mental health provider and managed care [Special issue]. *Psychoanalysis & Psychotherapy, 11*(2), 177–180.

Goldsmith, J. (1984, Fall). Death of a paradigm. *Health Affairs*, 12–14.

Haas, L. J. (1994). Managed outpatient mental health plans: Clinical, ethical, and practical guidelines for participation. In L. Lowman & R. J. Resnick (Eds.), *The mental health professional's guide to managed care* (pp. 137–149). Washington, DC: American Psychological Association.

Haley, J. (1976). *Problem solving therapy: New strategies for effective family therapy*. San Francisco: Jossey-Bass.

Harris, E. A. (1995). The importance of risk management in a managed care environment. In M. B. Sussman (Ed.), *A perilous calling: The hazards of psychotherapy practice* (pp. 247–258). New York: Wiley.

Hartmann, L. (1992). Presidential address: Reflections on humane values and biopsychosocial integration. 145th Annual Meeting of the American Psychiatric Association. *American Journal of Psychiatry, 149*(9), 1135–1141.

Hemenway, D., Killen, A., Cashman, S. B., Parks, C. L., & Bicksnell, W. J. (1990). Physician's responses to financial incentives. *New England Journal of Medicine, 322*, 1059–1063.

Himmelstein, D., & Woolhandler, S. (1995). Care denied U.S. residents who are unable to obtain needed medical services. *American Journal of Public Health, 85*(3), 341–344.

Hoyt, M. F. (1994). Characteristics of brief psychotherapy under managed health care. In M. F. Hoyt (Ed.), *Brief therapy and managed care: Readings for contemporary practice* (pp. 1–8). San Francisco: Jossey-Bass.

Karon, B. (1995). Provision of psychotherapy under managed health care: A growing crisis and national nightmare. *Professional Psychology: Research and Practice, 26*, 5–9.

Katz, S. J., Hofer, T. P., & Manning, W. (1996). Physician use in Ontario and the United States. *American Journal of Public Health, 86*(4), 520–524.

Kerns, L. L. (1993). Avoiding liability in managed-care settings during patient transitions. In D. H. Ruben & C. E. Stout (Eds.), *Handbook of managed care for inpatient to outpatient treatment* (pp. 113–126). Westport, CT: Praeger Publishers/Greenwood Publishing.

Kissick, W. L. (1994). *Medicine's dilemmas*. New Haven, CT: Yale University Press.

Koss, M., & Shiang, J. (1994). Research on brief therapy. In A. E. Bergin & S. L. Garfield (Eds.), *Handbook of psychotherapy and behavior change* (pp. 664–700). New York: Wiley.

Lambert, M. J., & Bergin, A. E. (1994). The effectiveness of psychotherapy. In A. E. Bergin & S. L. Garfield (Eds.), *Handbook of psychotherapy and behavior change* (4th ed., pp. 143–189). New York: Wiley.

Morris, J. A. (1994). The history of managed care and its impact on psychodynamic treatment. Psychoanalysis and dynamic psychotherapy, the mental health provider and managed care [Special issue]. *Psychoanalysis & Psychotherapy, 11*(2), 129–137.

Nash, D. B., Markson, L., Howell, S., & Hildreth, E. (1993). Evaluating the competence of physicians in practice: From peer review to performance assessment. *Academic Medicine, 68*(2), 19–26.

Navarro, V. (1992). *Dangerous to your health: Capitalism in health care*. New York: Cornerstone Books.

Newman, F., & Tejeda, M. (1996). The need for research that is designed to support decisions in the delivery of mental health services. *American Psychologist, 51*, 1040–1049.

Newman, R. (1994). Parameters of managed mental health care: Legal, ethical, and professional guidelines. In R. L. Loman & R. J. Resnick (Eds.), *The mental health professional's guide to managed care* (pp. 211–220). Washington, DC: American Psychological Association.

Olfson, M., & Pincus, H. A. (1994). Outpatient psychotherapy in the United States: I. Volume, costs, and user characteristics. *American Journal of Psychiatry, 151,* 1281–1288.

Olsen, D. P. (1995). Ethical cautions in the use of outcomes for resource allocation in the managed care environment of mental health. *Archives of Psychiatric Nursing, 9*(4), 173–178.

Patrick, C., Padgett, D., Burns, B., Schlesinger, H., & Cohen, J. (1993). Use of inpatient services by a national population: Do benefits make a difference? *Journal of the American Academy of Child and Adolescent Psychiatry, 32*(1), 144–152.

Phillips, L. (1985). *A guide for therapists and patients to short-term psychotherapy.* Springfield, IL: Charles C. Thomas.

Pipal, J. E. (1995). Managed care: Is it the corpse in the living room? An expose. *Psychotherapy, 32*(2), 323–332.

Quick, E. K. (1993). *Doing what works in brief therapy.* San Diego, CA: Academic Press.

Richardson, L. M., & Austad, C. S. (1994). Managed mental health care: Critical issues and next directions: Realities of mental health practice in managed care settings. In L. Loman & R. J. Resnick (Eds.), *The mental health practitioner's guide to managed care* (pp. 278–296). Washington, DC: American Psychological Association.

Rodriguez, A. R. (1994). Quality-of-care guidelines. In R. K. Schreter, S. S. Sharfstein, & C. A. Schreter (Eds.), *Allies and adversaries: The impact of managed care on mental health services* (pp. 169–185). Washington, DC: American Psychiatric Press.

Rodwin, M. (1993). *Money, medicine, and morals.* New York: Oxford University Press.

Sabin, J. E. (1994a). Caring about patients and caring about money: The American Psychiatric Association code of ethics meets managed care. *Behavioral Sciences & the Law, 12*(4), 317–330.

Sabin, J. E. (1994b). Ethical issues under managed care. In R. K. Schreter, S. S. Sharfstein, & C. A. Schreter (Eds.), *Allies and adversaries: The impact of managed care on mental health services* (pp. 187–200). Washington, DC: American Psychiatric Press.

Sands, H. (1994). Overview: Psychoanalysis and dynamic psychotherapy, the mental health provider and managed care [Special issue]. *Psychoanalysis & Psychotherapy, 11*(2), 107–112.

Scheidemandel, P. (1994). *Coverage for mental and nervous disorders: A compendium of public and private sector health insurance plans* (3rd ed.). Washington, DC: American Psychiatric Press.

Seligman, M. (1995). The effectiveness of psychotherapy: The Consumer Reports Study. *American Psychologist, 50*(12), 969.

Sleek, S. (1996). State laws are reining in managed care. *The American Psychological Association Monitor, 27*(11), 1, 34.

Shapiro, D. A. (1996). Validated treatments and evidence based psychological services. *Clinical Psychology, 3*(3), 256–259.

Simon, I. (1994). Ethics, psychodynamic treatment, and managed care. Psychoanalysis and dynamic psychotherapy, the mental health provider and managed care [Special issue]. *Psychoanalysis & Psychotherapy, 11*(2), 119–128.

Spencer, C. S., Frank, R. G., & McGuire, T. (1996). How should the profit motive be used in managed care? In A. Lazarus (Ed.), *Controversies in managed mental health care* (pp. 279–290). Washington, DC: American Psychiatric Press.

Starr, P. (1982). *The social transformation of American medicine.* New York: Basic Books.

Stechler, G. (1994). The blind oppressing the recalcitrant: Psychoanalysis, managed care, and family systems. Psychoanalysis and dynamic psychotherapy, the mental health provider and managed care [Special issue]. *Psychoanalysis & Psychotherapy, 11*(2), 229–239.

Stein, L. I. (1994). *Maturing mental health systems: New challenges and opportunities. New directions for mental health services.* San Francisco: Jossey-Bass.

Taube, C., Goldman, H., Burns, B., & Kessler, L. (1988). High users of outpatient mental health services: I. Definitions and characteristics. *American Journal of Psychiatry, 145,* 19–24.

Webb, W., Rothschild, B. S., & Monroe, L. (1994). Ethical codes of conduct in the medical profession. In R. E. Hales, S. C. Yudofsky, & J. A. Talbott (Eds.), Ethics and psychiatry (pp. 1341–1354). Washington, DC: American Psychiatric Press.

Welch, B. L. (1994). Managed care: The "basic fault." Psychoanalysis and dynamic psychotherapy, the mental health provider and managed care [Special issue]. *Psychoanalysis & Psychotherapy, 11*(2), 166–176.

Wilson, (1996). Empirically validated treatments: Reality and resistance. *Clinical Psychology, 3*(3), 241–244.

Zimet, C. (1989). The mental health care revolution: Will psychology survive? *American Psychologist, 44,* 703–708.

6

Ethics and Outcomes in Managed Behavioral Health Care: "Trust Me, I'm a Psychologist"

Sarah Pratt, William H. Berman, and Stephen W. Hurt

Outcomes management—the evaluation of the effectiveness of health-care delivery in natural settings—is the most recent in a series of innovations in the delivery of mental health and substance abuse services. Outcomes management as a scientific endeavor follows on the heels of the growth of behavioral and cognitive therapies, research demonstrating the efficacy of psychotherapy, and increased standardization of psychological treatments through manuals and controlled clinical trials. On the service delivery side, outcomes management is a natural outgrowth of changes in the process of treatment such as utilization review, reduced inpatient length of stay, and briefer, more focused outpatient treatment. On the service utilization side, growing concern about the convenience, effectiveness, and satisfaction with services has created demand for outcomes data. Increased emphasis on the prepayment of behavioral health services through capitation (paying fees on the basis of the number of patients available independent of whether they seek services), case rates (paying a fixed fee for each case regardless of duration or type of treatment), and other methods of predictive costing has also contributed to purchaser and payer interest in outcomes data.

Until Eysenck's review in 1952 suggesting that psychotherapy was no more effective in ameliorating emotional distress than no treatment, effectiveness of mental health treatment was not questioned or perhaps even considered. Since that time, the efficacy of psychotherapy has been well demonstrated (e.g., Crits-Christoph, 1992; Shadish et al., 1993), and its value to many consumers has been documented (e.g., Seligman, 1995). Assessment of the effectiveness of psychotherapy as it is practiced in a variety of real-world settings, however, is not yet a routine part of the administration and review of mental health treatment. The reality of mental health care is that most patients enter therapeutic relationships without knowing whether the treatment they will receive has been demonstrated to be effective with individuals having similar problems. Most patients have sought therapy from clinicians whose skills and expertise were judged solely by referral or word of mouth.

The impetus for increased emphasis on evaluating outcomes in behavioral health care has come from several sources. First, sophisticated purchasers of health-care services, such as corporations insuring their employees, have required specific data regarding not only the types of services provided but also the effectiveness of those services (Darling, 1995). Second, third-party payers, specifically managed care organizations, have exerted increased pressure on health-care providers to control costs, practice brief approaches to treatment, and demonstrate that the services they provide are not only efficient but also cost effective (Giles, 1993). Third, primary consumers of mental health services have become more aware of the many treatment options available and desire documentation of the quality of the care they will receive (Shern & Flynn, 1996).

Outcomes management serves several important functions in the mental health field, including evaluating and refining treatments, enhancing the credibility of psychotherapy, identifying the most effective treatments, and providing clear descriptions of therapeutic procedures (Pekarik, 1993). Information obtained from outcomes management may also be instrumental in moving the intense debate about the quality of treatment in managed care settings from opinion and individual experience to substantive knowledge and informed policy.

The current marketplace of mental health care increasingly demands greater accountability on the part of its caregivers. As noted earlier, mental health professionals are accountable both to purchasers and to consumers of health care, as well as to managed care organizations. The demonstration that psychotherapeutic treatments are effective through evaluation and assessment of outcomes will provide needed data for purchasers and managed care organizations. More important, mental health professionals are accountable to the patients they treat. They have an important ethical responsibility to provide services that can be expected to be effective in ameliorating psychological distress. Ongoing assessment of outcomes is an ethical response to the expectation that psychologists provide treatments that have a reasonable potential for success. This includes the assessment of treatments as they are practiced in real-world settings (effectiveness) and in the laboratory (efficacy).

The measurement, collection, and use of outcomes data in standard clinical practice have been described extensively in other publications, and are beyond the scope of this chapter. Readers seeking more in-depth information can find extensive references on the basics of outcomes (e.g., Mirin & Namerow, 1991; Sederer & Dickey, 1996), conceptual models of outcomes (e.g., Berman, Rosen, Hurt, & Kolarz, 1998), reviews of outcomes data (e.g., Speer & Newman, 1996), and outcomes in the broader human services fields (e.g., Mullen & Magnabosco, 1997).

Is Outcomes Management Research?

Outcomes management is the assessment of patient clinical status over time (Berman et al., 1998). It may vary with respect to its goals, the domains being assessed, who provides the data, and when the data are collected. What is consistent across outcomes efforts are the methods and procedures. The methods of outcomes management are both familiar and confusing to many psychologists (Berman, Hurt, & Heiss, 1996). It is important to differentiate psychotherapy outcome research from mental health outcomes management, or *mental health services research*, as it is sometimes called. The distinctions between outcome research and outcomes management are highlighted in Table 1.

Most psychologists' training has emphasized the value of research with a true experimental design, including randomized, controlled clinical trials. In accordance with this, research on the effects of psychotherapy was deemed valuable only if it resembled outcome research as outlined in Table 1. In other areas of the social sciences, however, naturalistic evaluation research has enjoyed a long and respected tradition. Health services research, which often includes naturalistic evaluation, has had many proponents and has played a major role in public policy regarding health care on the state and federal levels.

The most important distinction between outcome research and outcomes management is the difference in their basic goals. Outcome research attempts to answer the question, "Is treatment X better than treatment Y (or no treatment)." This can best be demonstrated by using a true experimental design, with small, homogeneous samples and specific, highly standardized interventions. This type of research does not address issues of risk adjustment (Iezzoni, 1994) such as different severity mixes, symptom profiles, and sociodemographic characteristics; profiling of providers (Lasker, Shapiro, & Tucker, 1992; Welch, Miller, & Welch, 1994); or quality improvement efforts (Berwick, Godfrey, & Roessner, 1990). More important, outcome research does not answer questions raised by many clinicians in the course of real-world clinical practice, such as "How am I doing? Is therapy working with the particular population I see? Can I predict who will do well? and What can I do to get better results with my patients?" These questions can only be answered through outcomes evaluation (Berman & Hurt, 1996). Outcomes management that is naturalistic and longitudinal is essential to answer the important question, "Is treat-

Table 1. Distinguishing Outcome Research From Outcomes Management

Outcomes research	Outcomes management
Random assignment to treatments	Treatment assignment by clinical judgment
Homogeneous samples	Heterogeneous samples
Discrete diagnostic groups	Broad spectrum of problems and diagnoses
Manualized treatments, supervised clinicians	Treatment "as usual"
Single treatments	Multiple interventions based on need
Emphasizes reliability and internal validity over external validity	Emphasizes external validity over internal validity

ment X effective as delivered in my mental health setting by my providers and with my population of patients?"

The ethical and practical implications of research studies, evaluation studies, and assessment of standard clinical care are different. Therefore, it is important to determine how outcomes management resembles these more traditional areas before discussing the ethical issues that may arise in collecting patient data.

Research studies commonly address a discrete question or set of questions that is examined in a specific population for a limited period of time. In general, they include predetermined groups or randomized assignment to treatment groups. Research studies have implications for general knowledge or future practice rather than for individual treatment or current practice. By emphasizing statistically significant differences among treatment groups, research studies often overlook treatment effects on individual patients (Beutler, Williams, Wakefield, & Entwhistle, 1995). In addition, research typically involves homogeneous groups of participants with a "pure" form of a disorder in order to refine understanding of the disorder. Such homogeneity is not typical of the general population of patients, who commonly present with multiple problems (Seligman, 1995).

Psychologists conducting research studies on treatment outcome must adhere to the ethical standards established regarding the use of human participants in research. Researchers at universities, hospitals, and other large mental health facilities also face scrutiny by institutional review boards responsible for ensuring that study procedures are designed and implemented in an ethically responsible manner.

Naturalistic outcomes evaluation studies, on the other hand, typically involve assessment of a specific program or activity and analyze the process as well as the effectiveness of the services offered (Speer & Newman, 1996). This type of research typically uses retrospective designs and archival data collected for other purposes. Follow-up data collection, including clinical interviews and questionnaires, is also a frequent component of an evaluation study. Retrospective data analyses, reviews of claims data, or chart reviews typically do not raise as many ethical concerns as outcome research. For example, these types of reviews do not require informed consent, as long as they are conducted by individuals who are involved in the treatment process, such as hospital staff or private mental health practitioners.

Unlike treatment outcome research or evaluation studies, outcomes management relies on data that are collected as a standard part of the administration of services to patients seeking treatment in real-world settings and that benefit the individuals on whom the data are collected. Traditionally, research studies in psychology have had a clear beginning and end, with conclusions drawn at the close of the study. The knowledge gained from research, if utilized at all, was often applied to populations other than those who participated in the research. Psychologists conducting outcomes management, however, may use the data on a case-by-case basis or sometimes analyze data several times during an ongoing process of data collection. If researchers determine through such analyses that treatment could be improved in some way, they may have an ethical responsibility to their patients or clients to improve the quality of the treatment they are receiving even as they are receiving it (Gordon, Hursch, & Gordon, 1988; Morrison, 1993; Sieber, 1992).

Conducting outcomes management as part of the routine process of treating patients can be scientifically rigorous and provide invaluable data if the study procedures are well designed and consistent and include adequate controls for reliability and validity. Outcomes management that is regarded as treatment research must adhere to the stringent ethical requirements established by law and professional codes of ethics for research with human participants.

Collection of outcomes data may be considered standard practice if the data have specific relevance to the patient's care and are used to improve individual treatment or general treatment procedures. The ethical standards for this type of investigation may be different than those required for discrete studies with a more specific focus. For example, informed consent is only necessary to the extent that consent is required in the context of routine clinical care. Ultimately, application of the appropriate ethical standards, either those that must be followed in routine administration of treatment or the more stringent standards required by research with human participants, depends on the nature of the outcomes investigation.

In summary, we distinguish among experimental outcome research, naturalistic outcomes evaluation, and outcomes management. Experimental research involves specific protocols for treatment, inclusion and exclusion criteria, and typically uses random assignment to treatments. Naturalistic outcomes evaluation uses none of these procedures but rather examines a specific hypothesis or question by using naturally occurring populations and groupings of treatments. Outcomes management involves the collection and use of standardized measures of clinical state over time as a part of regular patient care. The ethical standards that apply in each of these cases may be somewhat different. We recommend that, when available, institutional review boards review all types of data collection procedures to ensure that the information is collected appropriately, managed carefully, and handled consistently with the goals of the effort.

Professional Standards and Outcomes Management

Mental health professionals are bound by state and federal law and regulations, as well as professional standards, to deal with patients in an ethically responsible manner, which includes selecting treatments that are expected to be effective in reducing suffering. In planning any type of ethically responsible research, psychologists are guided by several standards in the "Ethical Principles of Psychologists and Code of Conduct" (Ethical Principles; American Psychological Association [APA], 1992). Investigations of treatment that are supported by any federal department or agency are also subject to federal regulation by the Department of Health and Human Services (DHHS) and therefore must comply with the standards in the *Protection of Human Subjects Code of Federal Regulations* (Publication No. 45 CFR 46; DHHS, 1995).

The expectation that clinical facilities be able to demonstrate effectiveness of treatments is rapidly becoming a part of the accreditation standards for the Joint Commission on the Accreditation of Healthcare Organizations (1998) and the National Council on Quality Assurance (1998). Demonstrating favorable results of mental health services may soon become one of the benchmarks by which therapists' competence is measured. Clinicians' proficiency and success cannot be determined solely by the positive effects of treatment on their patients. In the absence of objective assessment of change in their patients, it is difficult for clinicians or third parties to know whether psychotherapy as they practice it produces consistent and demonstrable improvements.

The development, implementation, and analysis of data from outcomes management require training and expertise. Psychologists are ethically bound to engage only in activities within their scope of expertise (APA, 1992). Many clinicians primarily engage in clinical service and may not have the background or expertise needed to conduct outcomes management according to proper, ethically responsible, scientifically sound procedures. The best outcomes management requires both clinical and research skills, but clearly the "grand aspiration [of training professionals to be scientists and practitioners], rarely has been achieved in individual psychologists, . . . few of whom, despite lip service, genuinely contribute in both research and practice venues" (Stricker & Trierweiler, 1995, p. 995).

The Ethical Principles (APA, 1992) include several general standards regarding competence, maintenance of knowledge, and sharing of information, all of which have implications for outcomes management. Ethical Standard 1.04 pertains to psychologists' responsibility with regard to their level of competence in performing their duties. It requires that psychologists be skilled in the services they provide in order to protect patients, clients, research participants, and others from harm. Standard 1.04 may be interpreted as requiring psychologists to demonstrate competence in conducting outcomes evaluation when such evaluation is a part of standard clinical service. Other standards regarding competence in conducting research remind psychologists to perform "only those tasks for which they are appropriately trained and prepared" and to seek consultation when studying special populations for whom additional expertise is needed (Standard 6.07; APA, 1992). Unfortunately, the principles do not specify how competence should be assessed, so clinicians usually determine their own competence (Haas, Malouf, & Mayerson, 1986).

Ethical Standard 1.05 requires psychologists to maintain competence and expertise in their area of practice and recognize the need for ongoing education (APA, 1992). Knowledge gained from outcomes management can and should be utilized to continually improve the treatment administered by mental health professionals. We have written elsewhere that outcomes management is a tool to be used in the pursuit of continuously improving quality (Berman & Hurt, 1996).

The Ethical Principles also require psychologists, in Standard 1.06, to "rely on scientifically and professionally derived knowledge when making scientific or professional judgments" (APA, 1992). Decisions about treatment planning and appropriate psychotherapeutic technique certainly qualify as "professional judgments," and outcomes management may be considered "scientifically and professionally derived knowledge." The knowledge behind professional judgments is increasingly derived from empirical data. The collection and dissemination of outcomes data will increase this knowledge base and enhance outcomes for all patients. A logical interpretation of this standard is that psychologists have an ethical responsibility to administer treatments that have been proven effective by outcomes management in a variety of clinical settings, including their own practices.

Psychologists have a responsibility, under Principle F of the Ethical Principles, to "apply and make public their knowledge of psychology in order to contribute to human welfare" (APA, 1992). In the context of outcomes management, effectiveness data for different disorders, for different treatment approaches, and for different provider organizations will contribute to human welfare. It certainly is reasonable to suggest that the collection of outcomes data is an ethical activity for the mental health profession.

The process of conducting outcomes management is complex but is manageable by individual practitioners without retraining or expensive consultations. The crucial issues for individual practitioners include the use of highly reliable instruments, implementation of standardized data capture procedures, and sensitivity to the uses of outcomes data. For group practices and larger service delivery organizations, these issues may be too complicated for psychologists who do not have training or experience in conducting this type of research. Unlike individual practitioners, large mental health care facilities must consider differences between multiple providers, multiple clinical populations, and provision of a full continuum of care. A number of software packages, outcomes services, consultants, and researchers are available to assist larger organizations in conducting ethical outcomes management.

Planning Ethically Responsible Outcomes Management

Before commencing research on psychotherapeutic treatments, psychologists "should consider the full range of ethical issues when deciding which clients to use for research participants, which problems to target for change, [and] which measurement procedures to use" (Nelsen, 1994, p. 140). The same can be said for outcomes management. Despite the fact that outcomes management may not always be considered research per se, in planning any type of ethically responsible investigation of outcomes, psychologists should consider several standards in the Ethical Principles (APA, 1992) that may be construed as guidelines for the design of outcomes management.

Standard 6.06 of the Ethical Principles addresses ethical responsibilities of researchers in a broad sense, advising psychologists to "take reasonable steps to implement appropriate protections for the rights and welfare of human participants" (APA, 1992, p. 1608). Psychologists are also
advised to design, conduct, and report research "in accordance with recognized standards of scientific competence and ethical research" and to
"conduct research competently" (Standards 6.06 and 6.07, p. 1608). The
Ethical Principles address specific responsibilities with respect to such
matters as informed consent, confidentiality, and financial inducements
offered to participants (a common practice in consumer survey research
such as Neilson ratings and product satisfaction surveys). Issues such as
respondent burden, clinical and personal relevance, focus of the research,
and insurance coverage should also be considered in planning ethically
responsible outcomes management.

Informed Consent

Psychologists have an ethical responsibility to inform patients about the
nature of their care and to obtain their informed consent for that care
(Standards 4.02 and 6.11; APA, 1992). They should also inform patients
about potential risks and benefits, treatment alternatives, and standard
administrative, financial, and clinical procedures involved in their care.
Outcomes management is no different in this regard. If a clinical setting
engages in routine outcomes management that is used for patient care as
well as quality improvement, the informed consent used by that clinical
setting should indicate such use of the data. If the outcomes management
is a part of ongoing clinical practice, the consent should include a description of the process, the benefits and risks, and the use of the information.
Any efforts at posttreatment follow-up should be explained in advance and
at the time of the follow-up, and patients should be given the opportunity
to refuse posttreatment follow-up. If the data from outcomes management
are expected to have a real impact on the patients' treatment, the patients
should also be informed of that.

When data are collected as part of a discrete time-limited study of a
particular treatment that resembles true experimental research, a separate informed consent should be provided. The clinician or facility should
explain to patients, in language that is comprehensible, the nature of the
study, including risks, benefits, adverse effects, alternative treatments,
limits of confidentiality, and potential discomfort. Consent should include
information regarding how data will be used and who will see the results
(APA, 1992; DHHS, 1995; Gordon et al., 1988; Nelsen, 1994). Patients
should be informed of deviations from expected practice; for example, if
treatment is determined by something other than clinician judgment, such
as random assignment to treatment type.

The requirements for informed consent may present particular problems with patients who are unable to give truly informed consent, such as
children or persons with severe mental illnesses (Sieber, 1994). For ex-

ample, the power differential between psychologist and child may make refusal to participate in outcomes management difficult for children, which increases the ethical risk of having participants who are uncomfortable and yet reluctant to withdraw from a study (Weber, Miracle, & Skehan, 1994). In such cases, the Ethical Principles advise obtaining consent from a "legally authorized person" (Standards 4.02 and 6.11; APA, 1992).

Confidentiality

Standards 5.01, 5.02, 5.03, 5.04, 5.05, 5.06, and 5.07 concern psychologists' responsibilities with respect to protecting the privacy and confidentiality rights of individuals with whom they work, including participants in outcomes evaluation. Psychologists have an ethical duty to inform participants of the limitations on confidentiality, preferably at the beginning of a contact (study or episode of care). Patients involved in outcomes management are entitled to the same confidentiality rights as any other consumer of mental health services. Likewise, the same limits on confidentiality apply, and data collected should become a part of the patient's chart.

The potential impact of the electronic management of information on confidentiality must be considered by mental health professionals conducting outcomes management. Currently, an increasing percentage of clinical, billing, and outcomes data are entered into some type of electronic database. Computer technology enables mental health professionals to maintain permanent records on all patients, which may be pooled periodically and analyzed for trends (Gordon et al., 1988; Morrison, 1993). The use of computer technology in the mental health field greatly facilitates the outcomes management process; in fact, computers may serve as a bridge for connecting research and practice (Bongar, 1988).

Although computers are invaluable to the outcomes management process, they also create a number of ethical concerns, particularly those that threaten confidentiality. The ease with which computer files can be examined leaves them vulnerable to loss, theft, and unauthorized duplication. The ability to transmit data via modem also risks confidentiality. The simplicity of producing computer-generated analyses may risk misuse of research results by uneducated users (Bongar, 1988; Schlosser, 1993).

A number of protections can be implemented to reduce threats to confidentiality. Encryption of files and password protection both at the general computer level and the program or application level are necessary. Patient data from computer databases that have been backed up onto computer disks should be stored carefully, either with separate storage companies or in secure facilities within the clinician's area of practice (Bongar, 1988). The use of a removable hard drive limits access to records and therefore increases the security of patient data (Bongar, 1988; Schlosser, 1993). Finally, copy protection devices may be used to prevent unauthorized duplication of data (Bongar, 1988).

Financial Inducements

One of the most important aspects of outcomes management is obtaining adequate numbers of participants for the questions being analyzed. The possibility of offering financial or other inducements to patients for these data is frequently considered. The fundamental ethical issue with regard to inducements is that of coercion; in other words, is the amount of the inducement sufficient to compel some to participate who would not otherwise do so (Ethical Standards 6.14 and 1.19; APA, 1992). In general, this means that financial remuneration should be commensurate with the duration and the risk of the procedures. This issue of coercion may be particularly important when the outcomes management involves patients who do not directly consent, such as minors. If the inducements are kept to the type and size typically found in survey research (less than $5), the risk of coercion is relatively minor.

In the context of outcomes management, the ethics of inducements is related to the nature of the investigation. If the outcomes management is part of a specific study, then financial or treatment inducements are probably within ethical boundaries. If the outcomes data are collected as a standard part of treatment, however, it would not be appropriate to provide inducements such as high payments or free treatment. Small inducements are probably sufficient to obtain reasonable posttreatment response rates, but if the treatment is part of standard clinical practice, the institution in which the outcomes management is conducted should carefully consider the pros and cons of financial inducements. In some cases, the benefits of financial reimbursement in terms of the value of the information obtained may outweigh the costs of potential coercion, but this cannot be established without careful consideration of the particulars of each case. The ethical guidelines should emphasize the balance of gaining knowledge about treatment effectiveness against the possible risks to the participant (Sieber, 1994).

Burden

Outcomes management usually requires patients to complete numerous questionnaires designed to assess improvement, often at several points during the treatment process. Although "self-reports are the blood and guts of a clinical diagnosis" (Seligman, 1995, p. 972), there is some ethical concern in asking patients to comment on their own mental and emotional state. When the patient's level of distress is severe, it may be unethical to place this burden on individuals until they have found some relief. Clinician-based data may be more ethical (and more appropriate) for patients who are too disturbed to effectively attend to, or effectively complete, standardized instruments.

The burden of paperwork does not rest solely with the participants in outcomes management. Both clinicians and support staff are also called on to complete and manage greater than normal amounts of treatment forms, which may adversely affect service delivery, representing a potential ethical question in terms of the effect on patients. It is likely, given the additional burden outcomes management places on their practices, that many clinicians will resist the mandate to assess their treatment. However, those who rely on reimbursement from third-party payers, particularly managed care companies, will increasingly be called on to demonstrate that the services they provide are cost effective. All mental health care providers, even those who do not face pressure from managed care, ought to include some type of outcomes management as part of their routine administration of services because they have an ethical responsibility to their patients to offer treatments that have been proven effective through a process of evaluation, modification, and reevaluation (Morrison, 1993).

Personal and Clinical Relevance

The measures and procedures for measurement are of particular concern in outcomes management. If outcomes management is conducted as a standard part of treatment, it is important that the data collected be both relevant to the individuals being evaluated and have some relationship to the clinical phenomena being treated. The evaluation of risk adjustment factors, and the examination of clinical processes, should be determined either by prior research or by clear clinical indications of relevance. Screening tools, such as general symptom inventories, are useful and necessary, but it is important that measures and instruments be carefully selected. A combination of minimal burden, minimal redundancy, and some relationship to the patient's subjective experience are basic guidelines for selecting the total set of measures in outcomes management. It is also valuable to include some idiographic measure, such as goal attainment scaling (Kiresuk, Smith, & Cardillo, 1993; Lewis, Spencer, Haas, & DiVittis, 1987) or a current problem narrative, to enhance focus on the patient's experience.

Follow-Up Evaluations

Assessment of patients after treatment has been terminated can provide invaluable information about the long-term effectiveness of therapy (Johan, 1989). Empirical research in mental health care has included increasingly long periods of posttreatment follow-up. It has been suggested that patients be asked to return to clinicians every 6 months to follow up on the effectiveness of treatment (e.g., Gordon et al., 1988). It is more feasible to argue that outcomes management should include follow-up assessment for periods of time consistent with the goals of the treatment being provided. Inpatient treatment may only need follow-up after the first month, for example, whereas outpatient therapy may require 6-month or 12-month follow-up points.

Although information about long-term functioning is crucial to understanding the process and evaluating the effectiveness of psychotherapy, follow-up contact with patients raises a number of ethical concerns (Johan, 1989). Scheduled follow-up of which the patient is aware, and therefore anticipates, may hinder separation from the therapist. Continued reliance on the therapist may prevent the patient from developing a sense of autonomy during and perhaps even after the follow-up period. Likewise, follow-up may cause a therapist to needlessly hang on to patients, which could discourage growth and independence. Patients may be left with a false sense that the therapist will continue to take care of them, thereby forestalling the necessary closure of the therapeutic relationship. Many of these issues can be handled by delegating the follow-up assessments to another individual. This, however, raises issues of confidentiality and privacy.

Follow-up assessments potentially threaten the patient's privacy and confidentiality rights in at least three ways. First, their identities must be known in order to reestablish contact. Second, the amount of data on patients in computer files obviously increases with the addition of follow-up data. Third, staffing changes over time may mean that patients are contacted or seen by several different mental health professionals over the course of the research (Johan, 1989). We do not see these problems as prohibitive. Rather, these are issues that require sensitivity, open information to the patient regarding the need for and uses of outcomes data, and clarity of intent and goals.

Individual or Group Focus?

To what degree outcomes management focuses on the individual or aggregate groups is a question that evaluators must face. There may be times when research to benefit a group conflicts with the needs and concerns of individual participants. In this vein, the psychologist designing and implementing outcomes management must balance the needs of the individual patient and the needs of the rest of the population being served. Although outcomes management should benefit individual patients, they may also be used to assess practice patterns, the effectiveness of treatments for specific subpopulations, and the processes of care in the clinical setting. The needs of a population (e.g., a community, employees of a corporation, or state residents) must enter into research planning and decision making in ways that have not previously been considered (Austad, 1996).

Insurance Coverage

Psychologists practicing in any setting involving third-party payment, including managed care environments, are constrained by the coverage provided by individual insurance plans. An ethical dilemma may arise if outcomes data suggest that patients would benefit from more services than those provided by their insurance plan. In other words, ethical problems may be raised by conflicts between data regarding the effectiveness of mental health treatment and the availability of third-party funds to pay for that treatment. This type of phenomenon has been documented already by research on the treatment of depression (Sturm & Wells, 1995). In the short run, clinicians may be in the position of having to continue with a patient despite a lack of insurance coverage. In the long run, clinicians will be responsible for providing data regarding additional need for services to managed care companies in efforts to alter benefit plans.

Who Conducts and Uses Data From Outcomes Management?

The issue of who collects, analyzes, and reports the data from outcomes management has obvious ethical implications. In some cases, managed care facilities hire outside consultants to coordinate outcomes management. Under this scenario, clinicians and health-care staff are responsible only for requesting that patients complete assessment instruments and sending the data to the consultants, who maintain and analyze the data.

Clinicians conducting outcomes management on their own patients have an ethical obligation to analyze data collected from them in a responsible manner and to report results accurately, despite the vested interest in finding that the treatment yielded significantly positive results. It would clearly be unethical for a clinician to present results from an outcomes management that was poorly designed or poorly controlled and that was based on data that were poorly analyzed, particularly if treatment decisions relied on or made use of the findings (Gordon et al., 1988). Clinical facilities conducting outcomes management as a standard part of practice have an ethical responsibility to enter these data in the patient record and to share the information with the patient as clinical judgment indicates. Psychologists should be attentive to the needs and expectations of all stakeholders in the outcomes management enterprise, including the patients, the clinicians, the managed care organizations, and the purchaser–employers (Sieber, 1994).

The application of results of outcomes management to daily practice is as much a concern for psychologists as the results themselves. The ethical implications of the many possible uses of the data on treatment effectiveness should carefully be considered. Given the concern for cost containment, managed care companies may use outcomes management to make financial decisions. Many stakeholders, including clinicians, patients, and insurers, hope that health care may become more effective by becoming more efficient. When this is not possible, however, the balance of cost and treatment effectiveness becomes an ethical and moral decision more than a scientific one.

Health-care professionals must be acutely aware of the meaning of outcomes data and its potential uses in the current economic climate. Some mental health providers fear that information from outcomes management will be used to scrutinize and perhaps weed out providers deemed ineffective (Morrison, 1993). This is already occurring in several large managed care organizations (Marques, 1996). Both the quality and the validity of the data used in these contexts must be impeccable or else they should not be used in this way.

Summary and Recommendations for Ethical Outcomes Management

Information about the effectiveness of treatments needs to come from well-designed, ethically responsible, systematic evaluation designs. These designs must include a clearly articulated plan that specifies whom the study is targeted to serve, what the goals are, how the constructs will be measured, how the measures relate to the goals, and how the data will be used. They should also include measures that are specific to the population being evaluated and analyses that are appropriate to the data and the questions being addressed. Outcomes management should include not only measures of treatment results but also of case-mix or risk-adjustment variables, such as age, gender, and ethnicity, that help to equate or differentiate patient populations. Process variables such as duration of treatment, type of treatment, intersession time period, and the like facilitate the understanding of both individual differences and provider or facility-based domains of improvement.

Whether outcomes management is included as part of routine practice or resembles a tightly controlled experimental study, it should be planned and conducted in an ethically responsible manner. Researchers or clinicians should consider the ethical implications of the focus and rationale of the study. And, as described earlier, psychologists should obtain informed consent, providing information about risks, benefits, confidentiality, use of data, potential adverse effects of treatment, alternate treatments, and follow-up contact.

To ensure that psychologists uphold their ethical responsibility to perform their duties in a competent manner, they should be familiar with the psychometric properties of the measures designed to assess treatment effectiveness or retain appropriate consultation from experts. In general, psychologists conducting outcomes management should use measures that are short, designed for repeated administration, and sensitive to change. Researchers should also be familiar with appropriate data-analytic techniques required for competent data analysis or they should obtain counsel from knowledgeable professionals.

The confidentiality of research participants must be maintained. The current computer technology requires that psychologists use a variety of security techniques, such as removable hard drives, coding of data, passwords and data encryption, proper training of computer operators, and closely monitored access to computer files.

Most important, researchers must be careful to guard against unethical misuse of data, including any use resulting in the reduction of quality care for patients. Ethically responsible research is that which is designed to gain valuable information about patient, therapist, and treatment variables and which may be used to improve psychotherapeutic treatments. Researchers conducting outcomes management have an ethical responsibility to improve psychotherapeutic interventions by feeding results from studies back into treatment.

Conclusions

Despite the difficulty in addressing the numerous ethical issues that must be considered in planning outcomes management, "simply foregoing . . . objective evaluation of practice is not the best way to respond to these various ethical issues" (Nelsen, 1994, p. 139). Mental health professionals are encountering mounting pressure for accountability from managed care companies and "accountable practice has come to mean making some systematic effort to measure client's responses to service" (Nelsen, 1994, p. 139). It is therefore becoming increasingly necessary for mental health professionals and staff to incorporate measurement and assessment of treatment as part of the normal process of doing business (Morrison, 1993). By conducting outcomes management, psychologists will also be fulfilling an ethical responsibility to administer treatments that have been proven effective.

Psychologists have an ethical responsibility not only to assess their treatments but also to keep themselves informed of outcomes investigations performed by their colleagues. Currently, despite the existing body of research on psychotherapeutic treatment of mental and emotional disorders, "success and failure of different types of treatment [demonstrated by empirical studies] seem to have little influence on practitioners" (Eysenck, 1994, p. 491). This point is illustrated by the empirical research on enuresis, which has repeatedly demonstrated the effectiveness and superiority of the bell-and-pad method over psychotherapy. In spite of these findings and the absence of studies demonstrating the effectiveness of psychotherapy, a significant majority of therapists continue to treat enuresis with psychotherapy. Often, this occurs because of therapists' allegiance to, comfort with, and confidence in a particular treatment orientation (Giles, 1993). The ethical implications of deciding to treat a disorder with demonstrably less effective treatment in light of evidence supporting the success of another, however, are considerable. It may become more apparent as the volume of outcomes data mounts that "it is unethical to engage in practices that fly in the face of scientific evidence" (Stricker & Trierweiler, 1995, p. 998).

It is becoming increasingly clear that the opinions of individual health-care providers may not represent sufficient justification for treatment decisions in the eyes of purchasers and managed care administrators. Although "requiring randomized controlled trials to justify every intervention would set too high a hurdle" (Sabin, 1994, p. 860), some balance will have to be struck between blind acceptance of clinical judgment and complete reliance on the results of experimental data. The future of individual clinical decisions may depend on outcomes management as a means of demonstrating the overall effectiveness of psychotherapeutic interventions and upholding the ethical responsibility to provide treatment that has a demonstrable likelihood of succeeding.

References

American Psychological Association. (1992). Ethical principles of psychologists and code of conduct. *American Psychologist, 47,* 1597–1611.

Austad, C. S. (1996). *Is long-term psychotherapy unethical?* San Francisco: Jossey-Bass.

Berman, W. H., & Hurt, S. W. (1996). Talking the talk, walking the walk: Implementing an Outcomes Information System. *Behavioral Healthcare Tomorrow, 5,* 39–43.

Berman, W. H., Hurt, S. W., & Heiss, G. (1996). Outcomes assessment in behavioral healthcare. In C. E. Stout, J. Theis, & J. Oher (Eds.), *The complete guide to managed behavioral care* (2nd ed., pp. 1–6). New York: Wiley.

Berman, W. H., Rosen, C., Hurt, S. W., & Kolarz, C. (1998). Toto, we're not in Kansas anymore: Measuring and using outcomes in behavioral health care. *Clinical Psychology: Science and Practice, 5,* 115–133.

Berwick, D. M, Godfrey, A. B., & Roessner, J. (1990). *Curing health care: New strategies for quality improvement.* San Francisco: Jossey-Bass.

Beutler, L. E., Williams, R. E., Wakefield, P. J., & Entwhistle, S. R. (1995). Bridging scientist and practitioner perspectives in clinical psychology. *American Psychologist, 50,* 984–994.

Bongar, B. (1988). Clinicians, microcomputers, and confidentiality. *Professional Psychology: Research and Practice, 19,* 286–289.

Crits-Christoph, P. (1992). The efficacy of brief dynamic psychotherapy: A meta-analysis. *American Journal of Psychiatry, 149,* 151–158.

Darling H. (1995). Market reform: Large corporations lead the way. *Health Affairs, 14,* 122–124.

Department of Health and Human Services. (1995). *Protection of Human Subjects Code of Federal Regulations* (DHHS Publication No. 45 CFR 46, Subparts A and D). Washington DC: U.S. Government Printing Office.

Eysenck, H. J. (1952). The effects of psychotherapy: An evaluation. *Journal of Consulting Psychology, 16,* 319–324.

Eysenck, H. J. (1994). The outcome problem in psychotherapy: What have we learned? *Behaviour Research and Therapy, 32,* 477–495.

Giles, T. R. (1993). Consumer advocacy and effective psychotherapy: The managed care alternative. In T. R. Giles (Ed.), *Handbook of effective psychotherapy* (pp. 481–488). New York: Plenum Press.

Gordon, R. E., Hursch, C. J., & Gordon, K. K. (1988). *An introduction to psychiatric research.* New York: Cambridge University Press.

Haas, L. J., Malouf, J. L., & Mayerson, N. H. (1986). Ethical dilemmas in psychological practice: Results of a national survey. *Professional Psychology: Research and Practice, 17,* 316–321.

Iezzoni, L. I. (1994). *Risk adjustment for measuring health care outcomes.* Ann Arbor, MI: Health Administration Press.

Johan, M. (1989). Evaluation of outcome of psychoanalytic treatment: Should follow-up by the analyst be part of the post-termination phase of analytic treatment? *Journal of the American Psychoanalytic Association, 37,* 813–822.

Joint Commission on the Accreditation of Healthcare Organizations. (1998). *Comprehensive accreditation manual for behavioral healthcare.* Oakbrook Terrace, IL: Author.

Kiresuk, T. J., Smith, A., & Cardillo, J. E. (Eds.). (1993). *Goal attainment scaling: Applications, theory and measurement.* Hillsdale, NJ: Erlbaum.

Lasker, R. D., Shapiro, D. W., & Tucker, A. M. (1992). Realizing the potential of practice pattern profiling. *Inquiry, 29,* 287–297.

Lewis, A. B., Spencer, J. H., Jr., Haas, G. L., & DiVittis, A. (1987). Goal attainment scaling: Relevance and replicability in follow-up of inpatients. *Journal of Nervous and Mental Disease, 175,* 408–418.

Marques, C. (1996, June). *How to use profiling for network improvement.* Paper presented at the Behavioral Healthcare Quality and Accountability Summit, Chicago.

Mirin, S. M., & Namerow, M. J. (1991). Why study treatment outcome? *Hospital and Community Psychiatry, 42,* 1007–1013.

Morrison, D. (1993). Clinical outcomes. In B. Schlosser & K. Moreland (Eds.), *Taming technology: Issues, strategies and resources for the mental health practitioner* (pp. 66–68). Phoenix, AZ: Division of Independent Practice of the American Psychological Association.

Mullen, E., & Magnabosco, J. (Eds.). (1997). *Outcomes in behavioral health, child health, and social service settings.* Washington, DC: National Association of Social Workers Press.

National Committee for Quality Assurance. (1998). *Standards for the accreditation of managed behavioral health care organizations.* Washington, DC: Author.

Nelsen, J. C. (1994). Ethics, gender, and ethnicity in single-case research and evaluation. *Journal of Social Service Research, 18,* 139–152.

Pekarik, G. (1993). Beyond effectiveness: Uses of consumer-oriented criteria in defining treatment success. In T. R. Giles (Ed.), *Handbook of effective psychotherapy* (pp. 409–436). New York: Plenum Press.

Sabin, J. E. (1994). A credo for ethical managed care in mental health practice. *Hospital and Community Psychiatry, 45,* 859–860, 869.

Schlosser, B. (1993). Implementing computer-based assessment services: An outline of considerations. In B. Schlosser & K. Moreland (Eds.), *Taming technology: Issues, strategies and resources for the mental health practitioner* (pp. 86–90). Phoenix, AZ: Division of Independent Practice of the American Psychological Association.

Sederer, L. I., & Dickey, B. (Eds.). (1996). *Outcomes assessment in clinical practice.* Baltimore, MD: Williams & Wilkins.

Seligman, M. E. P. (1995). The effectiveness of psychotherapy. *American Psychologist, 50,* 965–974.

Shadish, W. R., Montgomery, L. M., Wilson, P., Wilson, M. R., Bright, I., & Okwumabua, T. (1993). Effects of family and marital psychotherapies: A meta-analysis. *Journal of Consulting and Clinical Psychology, 61,* 992–1002.

Shern, D. L., & Flynn, L. M. (1996). The Outcomes Roundtable. Developing, evaluating, and disseminating outcomes monitoring technology. *Behavioral Healthcare Tomorrow, 5,* 24–30.

Sieber, J. (1992). *Planning ethically responsible research.* Newbury Park, CA: Sage.

Sieber, J. (1994). Will the new code help researchers to be more ethical? *Professional Psychology: Research and Practice, 25,* 369–375.

Speer, D. C., & Newman, F. L. (1996). Mental health services outcome evaluation. *Clinical Psychology: Science and Practice, 3,* 105–129.

Stricker, G., & Trierweiler, S. J. (1995). The local clinical scientist. *American Psychologist, 50,* 995–1002.

Sturm, R., & Wells, K. B. (1995). How can care for depression become more cost-effective? *Journal of the American Medical Association, 273,* 51–58.

Weber, L. R., Miracle, A., & Skehan, T. (1994). Interviewing early adolescents: Some methodological considerations. *Human Organization, 53,* 42–47.

Welch, H. G., Miller, M. E., & Welch, W. P. (1994). Physician profiling: An analysis of inpatient practice patterns in Florida and Oregon. *New England Journal of Medicine, 330,* 607–612.

7

Which Master's Voice? Ethical Dilemmas for Managed Care Reviewers

Ethan Pollack

Since its inception managed care has brought forth a multitude of ethical dilemmas for psychologists who choose to practice within such systems. Most often the focus of this attention has been on the predicaments facing practitioners who on a daily basis have to confront significant ethical dilemmas. Issues of confidentiality, informed consent, and competence, just to name a few, create substantial tensions for today's psychologists.

There is, however, another group of psychologists that must also confront these matters and often must do so with far more limited support and guidance—the managed care reviewer (MCR). In this chapter I explore ethical dilemmas faced by MCRs, examine the applicability of the "Ethical Principles of Psychologists and Code of Conduct" (American Psychological Association [APA], 1992) for MCRs, and propose remedies to address these dilemmas.

No discussion of managed care review would be complete without addressing, at least briefly, the historical context in which it occurs. The grandparent of the current managed care review process was something called *Professional Standards and Review Organizations* (*PSROs*). These groups, organized along regional lines in order to recognize and validate differing models of practice, came into being in the early 1970s under the auspices of what was then the Department of Health, Education, and Welfare during the Nixon administration.

The impetus for creating PSROs was the federal government's concern that medical services were being overutilized and there was no structure in place that could provide and apply standards for the delivery of these services. About the same time, Congress became aware of examples of significant fraud and abuse in the Civilian Health and Medical Program of the Uniformed Services (CHAMPUS), in which there was the provision of much unnecessary hospitalization and the overutilization of a range of treatment modalities, particularly in the residential and inpatient treatment facilities for emotionally disturbed adolescents.

As a result of the Congressional investigations, review programs were created whose mission it was to review treatments for their appropriateness and to weed out fraud and abuse. Organized psychology under the auspices of APA developed such a review program for CHAMPUS and a few commercial insurers. Importantly, the APA/CHAMPUS review program had explicit requirements for its reviewers that included prior experience in peer and utilization review and mandated participation, at regular intervals, in peer review procedures and training. The peer reviewer's work was also reviewed by more senior reviewers, thus assuring some quality control and consistency. The APA/CHAMPUS program also developed criteria for treatment on which protocols could be based. The reviewers were compensated for their work, and although there were some grumblings from practitioners, the program seemed to work well and did not create problems with the delivery of clinical services.

Most important, the APA/CHAMPUS reviewers addressed only the treatment provided and the plans for continued care—they made no benefit determinations. Unfortunately, the APA lost the contract for this review program, and with the loss of funding it could not be sustained.

As a participating reviewer in the APA/CHAMPUS program, I recall very little discussion, if any, regarding the application of ethics to our work. Although there were the typical cautions regarding confidentiality of the information reviewed, the application of ethical conduct was assumed and not elaborated on to any substantial degree, and all identifying information for both patient and providers was deleted from the materials submitted by providers. When reviewers encountered an ethical dilemma they could consult with other reviewers or with one of the supervising staff for guidance, but as noted earlier, such instances were rare.

The Present

For the MCR in 1998, the situation is far more complex than it was in the 1970s and 1980s. The profession of psychology has vastly changed, practitioners' awareness of ethical issues is more informed, and the ethical challenges are far greater, with consequences to match. However, if the MCR turns to the current Ethics Code, he or she finds precious little to inform or guide his or her thinking. In fact, the current code contains no direct reference regarding the application of the code to review activities, regardless of the entity for whom the review is being conducted.

Clearly those who developed the new Ethics Code either overlooked the need for specific standards or chose not to include such standards. I suspect the daunting complexity faced by the framers of the 1992 code was so great that the need to create ethical standards for reviewers appeared to be minor and was, therefore, not addressed. However, other possible explanations include the ambivalence of the profession toward review activities that lead to no specific standards being developed or the reality that most psychologists are not reviewers and therefore the demand is too small to warrant standards. I, however, argue that given the far-reaching implications of managed care review, and its capacity to affect large numbers of practitioners, the absence of specific ethical standards for reviewers creates dilemmas and forces psychologists to apply an Ethics Code in ways it may not have been intended and thus serves to create confusion for both practitioners and reviewers alike.

Before beginning the discussion of the application of the APA's 1992 Ethics Code to the dilemmas faced by MCRs, it is important to share the data sources used in the development of this chapter. I conducted a series of interviews with eight present and past MCRs.

The MCRs' experiences represented a wide range of the reviewer population: Three had been reviewers for more than 15 years, two for 5 to 10 years, and three for less than 2 years. Three reviewers worked for one managed care company, three for another, and two had worked for one or more companies. All of the reviewers had significant clinical experience (ranging from 5 to 25 years) and in addition to their review work also had active clinical practices. Although no data were gathered on the number of cases reviewed on the basis of the workloads reported, a full-time reviewer might review as many as 25–50 cases per day either by telephone or in written form.

They were asked the general question, "What ethical dilemmas have you encountered as a managed care reviewer?" and on the basis of their responses additional inquiries were made to allow for more elaborated responses. The data gathered from those interviews generated a number of themes that served as the focus for the dilemmas that are described later.

Applicability of the APA Ethics Code to Peer Review

Relevant General Principles

Although the General Principles of the APA (1992) Ethics Code are regarded as aspirational and are not enforceable and may not be used to resolve formal complaints, they do provide a framework that is elaborated on in the Ethical Standards. Therefore, a brief citation of the relevant portions is undertaken here to provide and to help establish the applicability of this code to the activities of MCRs.

It is also worth noting that the preamble to the code cites the many roles a psychologist can play, including that of consultant, which is the role that comes the closest to the duties of an MCR. The General Principles (APA, 1992) most relevant to the work of an MCR include the following: *competence*, in which psychologists are urged to "provide only those services and use only those techniques for which they are qualified by education, training, or experience" (p. 1599); *integrity*, when psychologists are asked to be "honest, fair, and respectful of others" and "attempt to clarify for relevant parties the roles they are performing and to function appropriately in accordance with those roles. Psychologists avoid improper and potentially harmful dual relationships" (p. 1599); and *concern for others' welfare*, which encourages psychologists to be alert to "when conflicts occur among psychologists' obligations or concerns they attempt to resolve these conflicts and to perform their roles in a responsible fashion that avoids or minimizes harm" (p. 1600).

These aspirational goals, despite their lofty ideals, establish the overriding principles upon which the more specific Ethical Standards are based. Rather than elaborate on these matters in any additional detail, let us recognize that the framers of the code envisioned its applicability to include the wide range of psychologists' activities, that psychologists should thoroughly consider how their functioning has a significant influence over others, and that they should be wary of any situations in which their knowledge and influence may be applied in other than the highest moral purpose.

Relevant Ethical Standards

In this section I explore the responses of the MCRs interviewed, the themes derived from these responses, and the Ethical Standards that likely apply. Perhaps most important at this time is the need to recognize and acknowledge that peer review in and of itself is a legitimate function of the psychologist, drawing as it does on the knowledge and application of psychological principles and theories. Standard 1.01 clearly states that "the activity of a psychologist to the Ethics Code may be reviewed under these Ethical Standards only if the activity is part of his or her work-related functions or the activity is psychological in nature" (APA, 1992, p. 1600). Thus, when functioning as MCRs, psychologists have an ethical responsibility to adhere to the standards set forth in the code.

Despite my position taken earlier with regard to the legitimacy of peer review as a psychological activity, there are some psychologists who argue that by participating with managed care as an MCR those individuals are serving to perpetuate an inherently unethical system. Although there may be some accuracy to such a stance, it is critical to recognize that the review functions will continue with or without psychologists' participation, and if we choose to "opt out" of such activity we will be abdicating a responsibility to our profession and turning over more control and regulation to others who are not subject to the same professional and ethical standards that we must uphold. If psychologists do not participate in review procedures, we relinquish long-held positions and roles as teachers, researchers, and professionals who actively integrate psychological theory and research into practice.

Competence. Many of the MCRs interviewed raised concerns regarding requests from their employers to review cases that were outside their areas of training and experience. The examples these MCRs provided included reviewing child therapy cases when they lacked experience with that population, cases involving patients with eating disorders, and cases for patients who manifested severe psychopathology when reviewers felt they lacked the appropriate training. These situations placed reviewers in the dilemma of potentially violating Standard 1.04: "Psychologists provide services only within the boundaries of their competence, based upon their education, training, supervised experience, or appropriate professional experience" (APA, 1992, p. 1600).

Faced with this dilemma, MCRs reported that they sought consultation with other MCRs or with their supervisors. This consultation often provided the knowledge specific to the case under review but did not fully address the ethical dilemma created. All of the MCRs interviewed agreed that a more responsible and effective system could be created by designating "experts" on the review staff who would automatically be referred cases in their specialty areas. However, these same MCRs acknowledged that the administrative requirements of such a system would possibly be seen as too cumbersome, costly, or both by managed care supervisors who would likely argue against adoption of such a program. Thus, although not perfect or preferable, the MCRs interviewed felt that the current system of seeking supervision when needed allowed them to cope with the dilemmas of providing services outside their area of competence.

Training. Closely related to the competence dilemma is the dilemma created by the limited generic training in peer review provided by managed care firms. MCRs frequently noted that once hired they were quickly put "on line" to conduct reviews, with their training primarily consisting of an orientation to the requirements and philosophy of the managed care firm and with scant attention given to the process of a review in and of itself. One could argue that such orientation and limited training is appropriate given the fact that the MCRs are working within and for a particular managed care setting and that more generic training would not be especially helpful or relevant. However, the MCRs spoken with frequently mentioned that they felt uncomfortable in their new position of reviewer given the relative absence of generic reviewer training. Here again they often turned to supervisors or more experienced MCRs in order to cope with the dilemma created by lack of knowledge, training, or both.

Emergency review. Worthy of special comment here was the dilemma created when a new MCR was asked to review an emergency situation, frequently one in which a decision regarding possible hospitalization was at issue. These situations often created the most intense conflict for new reviewers because they had to make difficult review decisions in situations (such as late nights or weekends) when backup consultation was difficult to obtain. The reviewers who mentioned this dilemma experienced very intense pulls at these times and had difficulty reconciling the demands of the managed care system with those of the provider, whom the reviewers knew was making crucial decisions and requests on behalf of their patients. At such times MCRs often reported that they relied on their clinical skills to arrive at a resolution, which enabled them to feel less in the midst of a dilemma.

Provider competence. An unanticipated finding from the interviews conducted with the MCRs was the frequent mention of their concern regarding the competence of the providers whose clinical work was under review. MCRs cited numerous instances in which a provider could not clearly articulate (or document) a treatment plan or provide a coherent rationale for clinical services. These instances, although certainly not applying to a majority of providers, did occur often enough to warrant comment. The MCRs reported that in these situations they often found themselves having to function more as supervisors and less as reviewers. The MCRs' discomfort in playing such a role emerged clearly in their interviews because they felt a confusion with regard to their role(s) with providers. Such confusion (and potential conflict) regarding roles was difficult if not impossible for the MCRs to address, and thus they often found themselves trying to straddle the line between reviewer and supervisor—a most difficult task. Moreover, in these instances the MCRs often felt that the quality and appropriateness of care being delivered to subscribers was of concern, but there was no available forum in which these matters could be addressed.

The MCRs felt that the potential problems they observed when they were concerned about a provider's competence were, in part, created by pressures placed on providers to accept almost any case that came their way. Such pressures may have been created by providers' economic concerns but also may have come from managed care organizations wanting their providers to treat cases without having to refer them to out-of-plan nonnetwork providers. The data derived from the interviews clearly suggest that ethical dilemmas regarding competency occurred for both reviewer and provider alike.

Conflict of interest. The area that has drawn some of the most intense focus and concern from both MCRs and providers is the potential for conflict of interest that MCRs face in their day-to-day review activities. Put more succinctly, is it possible for an MCR employed and supervised by a managed care firm to objectively review treatment for subscribers when they (MCRs) are simultaneously asked to make determinations regarding the number of treatment sessions or the form of treatment allowed or approved? It is argued, and with some justification, that such a demand on an MCR is inherently conflicted because if the reviewer does not follow the policies of his or her employer regarding the limitation(s) of care, his or her job could be at risk.

There are several General Standards (APA, 1992) that potentially could be used to guide MCRs in their attempts to resolve this dilemma. For example, Standard 1.15 (Misuse of Psychologists' Influence) alerts psychologists to guard against financial (and other factors) that might lead to a misuse of their influence, and Standard 1.16 (Misuse of Psychologists' Work) raises similar cautions. However, the standard most directly relevant is likely 1.17 (Multiple Relationships). Although this standard would appear to address some of the special problems created by practicing in a small community, it goes on to note the following:

> Psychologists must always be sensitive to the potential harmful effects of other contacts on their work and on those persons with whom they

deal. A psychologist refrains from entering into or promising another personal, scientific, *professional*, *financial*, or other relationship with such persons if it appears likely that *such a relationship reasonably might impair the psychologist's objectivity* or otherwise interfere with the psychologist's effectively performing his or her functions as a psychologist. (APA, 1992, p. 1601; emphasis added)

It is also worth recognizing here that all psychologists may find themselves in conflict when factors exist that might impair objectivity, especially during these times of demands, to maintain if not to increase the level of their clinical activity, and they may undertake cases that in a better business climate they might otherwise refer to a colleague more experienced in a particular population.

Dual-relationship conflict. All of the MCRs interviewed raised this concern regarding the conflict of the dual (or multiple) relationship in which they found themselves. All MCRs recognized and knew from the outset that their jobs would require them to set limits on clinical care approved. Additionally, the MCRs knew that managed care principles of a brief treatment model were something to which they would be charged to adhere. Nevertheless, among the MCRs interviewed, all reported that in the course of a typical day they found themselves in a conflicted position when only able to approve a limited number of sessions for cases in which the clinical rationale supplied by the provider indicated the need for extended treatment, and they could not approve visits beyond the limits created by their managed care employer.

The MCRs, while clearly uncomfortable in such situations, were able to resolve the ethical dilemma in several ways. First they noted that when providers "sign on" with managed care, they are aware of the philosophy of the brief treatment model and in fact often are accepted on managed care panels because they practice a brief treatment model. Second, MCRs pointed out that it is possible for providers to secure additional treatment sessions for their patients by requesting more sessions after the initial approval is used up or, if necessary, by appealing the managed care company's decision. Finally, the MCRs stated that if they felt a case warranted extended treatment they could make the request to a supervisor who would review such requests.

Despite these options, all MCRs spoke to the dilemma created when placed in the position of having to make benefit determinations in addition to addressing clinical needs. All reported feeling the substantial pressure of financial determinations affecting how they managed a case, and all felt compromised to some degree in this process. When reviewers are given the responsibility to make and render clinical case decisions based in substantial ways on financial factors (after all, they have jobs to keep), there exists a clear conflict of interest that has significant potential to impair the psychologist's objectivity. This is an ethical dilemma of the highest order, and one that MCRs struggled with most intensely.

Confidentiality. Much has been written regarding the dilemmas created by managed care review concerning confidentiality. In this section I do not reiterate the multitude of conflicts and problems but instead focus on some dilemmas raised by MCRs during the interviews. According to Standard 5.05,

> (a) Psychologists disclose confidential information without the consent of the individual only as mandated by law, or where permitted by law for a valid purpose, such as ... *to obtain payment for services*, in which instance *disclosure is limited to the minimum that is necessary to achieve the purpose.* (APA, 1992, p. 1606; emphasis added)

The MCRs interviewed for this chapter reported that concerns they had in this area frequently centered around information that was disclosed to reviewers and that exceeded the bounds of what was necessary to achieve the purpose of a review. Although the MCRs felt comfortable in receiving and handling such information, they frequently raised concerns about this information's residing in databases in which access was not well controlled. Additionally, and perhaps a necessity given the administrative needs and volume of reviews, there were very limited, if any, attempts made to disguise identifying information about patients.

The issue of access, however, was the dilemma most often noted by the MCRs. In most systems, when a client contacts the managed care company to secure a referral, the first person with whom they speak is often a clerk or receptionist. Not knowing who the person on the phone is, patients often will divulge personal information to the clerk, who is not clinically or professionally trained to deal with a patient in crisis or to deal with the information presented. Additionally, several MCRs reported instances that, while occurring infrequently, created significant concern. They told of situations, typically during times of limited reviewer staffing and high demand for reviews to be carried out, in which review responsibilities (and therefore sensitive information) were assigned to clerical staff who had little, if any, training or expertise in review work. Although these examples address issues of competence as well as confidentiality, they also point to the more dominant concern of the MCRs, which was that substantial amounts of sensitive clinical information could be accessed by individuals who were not professionally trained and not well schooled in the ethical issues related to confidentiality. This lack of appropriate administrative control over confidential information remained a significant ethical dilemma for the MCRs interviewed. Clearly the MCR needs to advocate, when appropriate, to ensure that clinical information is tightly controlled and to instruct nonprofessional staff in the requirements for maintaining confidentiality.

Ethical standards versus managed care requirements. Closely related to these concerns regarding confidentiality was the more overarching ethical dilemma for all the MCRs: How do we deal with the conflicts between our ethical standards and the requirements of our employers, the managed care companies? This quandary applies to all of the issues noted previously, and others that have not been discussed, and leads to the matter embedded in Standard 8.03—Conflicts Between Ethics and Organizational Demands—which states the following:

> If the demands of an organization with which psychologists are affiliated conflict with this Ethics Code, psychologists clarify the nature of the conflict, make known their commitment to the Ethics Code, and to the extent feasible, seek to resolve the conflict in a way that permits fullest adherence to the Ethics Code. (APA, 1992, p. 1611)

The MCRs interviewed struggled mightily with this dilemma. Although all reported having spoken with peers regarding the problem, few felt the degree of comfort and safety necessary to take up the matter with their superiors and therefore were left with disquieting feelings regarding their work. In part, several noted that the problem was due to the lack of an appropriate and sanctioned forum in which to raise such questions, whereas others spoke to a very clear but unverbalized prohibition about addressing such matters. The MCRs also noted that although they took their jobs as reviewers knowing what the managed care philosophy was, they did not fully appreciate how difficult it would be to work in settings in which their ethics and values would be subjected to such conflicts. In the final analysis the MCRs felt it was extremely difficult to raise, much less resolve, the conflicts between ethics and the organizations that employed them.

Some Modest Proposals

At this time some proposals, which one hopes will provide remedies for both the MCRs and the managed care companies that employ them, are suggested. Of primary import is the need to develop systems in which MCRs can conduct reviews without also making benefit determinations. This step, in and of itself, would significantly reduce the conflicts created under the current system because MCRs would feel freer to address relevant clinical issues in a more appropriate and comfortable fashion.

Such a proposed system would function in the following manner. The managed care company would routinely and automatically approve eight sessions for any patient who requested treatment. This number is suggested because research has demonstrated that approximately 75% of all patients seeking psychotherapy use fewer than eight sessions, and therefore, there is little, if any, advantage to be obtained from reviewing all patients' care at the initial entry point.

After four sessions the psychologist would determine whether the patient could be treated in the initially approved eight sessions. If the answer to that question is affirmative, then no further action is required. If the psychologist, in his or her best assessment, felt that treatment beyond the eight sessions was necessary, then the psychologist would be required to submit a treatment plan for review. The treatment plan would initially have to address the clinical necessity for treatment and then would focus on a clinically reasonable and appropriate treatment regimen for the patient in question. It is hoped that the reader has noticed that the focus here is on the development of a treatment plan that is based on clinical need and is clinically appropriate, and not on a predetermined theoretical focus.

Once this plan is drawn up and submitted, the MCR's task is to evaluate its clinical soundness and to determine if the plan is clinically appropriate for the patient. If the treatment plan is evaluated as appropriate by the MCR such approval is given and benefits are approved. Because all insurance has certain maximum limits (typically 20 sessions per year), the managed care company's fiscal exposure is clearly capped and should not present a hardship. For cases in which continuing care is necessary beyond 20 visits per year, that responsibility for reimbursement would rest, as it should, with the patient and psychologist to resolve.

The advantages to the MCRs of such a system are quite clear in that they would be doing what they are best trained to do, assess and evaluate the necessity for and appropriateness of clinical care. The insurance company (or managed care company) has the responsibility to manage the benefits by using the methods available to them through the mechanisms of premium determinations, benefit levels, and underwriting skills—all of which are appropriate areas for their expertise. Most of all, this system does away with the ethical dilemmas for the MCR of being caught up in conflictual and potentially harmful multiple relationships.

This review plan has other distinct advantages that would assist MCRs in dealing with the ethical dilemmas noted earlier. Without having to make benefit determinations, the MCRs are in an optimal position to address matters of quality of care. Managed care companies frequently underscore their concern for their subscribers receiving high-quality service. They address this by carefully selecting providers on the basis of the providers' training and expertise, but then the managed care system becomes complicated when its reviewers must also determine treatment limitations. The proposed review system encourages MCRs to examine the nature and quality of services provided to the patients without having to struggle with preimposed limits on the number of treatment sessions, thereby helping to ensure the highest quality of care.

A second proposal to remedy the ethical problems for MCRs is for the managed care companies to train adequately their reviewers in the process of conducting a generic peer review. Important in this process would be for the psychological community at large to develop sets of appropriate treatment protocols and standards for the conduct of treatment reviews. Such systems would need to acknowledge that there are many effective treatment approaches and that with some clear exceptions patients can effectively be treated by more than one approach. Therefore, MCRs could be trained to review cases to ensure that the treatment proposed for a patient was appropriate for his or her clinical needs.

If a proposed treatment was not appropriate, or if the MCR had concerns regarding the care being provided, he or she would now be in a far better position to address the concern because the focus would be on the treatment plan proposed and not on the reimbursement issue. The MCR's training could also include how to engage and work with psychologists in a matter designed to focus on patients' needs and care and to help ensure that the psychologist effectively addressed those issues.

In addition, the managed care industry could turn to the training standards and conduct standards developed by the APA's CHAMPUS review program. These standards focused on the criteria necessary to develop a treatment plan, as well as the process to be followed in conducting a review, and effectively maintained the focus on the clinical necessity and the appropriateness of the treatment.

If managed care companies wish to address the difficulties created by the conflict between their institutional criteria and psychologists' ethics, they must work to develop a safe and supportive atmosphere for the MCRs. Toward that end, it is incumbent on the managed care companies to develop in-house procedures and mechanisms that specifically encourage the MCRs to raise and hopefully resolve ethical dilemmas. Such a system should incorporate an internal ethics committee that would meet regularly and that would provide a forum and a resource for both management and staff to share ideas and develop ways to minimize the struggles faced by MCRs. For such committees to function in an effective manner, it would serve the managed care companies well to bring in an outside ethics expert as a consultant to such a committee. That individual would be in a position to provide a broad overview and would hopefully be free from the constraints with which both staff and management must deal.

To address the continuing concerns created regarding confidentiality, managed care companies should develop data-gathering mechanisms that require a minimum of intrusive personal information. In addition, patients should be identified by number only, and review materials should be handled only by the reviewers and should be under their strict control. A similar procedure should also be put into place for the reviewers, who should also be identified by an anonymous code. There are certainly enough security procedures readily available to protect and limit access to information contained in databases, assuming it is necessary to store information in such media.

Professional organizations also have responsibilities to the MCRs to assist and guide them. At the very least the professional organization's ethics committee should take the lead and develop guidelines, modify the existing code, or both, to address the dilemmas MCRs are forced to cope with. The absence of any mention of reviewer responsibilities in the current code is an oversight that should be addressed in a timely manner.

Furthermore, if managed care companies move toward capitated contracts with providers, the onus of conducting reviews will be placed squarely in the lap of the providers who hold such contracts. In these situations the dilemmas for MCRs, which were addressed earlier, will then be confronted by practitioners who will have to contend with the absence of guidelines or standards to direct them. Because these practitioners will be in control of the monies, the tension will be far more intense than that faced by the MCRs today.

Concluding Remarks

Although the purpose of this chapter was to call the reader's attention to the often overlooked difficulties MCRs experience in carrying out their responsibilities, it has also highlighted the inherent conflicts created when systems seek to address very different and certainly conflicting agendas simultaneously. Although some, if not many, would take strong issue with the basic premises of managed care, it is suggested that as psychologists we should consider the totality of the system and the historical issues that helped to create managed care as we now know it.

For many years psychologists practiced without giving adequate, or even any, attention to the development of general standards for care. Although most psychologists operated, if that is the correct word to use in this situation, with the assumption that people benefited from our services, we did not pay careful attention to when and which services benefited our patients the most. We did little, if any, outcomes research, and we were primarily held to account by free-market forces—if patients and referral sources felt you did high-quality work, you got referrals.

When the profession aligned itself with the health-care industry and obtained the right to bill insurance companies for services, things began to change, although too few of us realized it at the time. Insurance companies work from a medical disease-based model; that is, if there is a diagnosed disorder, there is generally a specific treatment for it and typically the treatment is limited. As we now know, psychological practice did not neatly fit that model, and we did not adequately address the needs of the insurers who were struggling to understand our model with an equal lack of comprehension.

Insurance companies, feeling the acute pressure to gain control over escalating costs, looked to the areas in which they could more easily assert themselves, and in part because of the great ambivalence held by the public regarding mental health and psychotherapy, psychologists were, and continue to be, an easy target. For legitimate concerns, psychologists have tended to cloak our procedures in some level of secrecy, and we have experienced difficulty in adequately defining our work, which has also served to make us more vulnerable to outside groups' attempts to control our professional conduct.

In response to the rapid and increasing anxiety created by managed care's entry into the marketplace, psychologists enrolled as providers, knowing full well that managed care policies very clearly stated that limited treatments would be the order of the day. Other psychologists, also anxious and looking for employment in a very uncertain environment, signed on with managed care as reviewers, and they too were very aware of managed care's philosophy of limited treatment.

Managed care, for its part, participated in this process of mutual denial. I have no doubt that, given the option, managed care would prefer not to have created these complex and costly review mechanisms and, if possible, from a legal perspective, would have simply limited care by restricting the number of sessions allowed in their policies and thus reduced costs in the most efficient manner possible. Instead, case managers and MCRs were hired in part to serve as a buffer, to deal with the public as well as providers and to serve a function similar to that of the heat-absorbing ceramic tiles on the space shuttle (physicists refer to this as a *heat sink*).

Despite the generally good intentions of all involved, it seems clear that the parties dealing with managed care are struggling with ethical issues, and for the MCRs these dilemmas may be the most troubling. Although the psychologist providers have readily available outlets and support (colleagues, the popular press, and others), the MCRs are seen more as "the enemy," and their struggles are more internal and without a great deal of empathy or sympathy from either the professional community or their own management. Although providers have to deal with the dilemmas created within their limited caseloads, MCRs must struggle with much larger numbers of patients and their needs. It is no surprise, therefore, that high turnover rates among MCRs exist, and without some modifications in the current system this is likely to continue.

As long as managed care continues to exist, it, of necessity, must employ reviewers. To help them in their ethical struggles the only reasonable step appears to be that of allowing them to function as clinicians and not as benefit managers. Whether managed care is ready to take such a step is most uncertain, and it will likely take the courage of one firm to lead the way or massive legislative initiatives to modify the system that has created these conflicts. Let us hope the needed changes occur soon.

Reference

American Psychological Association. (1992). Ethical principles of psychologists and code of conduct. *American Psychologist, 47,* 1597–1611.

8

Managed Health Care and the Ethics of Clinical Practice in Behavioral Medicine

Thomas F. Nagy

Behavioral medicine is a specialized area of practice in some ways more suited to the restrictions of managed health care than to any other area of clinical practice. Compared with psychological services offered in other settings, behavioral medicine has more clearly defined parameters in its scope and length of treatment. However, some of the rough waters encountered while navigating the shoals of managed health care in behavioral medicine may also pose significant problems for psychologists, and may even place them at risk of ethics complaints or civil lawsuits. Patients, too, may be affected negatively in this specialized area of practice without even being aware of the risks they encounter until it is too late.[1] In this chapter I focus on ethical issues in the behavioral medicine setting (and, indeed, virtually every clinical setting) as well as on the specific risks encountered there. The goal is to clarify the murky issues by using the American Psychological Association (APA) Ethics Code (APA, 1992), thereby reducing the risk of harm to both psychologists and their patients. The chapter is divided into three sections: the behavioral setting, managed health care contracts, and ethical issues in managed health care. These comments are based partly on my experience of over 10 years providing clinical services, teaching, and supervising in a behavioral medicine clinic, as well as my experience in chairing and participating in the work of ethics committees, including the APA's Task Force for the Revision of the Ethical Principles of Psychologists.

The Behavioral Medicine Setting

The reason that behavioral medicine may lend itself better to the constraints of managed health care is primarily due to two variables: (a) the

---

[1]As a companion to this chapter, the reader may find it useful to review preliminary ethical guidelines for managed health care settings (Nagy, 1993) and a brief overview of revisions to the APA "The Ethical Principles of Psychologists and Code of Conduct" (Nagy, 1994), henceforth referred to as the *Ethics Code*.

type of disorders treated and (b) the nature of interventions offered. Unfortunately, these same two factors may also place therapists and patients at risk, sometimes, of harming each other while attempting to carry out their roles on the platform of managed health care. In this section I explore the unique attributes of life in a behavioral medicing setting that facilitate work with managed health care and the risks of harm to both providers and consumers.

Part of the uniqueness of behavioral medicine, as mentioned earlier, resides in the types of problems that patients bring and the types of remedies that therapists offer. Typically, the types of problems treated in behavioral medicine clinics fall into the following categories: (a) anxiety disorders, (b) eating disorders, (c) chronic pain, (d) headaches, and (e) other physiological problems that are frequently stress related, such as gastric and intestinal disorders (e.g., irritable bowel syndrome [IBS]), Raynaud's syndrome, hypertension, sleep disorders, and hyperhydrosis, to name a few. Each of these categories could be treated as a presenting complaint in and of itself and could have highly successful treatment outcomes over time. If the patient also presents with an Axis II disorder, however, which is sometimes the case, then treatment may be more protracted and complex, and the differences between behavioral medicine and other settings then begin to disappear.

A predominant theoretical approach commonly used by therapists in behavioral medicine and pain clinics appears to be based on cognitive–behavioral psychology. Indeed, many presenting complaints of these patients lend themselves readily to the kind of focus brought by this approach (Barlow, 1985, 1988; Beck, Emery, & Greenberg, 1985; Meichenbaum, 1977; Turk, Meichenbaum, & Genest, 1983).

Other interventions in behavioral medicine include the relaxation therapies—progressive muscle relaxation being the oldest formally researched and taught intervention (Bernstein & Borkovec, 1973; Jacobsen, 1938). Diaphragmatic breathing has also been an extremely useful intervention, relatively easily taught, and readily applied in a variety of settings and activities (Benson, 1975). Hypnosis and meditation are also extremely helpful and, with individuals who have a good capability for these interventions, can have rapid and long-term effects (Benson, 1984; Brown & Fromm, 1987; Kroger & Fezler, 1976; Spiegel & Spiegel, 1978). Those who have a diminished ability to enter hypnosis may have much more success with biofeedback, utilizing a variety of modes, such as electromyograph, thermal, galvanic skin response, or electroencephalograph (Basmajian, 1983; Birk, 1973; Miller, 1974; Wickramaskera, 1976). Biofeedback has been a therapeutic tool for over 25 years and have proven to be a rich resource in aiding patients to learn about self-regulation and pain management (Miller, 1969, 1974).

Certainly, in providing services in behavioral medicine, psychologists must also be prepared to contend with Axis II disorders, in addition to treating presenting complaints with a physiological focus. This may considerably extend the treatment, and both patient and therapist must negotiate just what the focus should be. Is it enough to treat chronic pain without addressing the personality disorder? For some patients, these will be inextricably intertwined. This dilemma is further explored.

Another aspect of importance in providing competent treatment is collaboration with psychiatrists, or primary care physicians in some cases, for managing psychotropic medication. This may be a crucial aspect of treatment for the following two reasons: (a) Clinical depression is frequently associated with chronic pain and other chronic–somatic conditions, and (b) pain thresholds rise and fall along with depression levels and can greatly be ameliorated by antidepressants. The pharmacological management of anxiety or panic disorder, as well as eating disorders, may also be an intrinsic part of treatment, necessitating close coordination of a psychologist and physician. This is explored later.

Managed Health Care Contracts

It is important for practitioners to read the managed health care contract in its entirety in order to remain in compliance with its terms at all times. By being familiar with the contract, the practitioner will not be "surprised" later by a requirement, limitation, or exclusion that has been overlooked. Some contracts require that the provider carry a specified amount of malpractice insurance, for example, and to fail to do so could jeopardize his or her participation in the panel if there were ever a formal complaint from a patient. Other contracts require occasional reviewing of the therapist's actual progress notes. Most contracts and policies require therapists to meticulously observe deadlines, closely track the number of allocated and used sessions, and submit timely outpatient treatment reports. They will quickly learn that failure to observe these policies can result in a refusal to provide payment or loss of reimbursement to the patient. Providers should always be familiar with the formal or informal procedures for the petitioning of additional therapy sessions, over and above what has been allocated by the managed health care case manager. In fact, it is quite important that therapists seek additional sessions, if they feel they are warranted, rather than simply comply with limitations imposed by case managers. Failure to explore every recourse for increasing the number of sessions, in order to provide competent treatment, could well result in a civil suit by an angry patient who feels deprived, as discussed later (*Hughes v. Blue Cross of California*, 1988; *Wickline v. State of California*, 1986). In short, there are many reasons—ethical, legal, and clinical—for being very familiar with the language in the contract and with the implications it may have in the behavioral medicine setting.

The course of treatment can drastically be altered when either patient or provider participates in managed health care contracts. Such contracts limit treatment in several ways, but all are designed to control the flow of money from the administrator of the contract, or the *payer*, to the provider of psychological services, the *vendor*. This is accomplished by at least seven strategies: (a) limiting the fee that a provider may bill the payer for psychological services; (b) limiting the copayment that a provider may charge the patient; (c) limiting the number of sessions that will be reimbursed; (d) limiting the total amount of money to be paid out in a year; (e) refusing to pay or reducing the dollar amount for standard behavioral medicine interventions, such as hypnosis, biofeedback, or couples counseling; (f) objecting to the form of treatment for a particular patient, in preference to "quicker" or "more effective" methods; and (g) refusing to pay a provider for ongoing treatment unless progress reports are filed at regular intervals (e.g., after a certain number of sessions or a certain amount of time has elapsed).

Any combination of these strategies could apply to a psychologist who is on a panel of providers and could inhibit the manner in which therapy is traditionally conducted (i.e., in an open-ended fashion). Such policies likely change the way treatment progresses, in many cases, and also have immense implications for informed-consent procedures at the outset. Both ongoing treatment and informed consent are discussed in the next section.

Ethical Issues in Managed Health Care

Managed health care constraints pose many dilemmas to psychologists working in a behavioral medicine setting. They fall into the following categories: (a) informed consent, (b) assessment, (c) collaboration with other health-care professionals, (d) confidentiality and record keeping, and (e) termination and abandonment. Each of these areas is explored from the viewpoint of the APA's "Ethical Principles of Psychologists and Code of Conduct" (1992).

Informed Consent

Informed consent is an important aspect of all treatment, often beginning with the very first telephone call to the therapist. According to the APA Ethics Code (APA, 1992), psychologists are obliged to educate new patients not only about fees and confidentiality exclusions but also about what to expect from the therapy process itself. Standard 1.07, Describing the Nature and Results of Psychological Services, requires psychologists to give "appropriate information beforehand about the nature of such services," although it does not specify exactly what is to be discussed (APA, 1992). Standard 4.01 (a), Structuring the Relationship, is helpful in giving some examples of specific topics to be discussed at the outset, such as "the nature and anticipated course of therapy, fees, and confidentiality" and, in paragraph (d), requiring psychologists to "answer patients' questions and to avoid apparent misunderstandings about therapy."

At first glance these mandates appear straightforward, but complying with them may be problematical in treating patients with multiple diagnoses. A man with IBS who also has significant anxiety and a narcissistic personality disorder presents a significant order of complexity to the managed health care system and therapists within a behavioral medicine context. Consider the woman suffering from chronic neck and back pain for 4 years, who also has moderate depression, abuses alcohol, and has a borderline personality disorder. These are not uncommon presenting complaints for this setting, but they may raise considerable problems for therapists attempting to comply simultaneously with both the spirit and terms of the APA Code of Conduct and managed health care contracts.

Another factor to consider, which may affect informed consent and uniquely apply to a behavioral medicine setting, is the set of expectations that patients bring with them. The woman with chronic neck pain may actively seek out treatment only for her physical discomfort but not wish to address her chemical dependency, much less even consider other psychological disorders. However, if she had sought treatment in some other setting, such as a generalist's office or a mental health center, she may be more receptive from the outset to a variety of therapy goals and interventions. The therapist would naturally explore the goals and nature of treatment in any case, but he or she may encounter far more resistance to treating accompanying disorders within the specialized setting of a behavioral medicine clinic.

What exactly can or should be treated when therapy is severely limited by the third-party payer? How should patients be informed at the outset about the scope of treatment? The treating therapist is faced with the task of prioritizing presenting complaints or, at least, with negotiating with patients about which ailments to treat first, or at all, given the time constraints. In accepting the male patient mentioned earlier (the anxious narcissist with IBS), a therapist must decide which goals and interventions would clinically be indicated. The patient's wishes are primary, and he is in a position to know which symptoms inhibit functioning or make his life difficult. He may be unaware of the extent to which the underlying anxiety of his personality disorder contributes to his irritable bowel, or he may not care. Certainly, however, he is seeking reduction of his gastrointestinal discomfort, and that may be the only reason he would ever seek out a therapist. Reasonable interventions for his presenting complaint might include muscle relaxation training, biofeedback training, hypnosis, and cognitive–behaviorally oriented psychotherapy with anxiety reduction and stress management areas of focus. With a limited number of sessions, the therapist must make decisions at the outset about how to allocate these interventions so as to maximize success. The dynamics of the personality disorder may play a role in maintaining anxiety, hence contributing to the severity of the IBS. However, anxiety-management techniques may be taught without engaging a full psychotherapy for the treatment of narcissism. Depending on the theoretical orientation of the therapist, then, such an intervention may be appropriate and warranted. In providing informed consent, the therapist would discuss different levels of intervention and how therapy might have to be truncated because of the limitations of the managed health care contract. He or she may wish to explain how therapy might proceed if more sessions were permitted and how the focus might be broader or the treatment might be more resistant to relapse, if, in fact, this is the case. This allows the patient to have a full explanation at the beginning about the range, scope, and intensity of the planned therapy, what will be included, what probably will be excluded, and what might be included if additional sessions are allocated in the future. Informed consent further allows the patient a broader view of his problem and the factors that contribute to and exacerbate it. The patient becomes more of a "collaborator" in his own treatment and feels informed about the specifics of the therapy about to be undertaken if these matters are discussed at the outset.

Finally, it is also important to recognize that informed consent is a process that should continuously remain a part of treatment—whether or not a managed care case manager approves of the practice. Certainly treatment options are routinely discussed with the case manager or are described on monthly outpatient treatment report forms. However, it is advisable that the patient also be included in some of these discussions. Whenever there is a new direction in treatment, a different type of intervention (e.g., biofeedback, tape recording, patient behavioral homework assignment, including another family member in the treatment, and so forth), or some change in the focus of therapy (e.g., discussing secondary gains, the marital relationship, and so forth), it is important that the therapist help the patient to understand what is about to happen and that he or she always has options regarding participation. For example, consider the anxious male narcissistic patient with IBS who was treated by a therapist also skilled in object relations work and who thought that some psychodynamic therapy would be highly desirable, now that the initial eight sessions of relaxation therapy and hypnotherapy had begun having a beneficial effect. Instead of simply launching into this dynamic work, as it would represent quite a different way of interacting with the patient, the therapist should introduce this shift to the patient by explaining the different ways this method works and how it might affect the patient at this particular stage of treatment. The therapist should also describe new expectations or possible risks, such as extending the therapy commitment, exploring new psychological territory (with its attendant uncertainties), and a possible temporary increase in anxiety or conflict as a result of this new focus. Thus, the patient has a chance to make an informed judgment about whether to participate in this phase of treatment, and the therapist has effectively discharged his or her responsibility by not unilaterally imposing a form of therapy on an unwilling but compliant patient.

Assessment

For informed consent to be adequate, the therapist must have at least a preliminary diagnostic impression enabling him or her to estimate the focus and approximate duration of treatment. Certainly for some patients, 8 or 10 sessions may be adequate to reduce significantly both anxiety and the symptoms of IBS. However, it is also true that many patients would require a much longer course of therapy. These patients may be far more resistant to change for a variety of reasons, such as posttraumatic stress

disorder (delayed onset) from a history of significant child abuse, a life-
long duration of symptoms, frail health, low trust in therapists from prior
experience (or from prior abuse by a therapist), a concurrent long-term
stressor (e.g., a recent divorce, death of a family member, loss of job, etc.),
or some other reason. It is essential to assess the patient for factors that
are likely to retard the course of therapy in order for the therapist to
develop a treatment plan that is realistic and to provide informed consent
as well. According to Standard 2.01 (a) of the APA Ethics Code, "Evaluation, Diagnosis, and Interventions in Professional Context," psychologists
must base their "assessments, recommendations, reports, and psychological diagnostic or evaluative statements . . . sufficient to provide appropriate substantiation for their findings" (APA, 1992). It may be important to
use formal assessment measures, such as taking a formal history or using
psychological tests (Minnesota Multiphasic Personality Inventory [Hath-
away & McKinley, 1989], anxiety or depression inventories, stress inventories, etc.) or structured clinical interviews for diagnosing Axis II disorders, eating disorders, or dissociative disorders, if suspected. Such
measures may well allow for more accurate diagnostic impressions at the
beginning of therapy than informal history taking—ultimately enabling
the therapist to develop a treatment plan more consistent with a limited
number of sessions.

Another responsibility of the therapist during the assessment phase
may be to request that the patient obtain a complete physical examination
from his or her primary care physician. Indeed, there are many complaints
that may prompt a physical exam by a physician or may be diagnostic of
a serious medical condition, such as an eating disorder or chronic pain.
Certainly there are medical conditions, such as hypertension, which have
few or no symptoms at all. However, it is frequently essential for the psychologist to formally recommend an assessment by a physician and to establish a collaborative relationship with him or her—this facilitates a
clearer diagnostic impression, and thereby allows the therapist to provide
even better informed consent. Some patients may resist or sabotage such
recommendations, by lying or "forgetting" to follow up a referral, and many
patients will obtain no new useful information from such a consultation
with a physician. However, the small percentage who will learn of an ongoing medical condition may be significantly helped by medication, physical therapy, or some other regimen that will complement any psychological intervention offered by the provider.

Certainly, also, it is always wise to consider one's own ethical and legal
liability in overlooking a medical condition, such as a progressive disease
(e.g., thyroid disorders, diabetes, early stage cancer, and so forth), and
proceeding directly to the treatment phase without medical attention for
a treatable disease. Failure to request a medical assessment could well
result in the patient's further deterioration, or even death. This is tragic
enough in and of itself, but the therapist may well then be confronted by
an ethics complaint, civil suit, or state psychology board investigation for
malpractice in failing to recognize the advisability of a medical examina-

tion. Such actions can be initiated by the patient or by a surviving spouse or family members in the event of death.

Collaboration With Other Health-Care Professionals

Behavioral medicine may be the only area of psychological practice in which so many health-care practitioners simultaneously collaborate in attending to the needs of so few patients, at such great expense. A chronic pain patient may have a trail of multidisciplinary health-care professionals consisting of a primary care physician, psychiatrist, neurologist, surgeon(s), anaesthesiologist (pain specialist), gastroenterologist (for gastrointestinal pain), gynecologist (for pelvic pain), osteopath, physiatrist, physical therapist, chiropractor, acupuncturist, and various other specialists and generalists who have participated or who are currently participating in the patient's care. Each health-care professional has his or her own unique area of expertise, theories of etiology, methods of diagnosing and treating, and philosophical or theoretical orientation—and these are not necessarily complementary. Given this scenario, there is an increased likelihood for multiple diagnostic hunches by the treating health-care professionals and variability in treatments that may even contradict one another. This can result in fragmentation of the treatment that is far greater than when only one or two health-care professionals are involved. Furthermore, when the patient carries a borderline personality diagnosis he or she may be more likely to engage in "triangulation" or "splitting" when interacting with various providers. This essentially consists of resisting treatment in a sophisticated manner, distorting or otherwise misperceiving the motives and interventions of various treating providers, and attempting to control or manipulate providers by dividing and conquering them, resulting in discord among the treatment team and even feelings of impotence among those who are working so hard to help. Indeed, the psychologist may find her- or himself in the unique position, compared with everyone else on the treatment team, of exploring these complex relationships, and their overall effect on treatment itself, in addition to providing therapy for the original presenting complaint.

Certainly it is wise to seek the professional opinions of most or all other involved health-care professionals while clearly describing one's own treatment plans as well. Standard 1.20 of the Ethics Code, Consultations and Referrals, is a reminder that therapists must "arrange for appropriate consultations and referrals based principally on the best interests of their patients, with appropriate consent" (APA, 1992). This standard is straightforward in its message; however, it may necessitate spending a significant amount of time reviewing medical records, making telephone calls, writing psychological reports, or writing letters of inquiry.

Occasionally a patient begins treatment while already taking psychotropic medication, either prescribed by a psychiatrist or a physician (primary care physician, gynecologist, rheumatologist, etc.). In such cases, it would be wise not only to consult with the prescribing physician but also to consider seriously a psychiatric referral as well in order to involve a specialist in the area of psychopharmacology for monitoring the medication. Such a referral may well be resisted by a case manager, especially when a primary care physician is already prescribing and monitoring an antidepressant or an antianxiety agent. The additional expenditure of money on including yet another medical professional in the treatment will have to be justified by the psychologist. In so doing, it is important to remember that the class of medication, dosage, and chronicity all contribute to the beneficial effects in patients, and general practitioners are not necessarily equally well versed in administering psychotropic medication. In my view, patients are best served by having a specialist oversee the medication aspect of treatment; this is particularly apparent when medication has been ineffective and extensive, or experimental drug trials with the patient may be necessary, sometimes extending over many months. This is especially important in the following four scenarios: (a) patients with panic attacks or significant depression who may be at risk of suicide, (b) patients with chronic pain, (c) patients with a catastrophic illness, and (d) patients with chemical dependency (e.g., alcohol, prescribed narcotics, etc.) If patients carry one or more of these diagnoses, they may be especially in need of a qualified psychiatrist who can monitor the medication aspect of treatment.

Confidentiality and Record Keeping

The principles of patient confidentiality and privileged communication have historically had a high priority, with formal inclusion in ethical rules and legal statutes. The rationale has been to maximize the patient's ability to discuss freely a problem or concern, in all of its aspects, with a therapist, without fear or embarrassment that would result if others might learn of the disclosures. However, with the advent of managed health care, these principles seem to be at greater risk of being compromised. Also, as more professionals become involved in a patient's care, as mentioned earlier, threats to confidentiality may escalate exponentially, and it is increasingly unclear exactly how and where information flows, and who knows what about whom, at any given time.

It is useful to review the concepts of confidentiality and privileged communication. *Confidentiality* refers to patients' expectations that what is disclosed to a psychotherapist or physician will remain private, and not be revealed to any other person or entity. There are certain exceptions to confidentiality, and these are discussed later. *Privileged communication*, on the other hand, refers to the legal right of patients to control the dissemination of information that has already been disclosed to another person (e.g., psychologist, physician, etc.). Specifically, the patient holds this right and must give formal authorization, or signed consent, before a therapist may either disclose such information to anyone else (e.g., family member, physician, or case manager) or testify about the patient (or information he or she disclosed) in a legal proceeding (e.g., child custody assessment, disability litigation, etc.).

Any therapist who breaches confidentiality (i.e., discloses information to another without the patient's signed consent) does so at significant risk from both a legal and ethical standpoint. The APA Code of Ethics devotes an entire section to privacy and confidentiality, consisting of 11 standards, and the whole section is "potentially applicable to the professional and scientific activities of all psychologists" (APA, 1992). Standard 5.02, Maintaining Confidentiality, states that psychologists "have a primary obligation and take reasonable precautions to respect the confidentiality rights of those with whom they work or consult, recognizing that confidentiality may be established by law, institutional rules, or professional or scientific relationships." Standard 5.01, Discussing the Limits of Confidentiality, requires that psychologists tell patients at the outset of therapy exactly what the limitations of confidentiality are. These may vary somewhat from state to state but frequently include the following exclusions: allowing or requiring the psychologist to break confidentiality if (a) the patient is a danger to him- or herself or to the property or person of another; (b) there is a reasonable suspicion of child abuse or elder abuse; (c) the patient sues the therapist for malpractice or some other breach of duty owed to the patient; (d) the patient is under age 16 and the psychologist believes he or she has been the victim of a crime; (e) the psychologist is appointed by the court to determine mental competency; (f) litigation is pending, and the patient (or heirs) is raising his or her own mental or emotional condition as an issue in an action for injury (or death) of him- or herself; (g) the patient has died and survivors are engaged in litigation about some aspect of the estate that the psychologist is likely to have information about; and (h) other exceptions more technical in scope than would generally apply in this setting (Caudill & Pope, 1995). Certainly these exceptions should be explained to patients, and, preferably in writing, by means of a handout at the very beginning of treatment.

When requests for copies of the therapists' actual progress notes are made by the managed health care company, the therapist is placed in a dilemma. Certainly the APA has suggestions for how therapists document their work, and these are available in the "Record Keeping Guidelines" (APA, 1993). The Ethics Code, as well, in Standard 1.23, Documentation of Professional and Scientific Work, requires that "psychologists appropriately document their professional and scientific work in order to facilitate provision of services later by them or by other professionals, to ensure accountability, and to meet other requirements of institutions or the law" (APA, 1992). However, it is clear that in the current health-care environment, a therapist's notes can be accessed by the managed care company, stored electronically forever, and disseminated to others within the managed care hierarchy for review of benefits and for allocation of additional sessions. Certainly a therapist can write a summary of the treatment sessions, without literally photocopying the notes and sending them in, and often this will be sufficient. Although, technically, the therapist is not complying with a formal request for records by sending in a summary, he or she might offer to provide such a summary of treatment as a first response to such a request. If the managed care company persists in its request for actual records, and a signed consent exists from the patient, it must ultimately be honored, unless the therapist can justify refusing (e.g., on the grounds of harm to the patient or the therapy process).

It is important to note that supervision of the treatment by a case manager may have important implications for what a therapist may wish to include while documenting the course of therapy. If the therapist knows that the patient has formally given signed consent to the managed health care company to gain access to the notes at regular intervals (which usually is the case), and the therapist possesses a copy of the consent form, he or she would be well advised to limit these notes to concise representations of treatment interventions. It is crucial to bear in mind that every single word written by the therapist can become "grist for the mill" of a cross-examining attorney in the event of litigation or formal challenge to the treatment rendered by the psychologist. It is also important to remember that sometimes human resources departments may have casual practices in maintaining confidentiality of employees' records. It is not uncommon for patients to express concern about what is to be included on health insurance claims forms or other regularly submitted summaries of treatment. This may include anything from leaving patients' completed claim forms exposed on a secretary's desk top to unprotected entry of employee claims information into the company's administrative database so that others could easily access it. Specifically, it is wise to limit statements about diagnosis to the *Diagnostic and Statistical Manual of Mental Disorders* (4th ed.; American Psychiatric Association, 1994) code numbers, not diagnostic phrases. Therapists should take any reasonable steps that they can take to help protect the confidentiality of records against the prying eyes of supervisors, bosses, or colleagues—always keeping in mind the laws of the ubiquitous Murphy that assert that if anything can go wrong (about confidentiality), it eventually will. Again, the therapist could be liable if a confidentiality breach occurred, resulting in claims of damages by the patient.

Although time consuming, formal record keeping is an important activity for all therapists, and now that the risks to confidentiality are escalated to higher levels than ever before, it is incumbent upon therapists to be cautious and parsimonious in their documentation. In creating progress notes or filling out health-care forms, I suggest that the therapist always engage in the following fantasy exercise: Imagine that the patient is looking over one shoulder, the finest clinical supervisor is looking over another, and a lawyer is sitting across the table ready to poke holes in the therapist's logic or theoretical consistency. This somewhat vigilant stance may seem to be an unreasonable step to take for such a mundane activity as recording the progress of treatment. (And in most cases it probably would be unreasonable from the standpoint of the therapist's having to protect him- or herself against a complaint.) However, it only takes one litigious patient to bring an effective challenge to a therapist for malpractice, abandonment, or some other charge and cause a therapist to sincerely wish that he or she had chosen a different profession.

It is a challenging experience to be scrutinized by one's peers on an ethics committee, lawyers and jurors in a civil lawsuit, or board members of the state board of psychology. Certainly the challenge is weathered far better if the psychologist can refer to the history of treatment with progress notes or monthly reports that are accurate and thorough. It might be wise to remember that some patients take comprehensive notes about their own therapy, in the form of journal entries or diaries, and can easily cite their musings for practically any stage of treatment. It would be fortuitous indeed if the therapist were at least as well prepared as the patient in documenting the course of treatment.

Termination and Abandonment

A special problem faces the psychologist whose patient's psychopathology seems to burgeon during the course of therapy, instead of subsiding or yielding to the therapeutic process. This can be due to inadequate assessment at the outset, a focus on the somatic complaint to the exclusion of the psychological component (e.g., chronic pain), or some other factor that effectively masks the degree of mental disorder and hence the scope of psychotherapy required. In these cases the therapist, operating within the constraints of managed health care limits, may judge that having achieved some success with the presenting complaint, it is better to terminate treatment at that point than to embark on a necessarily limited course of therapy. After all, might it not be more harmful to the patient to interrupt psychotherapy in the middle, with many unresolved issues, than to avoid ever beginning in the first place?

In resolving such dilemmas, it is always crucial to consider the therapist's decisions from the patient's perspective. How would an individual diagnosed as a narcissistic personality disorder with some borderline features react to such a termination of psychological services, even though the patient may well be aware of the limitations imposed by his or her managed health care contract? Predictably, there could be a powerful, or even explosive reaction fueled by anxiety and anger, as this is perceived as yet another important loss in a life already filled with personal losses and abandonments.

In reviewing Standard 4.09 (a) of the Ethics Code, Terminating the Professional Relationship, therapists are reminded that "psychologists do not abandon patients or clients" (APA, 1992). It is arguably true that a therapist could not be thought of as truly abandoning a patient when both understand the terms of the contract at the outset, that a total of only 20 sessions will be paid for by a third party. However, it is more likely that the patient may entertain the perception of abandonment, which is the critical factor in whether a formal complaint will ensue. After all, in some sense, it may be true in businesses and service professions alike that "the customer is always right," even when he or she is wrong. It may indeed be a moot point which party is actually in the right. If the patient feels wronged, deprived, or ill-informed about the parameters of therapy at the outset, he or she may feel entitled to initiate a formal action against the therapist, regardless of the objective reality. Again, most patients would not take the time and effort to engage in such an energy-consuming adversarial action, as they are simply too involved in their own symptoms and suffering to embark upon such a venture. The chronic-pain patient wants relief, not the additional stress of following through with an ethics complaint or lawsuit. However, there are also those occasional high-energy patients with a deep well of dysphoric feelings, living in a large mansion on "Axis II Boulevard," who are ready and willing to follow through with a formal complaint if they feel they have been abandoned.

The patient may decide to sue both the therapist and the managed care company for failure to honor the terms of the contract as it is understood. There is some precedent for this, as mentioned earlier in *Wickline v. State of California* (1986), *Wilson v. Blue Cross* (1990), and other cases. Most of these cases involve physicians, rather than psychologists, yet the precedents have helped define the prudent course of action when a managed care company allocates only a limited number of sessions, and the therapist would recommend additional treatment. Each therapist should learn about the appeal process for additional sessions from the contract itself, the case manager, or some other source within the company. The therapist may then seek additional sessions, as he or she sees fit, according to the diagnosis and progress in therapy to date. Every step of this appeal should be documented in the patient's progress notes or else it should be carried out in the form of correspondence instead of only telephone calls. In short, a clear record of the process should emerge over the course of the appeal in order to document the psychologist's defense should questions or charges of abandonment ever be raised.

Another way to protect the patient's welfare, and therefore the psychologist's as well, is to formalize the termination process. Standard 4.09 (c), Termination of Services, reminds us that

> prior to termination for whatever reason, except where precluded by the patient's or client's conduct, the psychologist discusses the patient's or client's views and needs, provides appropriate pretermination counseling, suggests alternative service providers as appropriate, and takes other reasonable steps to facilitate transfer of responsibility to another provider if the patient or client needs one immediately. (APA, 1992).

This standard essentially requires that psychologists review the patient's concerns, ongoing needs, and wishes concerning further treatment and that they provide referrals as necessary. Such referrals could include a different type of intervention, such as marital therapy, group therapy, or even a low-cost or free support group (e.g., weight watchers or a 12-step program). In some cases, referral to a low-cost clinic or a mental health center might be appropriate, and within the financial resources of the patient. With such attention to the termination phase of treatment, the therapist reduces significantly the likelihood of discontent among patients and hence the probability of complaints or formal legal actions.

In the event that an unsuspected psychological diagnosis does emerge during therapy, the therapist has the obligation at the time to provide more informed consent concerning the need for extensive treatment. If the borderline aspect of the patient's problem was not evident to the therapist until the 7th of 10 allocated sessions, as the history taking was cursory and the focus until then had been on biofeedback training, the therapist would incur the responsibility of informing the patient about the need for more extensive treatment if it affected the presenting complaint (e.g., pain and depression). In short, informed consent is an ongoing process, as mentioned earlier, throughout the course of treatment, and is even implicit in the termination phase of treatment. The therapist should always be able to describe the array of possible therapeutic options that face the patient. This does not mean that the therapist must have a crystal ball to foresee the future. Rather, informed consent requires the therapist to draw continuously on his or her professional experience to help prepare and prompt the patient for a reasonable course of therapeutic experiences that might lie ahead. Obviously, theoretical orientation and diagnostic acumen play significant roles in providing informed consent; but, in any case, the attempt should always be made by therapists, in an ongoing sense, to protect patients from feeling that they have been exposed to interventions "by surprise" or that they have simply been abandoned.

Summary

It is clear that there are numerous unpredictable variables in navigating the seas of managed care in the behavioral medicine setting. These include informed consent, assessment, collaboration with other health-care professionals, confidentiality and record keeping, and termination and abandonment. Both psychologists and patients are at risk of being harmed by the restraints of managed health care in the form of reduced income for the psychologist, additional time and energy required for paperwork and reporting, and restricted number of allocated sessions, resulting in truncated treatment for the patient (to name a few). Psychologists and patients are also at risk of harming each other in the form of inadequate diagnostic assessment, improper treatment, confidentiality breaches, abandonment, and malpractice suits or ethics complaints. However, because the psychologist is vastly more experienced than the patient in working within the therapeutic milieu, he or she bears the burden of responsibility to provide adequate safeguards and, for the most part, has the knowledge of how to avoid these pitfalls along the way. Other examples of some of the pitfalls and problems that can occur in these and related situations are described in *Ethics in Plain English: A Vernacular Version of the Psychology Ethics Code, With Vignettes* (Nagy, 1998).

As in many areas of professional and ethical standards, it is important to note that it is the genuine attempt that psychologists make to adhere to a principle, and not necessarily the ultimate success of that attempt, that is most important. The psychologist must at least make an effort to right a wrong or address a problem; he or she need not necessarily succeed, however. Obviously there are many factors that are beyond the control of the psychologist that may make it impossible to guarantee an outcome. For example, a therapist can make a good faith effort at providing and documenting informed consent, yet can never be certain of the extent of the patient's comprehension. This standard mandates that the therapist should endeavor to provide informed consent and can prove this in some way by means of documented progress notes or handouts. This very theme—how the obligations of the ethics code can be fulfilled—is further explored in the book *Ethics for Psychologists: A Commentary on the APA Ethics Code* (Canter, Bennett, Jones, & Nagy, 1994).

There is much that psychologists can do to help the process of providing high quality of care in a behaviorial medicine setting while conforming to the requirements of managed care contracts. Certainly, by adhering to the APA "Ethical Principles of Psychologists and Code of Conduct," published APA guidelines and documents, and state and federal regulations (e.g., Veterans Administration settings), as well as keeping abreast of current literature in these areas, psychologists can vastly reduce the chances that significant problems will occur.

References

American Psychiatric Association. (1994). *Diagnostic and statistical manual of mental disorders* (4th ed.). Washington, DC: Author.

American Psychological Association. (1992). Ethical principles of psychologists and code of conduct. *American Psychologist, 47*, 1597–1611.

American Psychological Association. (1993). Record keeping guidelines. *American Psychologist, 48*, 984–986.

Barlow, D. H. (1985). *Clinical handbook of psychological disorders*. New York: Guilford Press.

Barlow, D. H. (1988). *Anxiety and its disorders*. New York: Guilford Press.

Basmajian, J. (1983). *Biofeedback: Principles and practice for clinicians*. Baltimore, MD: Williams & Wilkins.

Beck, A., Emery, G., & Greenberg, R. L. (1985). *Anxiety disorders and phobias*. New York: Basic Books.

Benson, H. (1975). *The relaxation response*. New York: Avon Books.

Benson, H. (1984). *Beyond the relaxation response*. New York: Times Books.

Bernstein, D. A., & Borkovec, T. D. (1973). *Progressive relaxation training: A manual for the helping professions*. Champaign, IL: Research Press.

Birk, L. (1973). *Biofeedback: Behavioral medicine*. New York: Grune & Stratton.

Brown, D., & Fromm, E. (1987). *Hypnosis and behavioral medicine*. Hillsdale, NJ: Erlbaum.

Canter, M. B., Bennett, B. E., Jones, S. E., & Nagy, T. F. (1994). *Ethics for psychologists: A commentary on the APA ethics code*. Washington, DC: American Psychological Association.

Caudill, O. B., & Pope, K. S. (1995). *Law and mental health professionals—California*. Washington, DC: American Psychological Association.

Jacobsen, E. (1938). *Progressive relaxation*. Chicago: University of Chicago Press.

Hathaway, S. R., & McKinley, J. C. (1989). *MMPI-2*. Minneapolis: University of Minnesota Press.

Hughes v. Blue Cross of California, 199 Cal. App. 3d 958, LEXIS 264 Cal. Rptr. 273. (Cal. Ct. App. 1988).

Kroger, W., & Fezler, W. (1976). *Hypnosis and behavior modification: Imagery conditioning*. Philadelphia: Lippincott.

Meichenbaum, D. (1977). *Cognitive–behavior modification*. New York: Plenum.

Miller, N. E. (1969). Learning of visceral and glandular responses. *Science, 163*, 434–445.

Miller, N. E. (1974). Biofeedback: Evaluation of a new technology. *New England Journal of Medicine, 290*, 684–685.

Nagy, T. (1993). Applying the new ethics code to practice. *The National Psychologist, 2*(5), 12–13.

Nagy, T. (1994). The ethical principles of psychologists and code of conduct (Rev. ed.). In R. J. Corsini (Ed.), *Encyclopedia of psychology* (2nd ed., pp. 504–508). New York: Wiley.

Nagy, T. (1998). *Ethics in plain English: A vernacular version of the psychology ethics code, with vignettes*. Sarasota, FL: Professional Resource Press.

Spiegel, D., & Spiegel, H. (1978). *Trance and treatment*. New York: Basic Books.

Turk, D. C., Meichenbaum, D., & Genest, M. (1983). *Pain and behavioral medicine*. New York: Guilford Press.

Wickline v. State of California, 192 Cal 3d 1630 (Cal. Ct. App. 1986).

Wickramaskera, I. (1976). *Biofeedback, behavior therapy, and hypnosis*. Chicago: Nelson Hall.

Wilson v. Blue Cross, 222 Cal. App. 3, 660, 2F1 Cal. Rptr., 876, 2nd Dept. (1990).

9

Mandated Addiction Services: Potential Ethical Dilemmas

Franklin G. Miller and Glenn A. Miller

An intake worker in a mental health center conducted an assessment on a client who was arrested for driving under the influence while using a company car. The referral was uncommon in two ways: First, it came directly from the judge rather than through the probation officer. Second, the referral was specifically for an intensive outpatient program rather than for assessment and treatment as recommended. Furthermore, the client also requested intensive treatment, explaining that unless the diagnosis indicated a dependence problem and he completed intensive treatment, he would have to be terminated from a long-term job against the wishes of his supervisor and the president of the organization. The client reported that the judge spoke to the employer and agreed to require intensive treatment. However, the intake worker's assessment revealed that the client did not meet diagnostic criteria for a substance use disorder and, therefore, should not be admitted to a treatment program for substance dependence. The judge referred the client to another agency that did enroll him in an intensive outpatient program. Subsequently, there was a decline in the number of referrals from the judge to the first agency.

Many ethical issues that commonly arise in health care are seen in unusual, bold forms of relief in providing treatment for substance-related disorders. This is due to the nature of the disorders, their impact on society, and the lack of consensus regarding what constitutes use and misuse of psychoactive substances. In this chapter we focus on ethical issues that arise from two facets of substance-related disorders: (a) Some people who suffer from misuse of psychoactive substances are not able or willing to acknowledge relevant behavior or modify their usage. (b) The negative impact of substance misuse extends beyond the individual to significant others and society. As a consequence of these two factors, people with substance-related disorders are often coerced into treatment, which gives rise to potential ethical dilemmas.

There have been a number of recent articles on the effectiveness of mandated addiction treatment (Berkowitz, Brindis, Clayson & Peterson, 1996; Hiller, Knight, Devereux, & Hathcoat, 1997; Lawental, McLellan, Grissom, Brill, & O'Brien, 1996; Wells-Parker, 1997). In this chapter we focus on ethical issues. Four specific questions are addressed: (a) What ethical issues arise as clients are required to participate in treatment and thereby lose power in the treatment setting? (b) How can therapists minimize the ethical problems associated with conflicts of interest that arise in providing addiction services that are mandated by a third party? (c) Are authorizations to exchange information really voluntary if clients are being coerced into treatment? (d) Do practitioners have an ethical obligation to address the unstated needs of clients who show clear evidence of serious life problems that are related to substance usage but who assert that they do not misuse psychoactive substances?

The fundamental ethical issue that arises for practitioners is recognizing and balancing stated and unstated needs of both the individual and the power that is mandating the treatment while also taking into account the interests of society. Additionally, practitioners should recognize that their decisions are affected by their own needs and by the preconceptions they bring to the situation. Practitioners have financial needs. The business of mental health relies on satisfying referral sources. However, there may be a conflict between the expressed needs of the client and the expressed needs of the referral source. Also, practitioners develop belief systems about substance-related disorders that color their view of clients and the circumstances that bring them to mandated treatment; there is a range of beliefs among practitioners about such things as denial, the impact of substance misuse, the severity of substance-related disorders, and the need for various treatment modalities.

By way of illustration, consider some of the forces that may be in play when someone is referred by a probation officer for assessment and treatment recommendations following a driving while intoxicated (DWI) violation. There is evidence of the possibility of a substance-related disorder. There may be conflicting and ambiguous evidence regarding the extent of symptoms. The client may present a variety of reasons why treatment is contraindicated. The probation officer, the presiding judge, and the practitioner each has a personal view regarding what constitutes a proper response to a DWI. The probation officer and other court personnel have a need to demonstrate that they have taken appropriate action to safeguard the community. The practitioner has a similar need—and a need to please the referral source. Ethical issues are intensified if the practitioner conducting the assessment has a financial stake in recommending a certain type of treatment. Practitioners may also face peer pressure from colleagues who embrace a particular approach to assessing and treating substance-related disorders.

Clients Referred Against Their Will

In presenting this chapter, our aim is to increase awareness of the forces at work and the issues that should be considered when a client presents for addiction treatment at the insistence of some other party. Ethical questions arise when there are multiple, conflicting needs. Appropriate resolution requires the ability to perceive, appreciate, and put into perspective the full range of various points of view. Although guidelines for resolution of ethical dilemmas are presented, it is recognized that the complexity and subtlety of the ethical issues that are being considered preclude stock solutions.

In this chapter we present the results of interviews with people who are involved in the process of referring clients for mental health services related to substance misuse. The intent is to provide practitioners with information that will broaden their perspectives and thereby help them maintain the highest possible ethical posture while providing services to these clients. We tried to select interviewees who represent a range of agencies that are involved in the process of referring people for addiction treatment; we do not view our list as comprehensive or methodically representative of a broad population of service agencies. The opinions expressed herein are solely those of the interviewees and should not be construed as official policies of their agencies.

In keeping with the recognition of the importance of practitioners' awareness of the preconceptions they bring to the process, we provide a brief introduction of ourselves. Glenn A. Miller and Franklin G. Miller are, respectively, the president and research director of the Substance Abuse Subtle Screening Institute. The Institute publishes the *Substance Abuse Subtle Screening Inventory Manual* (Miller, 1985). We both have training and experience in research and in clinical psychology. It is our view that substance-related disorders can have a devastating impact on the individual, significant others, and society as a whole. We believe that it is often difficult for people who suffer from substance-related disorders to recognize the problem. We believe that early identification and appropriate intervention can save lives. We believe that personal growth is facilitated in an atmosphere of respect, and we therefore place great importance on respecting the individuality, rights, and dignity of the client in the process of identification, assessment, and treatment.

The remainder of the chapter is organized on the basis of primary issues that emerged during analysis of the interview transcripts, which are as follows: voluntary consent for treatment, conflict of interest, information exchange, stated and unstated needs, and guidelines.

Voluntary Consent for Treatment

When voluntary consent for treatment is undermined by an element of coercion, clients lose power. Practitioners, whether they like it or not, become imbued with additional power that normally is not part of the treatment contract. In most of the coerced treatment situations that were described by the interviewees, clients have some element of choice. However, the choices may not always be perceived as appropriate and meaningful. For example, employees who are told that they must participate in treatment or they will be terminated may not view the situation as one of real choice. However, it is also important to recognize that, at some level, most referrals are precipitated by clients' behavior. Therefore, therapists have a responsibility to help clients assume responsibility for the choices they face. It is important for practitioners to understand the basis for the action that may be taken against their clients and to know the consequences clients face if they refuse treatment. In this section we present common circumstances in which the clients' freedom of choice in the treatment setting is limited.

In the criminal justice system, as described by James Swartz[1] and Ronald Dyson,[2] the context of required treatment is that the client has engaged in a criminal act and is liable to some penalty and that the treatment is an alternative to the penalty. Most assessments and treatment recommendations are made as part of presentence activity, and the client has the right to refuse treatment. The alternative is typically a heavier or stricter sentence.

Ronald Dyson indicated that all federal offenders are asked by a pretrial officer about the possibility of a substance-related disorder. Depending on whether the crime involved substance misuse and whether there was other evidence of a problem, the individual may be subject to further pretrial–presentence screening and assessment. The individual has a right to refuse, but he or she would face negative consequences, up to and including incarceration, in the course of the judicial proceedings.

Criminal justice clients are also assessed and referred for treatment as part of a postconviction process. There is a federal program that provides alcohol and drug services to individuals who are on parole. Subsequent to conviction and incarceration, there is typically ample evidence to indicate whether the individual has a drug problem. Thus, some people are paroled directly into a drug program. In addition, people on standard parole may be required to submit to urine screens if the parole officer suspects drug use. Parolees can refuse to participate in the drug program, but they face the prospect of being returned to court and possible further incarceration.

Daniel Lanier, Jr.[3] and David Bingaman[4] described an analogous scenario in workplace settings. A supervisor perceives deteriorated job performance, suspects that it may be related to substance use, and initiates a procedure resulting in assessment and possible treatment recommenda-

---

[1] James Swartz, Director of Research and Information Services at Treatment Accountability for Safer Communities, Inc. (T.A.S.C.). Swartz's primary responsibility is managing the research, evaluation, and information systems for the agency.

[2] Ronald Dyson, MSW, Administrator of the Substance Abuse Treatment Program, Administrative Office of the United States Courts. Dyson's primary responsibility is to oversee the provision of substance abuse and mental health treatment services to people under the supervision of the United States Courts.

[3] Daniel Lanier, Jr., DSW, ACSW, Certified Employee Assistance Professional, and Employee Assistance Program (EAP) Consultant, Human Resources, E. I. DuPont de Nemours & Company. Lanier's primary responsibility, along with several others in the department, is the administration of the EAP and the managed health care program for the company.

[4] David Bingaman, Employee Assistance Program Manager, Division of Federal Occupational Health. Bingaman's office is responsible for the administration and implementation of EAPs for the federal government.

tions. As in the criminal justice scenario, the referral is based on a behavior that could result in some form of consequence. The treatment is an alternative to that consequence. Also, EAP personnel attempt to establish and implement policies that facilitate entry into treatment before employer-mandated action occurs, which results in a forced choice between treatment and disciplinary action.

Sometimes employees are referred for addiction services if the supervisor suspects alcohol or other drug usage. For example, a supervisor may smell alcohol emanating from an employee or may observe the employee consuming a psychoactive substance. David Bingaman indicated that an employee who violates a code of conduct while under the influence on the job may face a choice between compliance with addictions treatment and disciplinary action up to and including termination.

Some employees are subject to random urine screens (Lawental et al., 1996). This is the case in safety-sensitive industries and in U.S. government jobs that have been classified for safety and security purposes as "Testing Designated Positions" (there are other workplace settings in which random drug screens are used). Positive urine screens can result in the same contingencies as impaired job performance. In both instances, personnel policies may require employees to comply with treatment as an alternative to a disciplinary action such as termination.

Lew Maltby[5] did not take comfort in the idea of a choice in situations in which the referral for treatment is based on evidence of usage rather than job performance. He pointed out that a positive urine screen does not necessarily signify a performance problem or a safety-security problem. Therefore, the choice between treatment and termination is inappropriate because a urine screen alone is not a justifiable basis for any job action. It is his opinion that the screening programs may be well motivated, but they are based on misinformation, a political agenda (the war on drugs), and a culture that does not adequately support individual liberties.

Applicants for public assistance may be required to participate in screening, assessment, and treatment as a requirement for receiving assistance. In those situations, a primary issue is determination of what constitutes adequate evidence of a substance misuse problem to warrant requiring applicants to participate in treatment.

School settings also refer people for assessment and treatment on the basis of observed usage, suspected usage, and positive urine screens. Frank Uryasz[6] reported that the National Collegiate Athletic Association (NCAA) conducts 9,000 urine screens each year, and student athletes who produce a confirmed positive drug test lose eligibility to participate in NCAA-sanctioned activities for a period of at least 1 year. Individual schools vary in terms of whether the student athlete is given an option to participate in treatment as an alternative to other consequences. Our clin-

---

[5] Lew Maltby, Director, National Task Force of Civil Liberties in the Workplace, American Civil Liberties Union. Maltby's primary responsibility is for all civil liberty issues that arise between employers and employees.

[6] Frank Uryasz, Director, Sports Sciences, NCAA. Uryasz's primary responsibility is directing the alcohol and other drug education and testing programs for the NCAA.

ical experiences include cases in which local public schools have required students who have been found using alcohol or other drugs to participate in treatment as a condition of continuing enrollment. Often, the students do not acknowledge a substance abuse problem and do not view the treatment as a choice but rather as a requirement that is at best irrelevant.

In summary, it is important to be familiar with common contingencies that result in coerced addiction treatment. Maintaining awareness of the circumstances that lead to a client being coerced into treatment allows practitioners to (a) acknowledge the extent to which clients' choices regarding treatment are constrained, (b) construe the situation in a manner that maximizes the clients' options, and (c) help clients recognize ways in which their behaviors may have precipitated the treatment recommendation.

Potential Conflict of Interest: Who Is the Client?

All of the interviewees acknowledged that practitioners may face conflicts of interest in providing addiction services when the treatment is initiated and mandated by a third party. James Swartz opined that such problems may be increasing because of growing economic pressures on practitioners, resulting in a greater need to cater to referral sources. Economic pressure has become part of the daily reality of most health-care practitioners as they face the broader realm of ethical dilemmas created by managed care. In this section we present interviewees' suggestions for resolving the ethical problems that arise from such conflicts of interest.

A common view was expressed clearly by Marc R. Kellams.[7] He emphasized that the needs of the individual receiving services are primary; therefore, the practitioner's responsibility to the referral source is to proceed in a professional manner in the interest of the client and to provide the referral source with all relevant information.

A fundamental challenge for practitioners is to be aware of conflicting needs that may not always be readily apparent. The interviewees presented a number of examples. Frank Uryasz discussed the circumstance in which practitioners are responsible to an agency to promote a message of abstinence, but they in fact believe that the message is not likely to have an impact within the context of the clients' culture. James Swartz noted that an agency's program admission criteria may not provide services to clients who could profit from some treatment. He also noted that the lack of tailoring of treatment to meet the particular needs of individuals sometimes causes clients to be required to participate in unnecessary treatment modules to satisfy the regulations of a referral source. This position was expanded by Lew Maltby, who expressed the view that practitioners are pressured to provide unnecessary treatment to meet the de-

---

[7]Marc R. Kellams, Circuit Court Judge, Division II, 10th Judicial Circuit in and for Monroe County, Indiana. Kellams presides over a unified court that includes criminal, civil, and domestic relations cases.

mands of the policies established in employment settings. In a similar vein, Daniel Lanier drew attention to the possibility that a referral in an employment setting may reflect an unstated agenda being promoted by a supervisor.

Sometimes the conflict involves interests in addition to those of the client and the referral source. A client's behavior may be interfering with the progress of other clients, or the client may be using scarce treatment resources unprofitably. The practitioner may feel constrained—in the interest of satisfying the needs of the referral source—to continue to serve the client at some expense to other clients. Judge Kellams's position is that the practitioner should rely on established principles of professional practice in determining the course of action. Ronald Dyson and Daniel Lanier also emphasized the practitioner's responsibility to maintain program standards, regardless of any perceived pressure to the contrary. Dyson indicated that it may be a burden for parole officers to return someone to court for noncompliance with treatment, but that the burden is part of the job and should not affect the clinical decisions of the practitioner. Ultimately, everyone's, including treatment providers', interests are best served by maintaining standards and by assuring quality programming.

The public sometimes has a significant stake in the treatment process. Judge Kellams refers people who are involved in custody disputes for addiction assessments to protect the interests of children. Some medical practitioners conduct addiction screenings as part of prepartum care to protect the interests of to-be-born children. Ronald Dyson and James Swartz pointed out that public safety is a significant issue when practitioners serve clients referred by the criminal justice system. Swartz expressed the opinion that much of the motivation and support for treatment within the criminal justice system is to avoid the broad costs of recidivism that accrue to victims and to society as a whole. Dyson reported that pretrial addiction assessments are used by judges to help determine the propriety of releasing or detaining the arrested individual. Similarly, some of the employment situations discussed by David Bingaman and Daniel Lanier involve issues of public safety and security.

Within the context of viewing public safety and security as a consideration in the assessment and treatment process, it is important to give careful consideration to Lew Maltby's position that much of the impetus for mandated screening, assessment, and treatment comes from a political agenda—the war on drugs. From Maltby's point of view, there is indeed a need to assure public safety, and most employers are well meaning in their attempts to establish and administer policies regarding drugs. However, it is important to scrutinize the extent to which drug screening and mandated treatment actually promote public safety. To the extent that they are accurate, urine screens reveal that the individual has used psychoactive substances, not that the individual is under the influence at the time of the screen. Also, evidence of usage is not a clear indication of an addictions problem. According to Maltby screening for motor skills impairment or other job performance indicators would be a more effective way to assure public safety while not infringing on individual liberties.

Christopher Lawson[8] discussed a situation involving a different type of public interest that may come into play when providing addiction assessments and treatment. In some public assistance programs, applicants who are identified as being at relatively high risk of having a substance-related disorder are required to participate in assessment and possible treatment as a condition of continuing in the assistance program. Lawson pointed out that in these situations, the practitioner has a responsibility to provide services that promote the health and well-being of the client and a responsibility to meet the requirements of the contract with the referring agency. Also, there is a responsibility to meet the needs of the citizens who express a desire that public funds not be used by drug-dependent people to support their addictions and thereby further the negative impact of the problem.

David Bingaman, Daniel Lanier, and Christopher Lawson stressed the importance of active recognition and acceptance of the fact that there are often multiple "clients." The two EAP professionals emphasized that it is important to view both the individual and the referral source as clients; practitioners have a clear responsibility to provide appropriate intervention for both parties. This posture requires careful adherence to established professional practices. During the interview, when Daniel Lanier was pressed with hypothetical cases involving potential conflicts of interest, such as a workplace supervisor using the EAP in an attempt to discharge an employee, his responses were invariably based on firm principles of professional conduct. He expressed a total willingness to intervene in the practices of the referral source, just as he is fully available to provide interventions for the identified client.

David Bingaman also indicated that practitioners have a responsibility to promote positive change for both the client and the referral source. When a client is in the office, the ethical demand on the practitioner is to accept his or her attitude toward the mandated treatment in a respectful and nonjudgmental manner and to help find a course of action that reflects the client's needs and values. Beyond that, the practitioner also has an ethical obligation to maintain contact with the employer and to advocate for policies on behalf of the employees' well-being.

Christopher Lawson had an exceptionally thorough analysis of the forces at play in the public assistance setting. He recognized the needs of the applicants for public assistance who misuse substances; it is important to intervene in the progressive process of substance-related disorders to avoid the horrendous cost to the individual. He recognized the needs of the public officials; it is an enormous challenge to provide and administer public services within the context of conflicting demands, conflicting values, and shrinking budgets. He recognized the desire of the public; it is important to provide the resources to help individuals who are in need while not allowing limited resources to promote rather than to solve per-

---

[8]Christopher Lawson, LCSW, San Diego County Alcohol and Drug Services, Department of Health Services. Lawson's office has primary responsibility for planning, coordinating, and monitoring alcohol and drug services contracts for San Diego County.

sonal and societal problems. Lawson expressed his view that it is vital to maintain a broad, thoughtful posture to reconcile satisfactorily the conflicting needs and values that operate in this type of situation.

In summary, in dealing with the possibility that a client's needs may not correspond with those of referral sources, it is important for practitioners to (a) give primary consideration to the needs of the individual receiving services, (b) maintain a high level of professional standards in all contacts with referral sources, (c) provide referral sources with all relevant information, (d) be aware of the possibility that there may be conflicts of interest that are not apparent, and (e) maintain program standards and established principles of professional practice.

Information Exchange

The related issue of authorization to exchange information may heighten the potential ethical problem of conflicting interests between the client and the referral source. Practitioners require a written authorization from the client to exchange any information. Such authorization is supposed to be voluntary, and treatment should not be contingent on a client's willingness to allow information exchange. However, as Lew Maltby emphasized, when treatment is mandated, the "voluntary" authorization may not actually represent an act of free will. This is similar to the ethical dilemma created by managed care programs that cover health-care costs only if the client signs authorizations to release information, and they then exchange the information in a manner that is not in keeping with the client's needs. In this section we present the interviewees' views regarding voluntary consent to exchange information when the client is required to participate in treatment.

To examine the implications of having consent to disclose information to an organization that has clear power over the client, consider a circumstance raised in the interviews with James Swartz and Ronald Dyson. A client who has been referred by the criminal justice system is progressing and is well motivated. In the course of treatment, the client acknowledges a criminal act or reports a slip. By virtue of the exchange authorization and the contract with the referral source, the treatment provider is under some obligation to report the information, even if they believe (rightly or wrongly) that the consequences of reporting the information are not in the best interests of the client. The practitioner must weigh the needs of the client, the needs of the referral agency, and his or her need to avoid potential liability and loss of reputation.

James Swartz and Ronald Dyson emphasized the value of a good working relationship between the practitioner and the referral source; a nonadversarial relationship between colleagues promotes consultation regarding the optimal course of action. Most court systems allow discretion on the part of the agencies involved with the client. Indeed, most court programs have explicit procedures for handling minor violations without returning the client to the court for further action. Also, if the agency that is responsible for assessment and referral is separate and distinct from the agency that provides the treatment (as is the case with T.A.S.C.), there is a further opportunity for professional consultation; the assessment agency can also function as an intermediary between the treatment provider and the primary referral source.

Decisions regarding disclosure of prior offenses can be turned into an opportunity for a therapeutic intervention. In keeping with his emphasis on maintaining a respectful posture toward clients, Ronald Dyson suggested that clients be given an opportunity to choose to disclose this type of information as part of a process of unloading guilt and learning the value of honesty. The therapist can be supportive of the client in the process of disclosing and can consult with other involved parties to help determine the optimal course of action. It has been Dyson's experience that progress in the therapy setting is enhanced if the client is thorough in dealing honestly with their past.

As practitioners face the responsibility of providing client information to referral sources, it is important to (a) establish a clear understanding with both the client and the referral source regarding the appropriate level of disclosure, (b) maintain good working relationships with the referral sources, and (c) support the client in the therapeutic process of disclosing relevant information.

Stated and Unstated Needs

As discussed in the introduction, there are two factors that lead to coerced addictions treatment: (a) the difficulty substance misusers have in acknowledging the problem and (b) the negative impact of substance misuse on society. The ethical dilemma addressed in this chapter is more fully revealed when the negative impact of substance use disorders on the individual is considered. Substance misuse can lead to serious emotional, social, familial, spiritual, and economic consequences to the individual. Therapists may therefore have an ethical obligation to address unstated needs of clients who show clear evidence of serious life problems that are related to substance usage but who assert that they do not have a substance-related problem.

There is scholarly controversy regarding the extent to which people who misuse psychoactive substances minimize their usage and related problems. Some researchers are exploring the proposition that people can be screened for substance use disorders by simply asking them about their usage (Otto & Hall, 1988; Otto, Lang, Megargee, & Rosenblatt, 1988; Sinnett, Benton, & Whitfill, 1991; Sobell & Sobell, 1990). From this point of view, it is adequate to address only the clients' stated needs regarding addiction services. However, people who misuse psychoactive substances may not invariably be completely forthright in reporting the problem, and some clients may be seen as needing addictions treatment, even though they do not articulate such a need.

Daniel Lanier and David Bingaman reported that resistance is com-

mon when employees are first referred into treatment as part of a requirement by an employer. They also indicated that in many instances
resistance diminishes, and employees often express gratitude for the intervention after they have been in treatment for awhile. Many EAP programs
are highly sensitive to the perceived needs of clients. This sensitivity is
manifested in programs and policies that are designed to provide employees with addictions and other forms of services before any need for disciplinary job action and forced referrals. It is important for service providers
to recognize the progressive, negative impact of substance use disorders
and to attempt intervention in the process as early as possible.

Chris Lawson expressed in a dramatic manner the importance of addressing unstated needs, to prevent clients from experiencing the full cost
of substance misuse. Some clients who are required to participate in treatment as part of a public assistance program may be quite vocal in express-
ing their beliefs that they do not need treatment, that they do not want
it, and that they consider it to be an unwelcome burden. Some of the people
who resist mandated treatment may be correct in their assessments that
they do not have a substance misuse problem. However, some may be
sincerely deluded and on a path of self-destruction. There is value in honoring each person's right to choose one's own path through life. However,
is the public being served by a drug addict suffering and dying in the street
or who is alone in the darkness of an overburdened, underfunded public
hospital? As unstated needs are considered, it is vital to recognize that
substance use disorders sometimes evolve within an individual and, in a
cunning and baffling manner, lead to suffering and premature death.

Three of the interviewees (Lew Maltby, Frank Uryasz, and James
Swartz) also focused on the responsibility of the therapist to be thorough
and methodical in understanding the reality that a client faces in his or
her daily life. This is not always an easy matter.

Lew Maltby stressed the importance of making no assumptions on the
basis of limited information. A positive urine screen is not an indication
of a substance use disorder. A screen alone does not provide sufficient
information to determine if a client meets admission criteria for a treatment program. It is important that a client not be placed in treatment
without adequate evidence that the treatment is necessary and serves the
individual's interests and values. If a client is referred by an employer for
mandatory services on the basis of something other than job performance,
a comprehensive assessment of the entire situation is essential to achieve
a reasonable perspective.

Frank Uryasz pointed out that practitioners may not have a full understanding of the motivation and basis of substance usage among
student-age clients. Performance-enhancing drugs are a case in point. Anabolic steroids and amphetamines, as they are used by many student athletes, may need to be addressed differently than marijuana and other psychoactive drugs. It is important to scrutinize the user in an effort to
understand the factors that underlie the usage. Student athletes are under
pressure to perform well and may believe that anabolic steroids can be
helpful. Student-age people are highly conscious of their appearance and

may therefore take steroids in an attempt to look better. It is also important to recognize that many youthful clients are unable to recognize and appreciate the significance and negative effects of long-term drug usage. In general, the practitioner should not proceed from a set of assumptions regarding the basis of the substance usage without determining if those assumptions are appropriate for the particular client.

James Swartz made a similar point. He expressed the opinion that rehabilitation programs often do not take into account the functional reality of the client's life. With the erosion of well-paying factory jobs in urban areas, the drug culture has taken on increased significance in many people's lives. Some people who receive addiction treatment while incarcerated leave jails and prisons to face a world in which drugs are the predominant economic and social force. Treatment programs do not address many of the factors that contribute to the clients' drug problems and may therefore raise hopes that are not likely to be fulfilled. Individual mental health practitioners cannot create the social and economic changes that are needed to support sobriety as a lifestyle among many criminal justice clients. However, to be as effective as possible and to respect clients, it is necessary to honor their reality and to appreciate their individuality.

Addictions counselors rarely work in what may be considered an ideal context for providing mental health services: (a) a common reference base regarding what constitutes problematic behavior, (b) self-referral and willingness to change, (c) a mutual contract of total honesty and forthrightness, and (d) an objective way to look at the evidence and thereby weigh the costs and payoffs of treatment options. Many people who misuse substances continue to do so for prolonged periods of time, despite negative consequences not only to themselves but also to others. Because substance misuse can exert a progressive negative impact on people's lives, it is important for practitioners to help some clients recognize the manner in which their substance use is affecting their lives. It is also important to endeavor to understand and to respect the reality that clients face and to place their needs above ideological positions.

Guidelines

The subtlety and complexity of the ethical issues that arise when clients are coerced into addiction treatment preclude a comprehensive listing of ethical issues and clear guidelines for resolution. However, the interviewees provided the following useful suggestions:

1. *Be aware of the circumstances that enter into the treatment contract and how they affect the relationship between clients and practitioners.* Often, addiction clients come to treatment with a sense of pressure from family members, employers, and legal authorities. They are likely to feel and express resentment toward practitioners. To be effective, practitioners need to recognize and acknowledge the pressures clients face.

2. *Be aware of potential conflicts of interest that may not be obvious.* Psychoactive substance abuse is a focal point in political and ideological

debates regarding social, moral, and economic issues. As we seek to serve people who may suffer from substance-related disorders, it is important that we recognize that our abilities to focus on their needs may be affected by an array of subtle, social, and economic forces.

3. *Maintain primary consideration for the identified client.* Regardless of the pressures that accrue as a result of having to satisfy the demands of referral sources, it is vital for practitioners to recognize that their primary contract is with the client and that their primary responsibility is to act in accord with the client's needs.

4. *Attend to the clients' unique profile of needs.* There are forces that may make it difficult for practitioners to adequately appreciate the reality of the clients' lives and circumstances. We bring our own assumptions about mental health and optimal functioning to the treatment process; those assumptions may not be relevant for our clients. We need to seek to understand the forces at work in their lives. We need to scrutinize the appropriateness of our treatment programs on a regular basis, and we should endeavor to tailor treatment to meet the specific needs of each client.

5. *Consider the extent to which clients' voluntary actions are indeed voluntary.* Clients who enter treatment to avoid job loss or severe legal penalties do not voluntarily consent to disclosure of information; they are coerced by the referral source into signing exchange authorizations. It is not always possible or even desirable to change the systems that affect our clients; it is our primary responsibility to help our clients learn to function effectively within the context of the reality they face. However, in the interests of honesty and respect toward our clients, it is important that we recognize and acknowledge the constraints that they face as they enter into a treatment contract with us.

6. *Scrutinize policies to determine if they address the problem rather than unnecessarily constrain individual liberties.* Because substance abuse is a focus of political and ideological debate, multiple agendas enter into the creation of public policy regarding substance abusers. As service workers, we incur an obligation to serve our clients' needs. We therefore have an obligation to develop and maintain service systems and programs that meet those needs.

7. *Seek appropriate consultation.* There are subtle pressures on practitioners who provide services for people who are coerced into treatment. We may not always be aware of conflicts of interest and unstated agendas. We may not always feel comfortable about our concerns in meeting the expectations of referral sources. Therefore, it is important for us to seek professional guidance and to be forthright in presenting relevant information to consultants.

8. *Act in accord with established professional principles and guidelines.* The case presented at the beginning of this chapter is an example of the complex needs and pressures that come to bear when clients are coerced into treatment. The client, the judge, and the employer wanted intensive treatment. The agency needed to maintain the good will of the judge. The intake worker wanted to accommodate the client's stated need.

The intensive outpatient program would not have harmed the client. However, the client was not diagnosed as having a substance dependence disorder and therefore did not meet admission criteria. The consensus among the interviewees is, regardless of the pressures to the contrary, to act in accord with established professional principles and guidelines.

9. *Be willing to intervene in an effort to modify the behavior of the referral source as well as that of the client.* Ethical behavior sometimes requires courage. Referral sources such as court programs or personnel offices may develop policies that lead to inappropriate treatment referrals. In the interests of clients, practitioners may incur an ethical obligation to promote change within the agencies that refer clients.

10. *Be aware of the extent to which the consent for treatment and authorization to exchange information are voluntary.* When you invite clients to sign forms indicating voluntary consent for treatment and authorization to exchange information, acknowledge the constraints they face and help them clarify their options.

11. *Maintain a positive, nonadversarial relationship with referral sources.* Forthrightness and honesty are the most important elements in navigating tricky ethical issues. Clients' needs are best served when all the service workers who are involved are able to define a shared mission and maintain a sense of collegiality.

12. *Try to use disclosure as an opportunity for positive therapeutic interventions.* Typically, clients who are coerced into treatment are required by the referral source to authorize the treatment provider to exchange information. This has an impact on the treatment setting; it brings a third party into the room. Before commencing treatment, be clear with all parties regarding what information you will and will not disclose. Furthermore, use the process of disclosure to help clients learn to deal honestly and effectively with the social systems that have an impact on their lives.

13. *Recognize that clients may have unstated needs.* When people are coerced into addiction treatment, resistance may be intensified. The coercion can engender feelings of powerlessness and a sense of being disrespected, which can lead to reactivity and an unwillingness to disclose. Also, it is often difficult for people who abuse substances to recognize and acknowledge the full extent of their substance misuse. Thus, therapists may incur an ethical obligation to help clients recognize the impact of their substance usage on their lives, even if the client does not initially perceive substance misuse as a significant problem.

14. *Conduct adequate assessments before making treatment recommendations.* Every service practitioner and every agency that is involved in referring and treating people with substance-related disorders has a point of view regarding what constitutes an appropriate response to substance misuse. We often become entrenched in our beliefs, and treatment plans may be based on preconceptions rather than on detailed assessment of the client's symptoms and needs. Comprehensive assessments are necessary to ensure that the client is the central consideration in the treatment planning process.

15. *Maintain a posture of respect toward the clients.* In all treatment

settings, the therapeutic alliance between practitioner and client is fostered by an attitude of respect. This is of particular importance when clients are coerced into treatment. They are likely to be angry and may enter the treatment setting with a sense that they are not respected. Also, addiction treatment often involves confronting clients regarding their tendencies to rationalize and to minimize the impact of their substance misuse. A fundamental ethical responsibility for the practitioner is to seek to understand and to respect the unique constellation of experiences, desires, and needs that each client brings to the treatment setting. It is important to help clients make the changes that are necessary to enhance the quality of their lives, and this can be accomplished most readily in an atmosphere of respect.

Each interviewee presented a unique way of conceptualizing and articulating basic ethical principles. They all recognized that, ultimately, decisions regarding ethical principles must rest on the judgment of the individual practitioners. As practitioners face the changing demands created by an evolving health-care system, the most important recommendation may be to periodically stand back from the day-to-day tasks of providing addiction services and to contemplate the ethical implications of our work, seeking to increase awareness and sensitivity to the range of needs that can enter into the treatment process.

References

Berkowitz, G., Brindis, C., Clayson, Z., & Peterson, S. (1996). Options for recovery: Promoting success among women mandated to treatment. *Journal of Psychoactive Drugs, 28*(1), 31–37.

Hiller, M. L., Knight, K., Devereux, J., & Hathcoat, M. (1997). Posttreatment outcomes for substance-abusing probationers mandated to residential treatment. *Journal of Psychoactive Drugs, 28*(3), 291–295.

Lawental, E., McLellan, A. T., Grissom, G. R., Brill, P., & O'Brien, C. (1996). Coerced treatment for substance abuse problems detected through workplace urine surveillance: Is it effective? *Journal of Substance Abuse, 8*(1), 115–128.

Miller, G. A. (1985). *The Substance Abuse Subtle Screening Inventory manual.* Spencer, IN: Spencer Evening World.

Otto, R. K., & Hall, J. E. (1988). The utility of the Michigan Alcoholism Screening Test in the detection of alcoholics and problem drinkers. *Journal of Personality Assessment, 52,* 499–502.

Otto, R. K., Lang, A. R., Megargee, E. I., & Rosenblatt, A. (1988). Ability of alcoholics to escape detection by the MMPI. *Journal of Consulting and Clinical Psychology, 56,* 452–457.

Sinnett, R. E., Benton, S. L., & Whitfill, J. (1991). Simulation and dissimulation on alcoholism inventories: The ALCADD and the MAST. *Psychological Reports, 68,* 1360–1362.

Sobell, L. C., & Sobell, M. B. (1990). Self-report issues in alcohol abuse: State of the art and future directions. *Behavioral Assessment, 12,* 77–90.

Wells-Parker, E. (1997). Mandated treatment: Lessons from research with drinking and driving offenders. *Alcohol Health & Research World, 18*(4), 302–306.

Part II _____

Business and Legal Issues

The business and legal context of clinical practice is becoming increasingly important to mental health practitioners. Clinicians need to understand these issues to determine how they will organize their practices and what alternatives are available. Many terms are included in the following chapters that may be unfamiliar to the newcomer or to the busy practitioner, so a brief guide is provided here.

Managed care is a generic term, rarely well defined, that refers to any third-party reimbursement system in which costs are actively controlled through limiting access, preauthorizing services, utilization review, capitation, or other means. These services may include something as minimal as examining and paying claims but often include some type of *utilization review*, which requires health-care providers to justify procedures and fees before services will be paid for. Sometimes utilization review includes *case management* in which the reviewer, or case manager, may ask details about the diagnosis and treatment plan and may require the clinician to report back after a few sessions to justify further treatment. If utilization review decides against reimbursing services, then sometimes the client can self-pay, but other times that too is prohibited by contract, so the clinician has the choice of terminating treatment or providing it without reimbursement. Some contracts even prohibit the clinician from providing free services. Although managed care organizations insist that they determine only what the benefit plan will cover—and not whether services will be provided, because that is up to the practitioner—in actual practice, services generally end when coverage is denied. Courts and legislatures are finally beginning to accept this reality leading to increased litigation and regulatory proposals.

Managed care organizations (*MCOs*) typically build networks of providers, often called *preferred provider organizations* (*PPOs*), in which providers are required to sign contracts with the MCO, which details *discounted fees* and procedures for working with clients and the MCO in the way in which they wish. *Health maintenance organizations* (*HMOs*) are MCOs that tend to be more tightly integrated than a PPO network, often hiring their own staff and having an actual clinic. Sometimes HMOs and PPOs include mental health services but often these are *carved out* (i.e., contracted for) to a specific mental health (or "behavioral health") PPO. A common arrangement that is confusing to clients (and sometimes to professionals) is a health-care benefit plan that includes a medical plan, usually a PPO or HMO, with mental services "carved out" to a mental health PPO.

Traditional indemnity insurance plans fund for services through insurance premiums, or they bill a consumer organization for costs as they are paid. HMOs and many PPOs are usually funded by *capitation*, in which the consumer organization pays a specific amount per member per month for services—in a sense, prepaying for the services. The HMO is then *at risk* for the services because it must provide the services regardless of how much it has taken in premiums. If the MCO/HMO/PPO can provide the services for less cost than it receives in capitation, then it increases its profit. Sometimes groups of providers can go at risk for services by accepting capitation payment. Another way that provider groups can assume risk is with *case rates*. MCOs can contract for providers to take cases for a certain fixed amount, a case rate (e.g., $300/case), which they would receive for every case that they would take—whether the client uses 1 session or 20 sessions. The practitioner then makes or loses money on the basis of how many sessions are used. Additional information on these matters is discussed in the chapters that follow.

10

Practitioner Legal Liability: When Utilization Review Says No

Thomas E. Sweeney, Michael J. Stutman, and Renee H. Martin

With the growth of managed care over the last several years, the potential for exposure to liability of behavioral health-care providers (e.g., psychologists, psychiatrists, social workers, and other therapists; referred to collectively as *practitioners*) has increased as well. Managed care has introduced new players into the field, including such managed care organizations (MCOs) as HMOs, PPOs, and third-party behavioral health administrators. The input of these MCOs into the process has added levels of review and decision making to behavioral health-care delivery and has increased the possibility that delivery of care from practitioners will be adversely affected.

In this chapter we explore the extent to which liability may be imposed on practitioners and MCOs in connection with the delivery of behavioral health care, as well as the alternatives available to practitioners who want to avoid such liability, while still providing adequate care. An exhaustive discussion of practitioner and MCO liability is beyond the scope of this chapter. Also, it must be emphasized that this area of the law is rapidly evolving, outcomes vary by jurisdiction, and judicial decisions rendered are highly fact specific. Practitioners should not assume that the legal principles enumerated in this chapter currently apply within their jurisdiction. Indeed, new case law and legislation may alter the practitioner's responsibilities and the principles discussed in this chapter. Our goals are to raise the consciousness of practitioners, to provide guiding principles to navigate the relevant issues, and to alert practitioners of the need to remain current with this changing area of the law.

The experience of psychiatrist Gordon Blundell introduces a managed care dilemma many practitioners struggle with each day. In the *Salley* case (*Salley v. DuPont*, 1992), DuPont, a large corporation, engaged Preferred Health Care (PHC), a third-party MCO, to curb the mental health care costs of its employees, which were rising 15% or more a year. Blundell had diagnosed Jack Salley's 13-year-old daughter, Danielle, as being severely depressed and recommended hospitalization. Salley's benefits covered his daughter's two initial hospitalizations. PHC, however, denied continued hospitalization for Danielle, despite Blundell's warning that she could seriously harm herself. Fortunately, Salley could afford to continue hospitalization for his daughter, but he sued DuPont in federal court for $40,000 in denied hospitalization care and won (*Salley v. DuPont*, 1992).

Salley did not sue his daughter's mental health practitioners—Blundell had documented his recommendations and discussions with PHC, and he had provided adequate recommendation for care. Yet, in day-to-day dealings with MCOs, practitioners must face and address their increased exposure to liability (Appelbaum, 1993). For instance, if a utilization reviewer refuses to approve a practitioner's clinical recommendations, the practitioner faces three professional choices: (a) continue treatment consistent with the practitioner's clinical judgment, although the MCO will not pay for services or the patient cannot pay for services; (b) terminate treatment and assume potential legal exposure; or (c) provide the services approved by the MCO, although they may be inconsistent with the practitioner's professional recommendations. There are no easy answers to these difficult options in a managed care environment. To explore the practical implications of this dilemma, in this chapter we first review managed care contracts, including the nature of those contracts that provide a framework for the practitioner–patient relationship. Second, we discuss traditional legal duties owed by the practitioner to the patient in the context of managed care. Third, we address the impact of the Employment Retirement Income Security Act (ERISA, 1974) on practitioner liability. The Appendix includes practical recommendations and guidelines for practitioners operating in the managed care environment.

Introduction to Managed Care

Managed care has many definitions. Applebaum (1993) pointed out that "managed care as a generic term subsumes a wide variety of practices designed to regulate the utilization of health care" (p. 251). The critical element is the prospective ability "to deny payment for care thought to be unnecessary or not cost effective" (Appelbaum, 1993, p. 251). One way to investigate the impact of managed care on the practitioner–patient relationship is to illustrate the network of contracts between the patient and his or her employer; between the employer and the MCO; between the MCO and the practitioner; and, finally, between the practitioner and the patient.

The contract between the provider and MCO is generally called a *participating provider agreement*. The participating provider agreement typically addresses the following: (a) services to be provided by the practitioner; (b) the covered person verification process; (c) practitioner payments and time frame; (c) the practitioner's appeal process for negative utilization review determinations; (d) the term and termination of the agreement; and (e) the utilization review, quality assurance, and case management processes. The agreement also often specifies that practitioners may not receive payments directly from the employee or patient for treatment, except if the service is deemed not medically necessary or not covered by the employer benefit plan, and only then under certain circumstances. Usually, the contracts require the written consent of the employee or patient before the provision of noncovered services. The following discussion provides a helpful framework for evaluation of the participating provider agreement.

In *Varol v. Blue Cross and Blue Shield of Michigan* (1989), 10 psychiatrists signed a provider agreement with Blue Cross and Blue Shield of Michigan (Blue Cross) to participate in the Blue Cross provider network. Once in the network, the psychiatrists challenged Blue Cross's utilization review mechanisms and asserted that these mechanisms violated state law by interfering with their medical judgment. The court in *Varol* rejected all of the psychiatrists' claims (see following discussion). The *Varol* case is especially instructive because it illustrates a classic network of contracts that forms the foundation for evaluating practitioner duties and responsibilities under managed care.

The basic health-care benefits at issue in *Varol* were funded for employees of General Motors (GM) under the GM Health Care Program (the employee benefit plan). Under the employee benefit plan, *enrollees* (i.e., GM employees, retirees, or eligible dependents) had the choice of selecting one of three health-care delivery options: traditional fee for service, an HMO, or a PPO. These employee benefit options are administered for GM by Blue Cross under an *administrative services only* (ASO) contract. Blue Cross served not as the insurer but rather as a third-party administrator, a common type of MCO. GM reimbursed Blue Cross for all covered health-care charges paid by Blue Cross on behalf of GM employees, and GM also paid Blue Cross a fee for administering the program.

Under the ASO agreement, Blue Cross agreed to administer the employee benefit plan established by GM and to perform certain administrative services such as billing; establishing a network of hospitals, doctors, and other behavioral health-care providers who can provide the services required by the employee benefit plan; and administering the prior authorization program, more commonly referred to as *utilization review*. Generally, utilization review determines the "medical necessity" of behavioral health services under the benefit plan. Utilization review comes in three basic forms: (a) *prospective approval*, the prior authorization of services before services are rendered; (b) *concurrent review*, the monitoring of medical appropriateness of services concurrently while such services are provided; and (c) *retroactive review*, the auditing of services already provided to ensure that they are consistent with the employee benefit plan. Benefit plans will cover only those services considered medically necessary.

The participating provider agreement between Blue Cross and the 10 psychiatrists was intended to achieve certain goals for both parties. From Blue Cross's perspective, it sought to establish a provider relationship that would complement the plans' attractiveness to employers and to establish a reimbursement and utilization review mechanism that would allow it to manage services in a cost-effective manner. The psychiatrists, alternatively, sought increased volume of patient referrals from the benefit plan, expedited payments of claims, and ease of administration.

Turning to some general, practical considerations, practitioners should read each agreement and, to the extent possible, seek to limit or mitigate problematic aspects of the provider agreement, such as hold-harmless clauses, reimbursement levels, timely processing of utilization review requests, reasonable and timely appeal procedures, and timely payment to the practitioner.

This is, of course, easier said than done. In the real world, solo and small group practitioners do not have sufficient bargaining power to insist on amendments to the model MCO participating provider agreement. Faced with limited bargaining power, the practitioner is faced with difficult choices. If a practitioner signs the agreement, a court will hold him or her accountable. As the court in *Varol* stated, "having sought to be members and contractually agreed to be members, how can [practitioners] be heard to challenge the provision to which they agreed? How can they voluntarily enter a contract bid then challenge its terms?" (*Varol v. Blue Cross and Blue Shield of Michigan*, 1989, p. 833). Alternatively, rejecting the agreement may not be an attractive alternative, especially in light of growing managed care and the virtual necessity to contract with MCOs. One solution to this dilemma may be to form or merge into a group practice, bolstering the practitioner's ability to negotiate effectively changes to the MCO's standard provider agreement.

Practitioner Legal Liability

In the *Salley* case, Salley did not sue the practitioners who treated his daughter. Yet, mental health professionals involved in the Salley matter probably faced the same multifaceted dilemma behavioral health practitioners face each time a utilization reviewer denies the recommended treatment. Should the practitioner appeal the decision? How aggressive should the practitioner be in the appeal? Is the practitioner free to terminate treatment? If the practitioner continues to treat the patient, may he or she bill for services? If the practitioner provides the treatment approved by utilization review, but not on the basis of his or her professional judgment, what is his or her liability? In this section we address these questions and outline clinical aspects of practitioners' legal obligations in the context of managed care.

Practitioner liability when utilization review says no arises in two legal frameworks: contract law and tort law. Generally, a contract is "an agreement between two or more persons which creates an obligation to do or not to do a particular thing" (*Black's Law Dictionary*, 1979, p. 291). Thus, if a practitioner signs a participating provider agreement with an MCO, the practitioner is obligated to provide medically necessary covered services to the patient. Payment for medically necessary services is often subject to preapproval of the MCO. If one party fails to comply with the terms of the agreement, the other party normally may terminate the agreement. Depending on the terms of the contract, an aggrieved party may sue for damages (e.g., practitioners might sue for nonpayment of services provided, and an MCO might sue for failure to provide required services).

The participating provider agreement does not establish the standard of care owed by the practitioner to the patient. This standard of care is established by that category of state law known as *tort* law. Tort law is a system of laws related to a private or civil wrong or injury (other than breach of contract), including malpractice liability, for which the court will provide a remedy in the form of *damages*. Malpractice of a psychologist may be defined as "an act or omission by a psychologist that causes the care he or she provides to fall below a standard considered reasonable among reputable psychologists of the same school of thought resulting in injury to a patient" (Post, 1984). In other words, negligence of a practitioner is established by comparing the behavior of the practitioner to that of a reasonable and prudent practitioner in the same area of practice (Post, 1984). Four legal elements are necessary for a patient to prove that a practitioner was negligent. Specifically, the plaintiff (i.e., the employee under the employee benefit plan) must prove, usually by expert testimony, that (a) the practitioner owed a duty of reasonable care, (b) the practitioner breached this duty, (c) this failure caused injury or harm, and (d) the patient was, in fact, harmed. We discuss in the following section the duties generally accepted as owed to the patient, regardless of the payment mechanism.

Duty of Care Regardless of Payment

The participating provider agreement executed by the practitioner does not change the basic legal duty owed to the patient. The practitioner must exercise reasonable care to prevent harm to the patient. As the court in *Varol* stated, whether or not treatment is approved, "the physician retains the right and indeed the ethical and legal obligation to provide appropriate treatment to the patient" (*Varol v. Blue Cross*, 1989, p. 834). In addition, courts have held that physicians owe the patient the same duty of exercising ordinary care, regardless of the payment source. Thus, the basic duty to exercise reasonable care to the patient exists whether the professional services of the practitioner are rendered for free or paid for by the patient or by a third-party payer (Post, 1984).

Consensual Relationship

The practitioner–patient relationship is based on the consent of both patient and practitioner. Consent may be written or implied. Thus, where the practitioner has rendered a bill, entered clinical notes in a chart, or otherwise established a therapeutic relationship, a court would probably find that a practitioner–patient relationship exists (Bennett, 1988). (An exception to the general rule applies when services are rendered to a patient in an emergency situation and when services are required to stabilize the patient.)

A similar but distinct duty is the doctrine of informed consent, which requires practitioners to explain, in understandable terms, the nature of treatment; the benefits and risks of such treatment; and alternatives to such treatment. The distinction between consent and informed consent is generally eroding in many state courts. For example, in Pennsylvania,

> Lack of informed consent is the legal equivalent to no consent; thus, the physician or surgeon who operates without his patient's informed consent is liable for damages which occur, notwithstanding the care exercised. Because a patient must be advised of those material facts, risks, complications and alternatives to surgery that a reasonable person in the patient's situation would consider significant in deciding whether to have the operation to give informed consent, the Superior Court appropriately made no distinction between consent and informed consent cases. (*Gousse v. Cassel*, 1992)

Although behavioral health services provided by practitioners differ significantly from traditional surgical care, the legal duty to inform the patient is the same. The American Psychological Association's (APA's) Ethical Standard 4.02, Informed Consent to Therapy, states that "Psychologists [shall] obtain informed consent to therapy using language that is reasonably understandable to the patient" (APA, 1992). Of course, the participating provider agreement does not negate this duty. If the MCO refers a patient to a practitioner, it is important to advise and to inform the patient the same as any other patient.

Confidentiality

State law provisions frequently provide that the practitioner–patient relationship must be kept confidential, and products of the relationship may be revealed by the practitioner under very limited circumstances. Such circumstances include situations in which the patient may pose a risk of danger to her- or himself or to others and situations in which the patient consents to the release of such information. Confidentiality of the practitioner–patient relationship might be placed in jeopardy when an MCO requires practitioners to provide it with information regarding their patients, but such concerns generally are alleviated by the patients' consent to the release of such information. Typically patients sign broad releases between the MCO or insurer when they enroll in the health-care plan.

Documentation

The importance of a practitioner keeping proper and thorough documentation cannot be overstated. If a patient is referred to the practitioner by an MCO, the practitioner should document, through the use of a consent form or clinical records, the basic elements of treatment discussed with such patient. However, the consent form should not be confused with informed consent. The consent form usually documents that the practitioner met and discussed the patient's treatment with the patient; informed consent is the actual discussion or process in which the practitioner explains to the patient the benefits, risks, and alternatives to treatment. This consent process should occur regardless of the patient's third-party insurance, including whether the patient was referred by an MCO (Bennett, 1988). The APA's "Ethical Principles of Psychologists and Code of Conduct" require psychologists to "appropriately document their professional and scientific work in order to facilitate provision of services later by them or by other professionals, to ensure accountability, and to meet other requirements of institutions of the law" (APA Ethical Standard 1.23; APA, 1992). Clinical records are also critical to the practitioner in the event he or she later needs to defend him- or herself. Clinical documentation allows the practitioner confronted with a negligence suit to show why he or she did or did not pursue certain treatments or courses of action.

Documentation under managed care arrangements is equally important. For instance, practitioners need to keep thorough, up-to-date treatment records, and they need to document discussions and correspondence with utilization reviewers. The *Salley* case, first discussed at the beginning of this chapter, is instructive regarding the role of medical record documentation.

In *Salley v. Dupont* (1922), the MCO utilization reviewer denied medical necessity for Danielle Salley's recommended third hospitalization stay. On the basis of Blundell's recommendations that Danielle remain in the hospital during her third admission, the utilization reviewer sent the case to a staff psychiatrist for review of medical necessity (a term, the *Salley* court pointed out, that was never defined). Although the treating and reviewing psychiatrists discussed the patient on the phone, the reviewing psychiatrist never examined Danielle or reviewed the medical records in connection with the second and third admissions. Luckily, however, Blundell had documented his recommendations and discussions with the MCO reviewing psychiatrist. During the Salley trial, the reviewing psychiatrist admitted that Blundell disagreed with the decision to discharge, and the documentation supported the disagreement. Ultimately, the court found DuPont abused its discretion by not examining Danielle or reviewing the medical records and denying benefits. Thus, thorough and complete documentation will play a large part in proving the medical necessity of certain courses of treatment.

As we have indicated, documentation plays a critical role in responding to the dilemma created when the utilization reviewer says no. In addition to documenting treatment decisions, examinations, and discussions with the utilization reviewer, the practitioner should also document discussions with the patient. The decision to proceed with treatment recommended by the practitioner or to accept the benefit levels, if any, approved by the utilization reviewer should ultimately be made by the patient. Practitioners should clearly document discussions with patients regarding the implications of proceeding or not proceeding with certain courses of treatment.

Termination of Treatment

When utilization review rejects the recommendations of the practitioners, they are often faced with an ethical and financial dilemma. Do their professional standards require continuation of services if the patient is unable or unwilling to pay for the services? If the practitioner terminates services, does this increase his or her legal exposure?

The case of *Muse v. Charter Hospital of Winston-Salem* (1995; Post, 1984) is instructive. Sixteen-year-old Delbert Joseph Muse, III (Joe) had been admitted to Charter Hospital for treatment of depression and suicidal thoughts. Joe's insurance coverage was to expire the day before a critical blood test. Joe's psychiatrist received permission to continue hospitalization for the two additional days that were necessary to take the blood test (Joe's parents signed a promissory note to pay the hospital for the two days not covered). However, Joe was discharged the day before receipt of the results of the blood test. Joe was referred to a mental health agency; after two sessions with a psychologist, Joe committed suicide by overdosing on one of his prescription drugs.

The family sued the hospital. The Muse family contended that the acts of the hospital constituted negligence in that the hospital's policy or practice required physicians to discharge patients when their insurance benefits expired, and the hospital allowed this policy or practice to interfere with a physician's medical judgment. At trial, current and former employees testified extensively that it was the hospital's policy to routinely discharge patients when their insurance expired. Numerous expert witnesses testified that the hospital's practices were below the usual standard of care. The jury awarded the Muses compensatory damages of $1,000,000 and punitive damages of $2,000,000.

The *Muse* case demonstrates that the termination of a patient's treatment on the basis of the availability of insurance instead of the clinical condition of the patient can result in serious legal liability exposure. In *Muse*, the jury was outraged, notwithstanding the transfer of the patient to a community mental center, because the hospital failed to make the patient's welfare its top priority.

The individual practitioner must carefully consult his or her code of professional ethics before terminating patient care, because the code will serve as an important benchmark for establishing the standard of care owed to the patient. Psychologists, for example, must carefully consult Ethical Standards 4.09 and 1.14 (APA, 1992), which provide that a therapist may initiate termination (a) when it is reasonably clear that the client is not benefiting from treatment, (b) if a dual relationship develops or is discovered after treatment has begun, or (c) if the therapist's competence is impaired. Moreover, careful documentation of the termination factors should be noted, in the record or files of the patient, if therapist-initiated termination is considered. Furthermore, as noted by Barnett and Sanzone (1995), basing termination on carrier reimbursement limitations is inconsistent with the APA standards (APA Ethical Standard 1.06) and "allows irrelevant, outside bodies of information to determine practice guidelines" (p. 11).

Finally, the rejection of a recommended course of treatment by a utilization review officer does not terminate the practitioner's therapeutic relationship with his or her patient. Perhaps ironically, in such a situation, the practitioner's traditional clinical duties are increased pursuant to the participating provider agreement. The practitioner's options vary but are broadly outlined as follows: Initially, after explanation of the utilization review denial, the patient should be apprised of his or her right to seek continued treatment, notwithstanding his or her benefit plan denial. Indeed, many participating provider agreements clearly state that a patient may seek treatment for services that are not "covered services" or that are determined not medically necessary. This decision should be documented in writing. In addition to documenting the patient's decision, the practitioner should discuss the patient's decision with the utilization reviewer (and document the discussion).

Furthermore, when utilization review rejects the practitioner's recommended course of treatment, the practitioner–patient relationship creates a reasonable duty to appeal or advocate for the patient. Generally, the duty arises out of the clinical relationship with the patient. However, an early managed care case has also suggested that this duty exists. In the California case of *Wickline v. State of California* (1986), the state Medicaid plan, Medi-Cal, rejected the continued hospitalization of a surgery patient as recommended by the patient's doctor. The surgeon testified that he felt compelled to go along with Medi-Cal's decision. The Court stated that the surgeon was not absolved from liability:

> The physician who complies without protest with the limitation imposed by a third party payor, when his medical judgment indicates otherwise, cannot avoid his ultimate responsibility for his patient's care. He cannot point to the health care payors as the liability scapegoats when the consequence of his own determinative medical decisions go sour. (*Wickline v. State of California*, 1986, p. 1646)

Although the same court in another important decision (*Wilson v. Blue Cross of Southern California*, 1990) retracted this statement, it remains an important warning for practitioners.

MCO Accountability

Despite the continued accountability of the practitioner in connection with the delivery of behavioral health care in the managed care era, courts have been split over the imposition of liability on MCOs; only under certain circumstances will an MCO be accountable for its utilization review decisions. In this section we highlight those situations in which the government and courts have determined that MCOs are immune to suit and situations in which liability may be imposed.

The Impact of ERISA

At some point in time, most psychotherapists have probably heard the term *ERISA* or the Employee Retirement Income Security Act of 1974. They know it refers somehow to pension and health and welfare plans, but most are probably unaware that this federal law has a significant impact on MCO liability.

Congress adopted ERISA primarily to protect participants in pension plans by establishing "standards of conduct, responsibility and obligation for fiduciaries of employee benefit plans, and by providing for appropriate remedies, sanctions, and ready access to the Federal Courts" (ERISA, 1974). As discussed previously, ERISA also governs employee benefit plans and medical benefit plans sponsored by employers. To assure nationwide uniformity and to protect these employee benefit plans from inconsistent state regulatory requirements, Congress adopted broad language known as the ERISA *preemption* provisions, which established that ERISA supersedes state laws that "relate to any employee benefits plan." The Supreme Court has stated that "the express preemption provisions of ERISA are deliberately expansive" and are intended to assure that plan regulation is exclusively a federal concern (*Corcoran v. United Healthcare, Inc.*, 1992).

ERISA (1974) preempts state law, including state tort suits, that "relate to" an employee benefit plan if it has "a connection with or reference to such a plan." If the state law is preempted, then it cannot be enforced. To determine if preemption exists, then, the crucial question that a court must decide is whether the tort suit "relates to" the benefit plan. To answer this question, courts generally analyze whether the claim is for a denial of the benefits due under the plan or whether the tort suit challenges the quality of the benefits provided. If the court determines that the tort suit is essentially a claim for the denial of benefits due, then the claim is not preempted, and the plaintiff is entitled to the benefits previously denied. However, should the court decide that the suit is really a claim concerning the quality of the benefits provided (i.e., a malpractice or negligence claim), then the claim is often deemed preempted.

Initially, MCOs enjoyed tremendous insulation from tort liability with ERISA preemption. Over time, this insulation has eroded; currently, the courts are divided on whether, and to what extent, ERISA preempts quality-of-care claims against MCOs. To date, the United States Supreme Court has not provided any guidance on this important issue. Regardless, two real-life examples found in the *Corcoran* and *Dukes* cases illustrate the basic approaches utilized by courts in deciding ERISA preemption.

In *Corcoran v. United Healthcare, Inc.* (1992), Florence Corcoran's physician recommended that she have complete bed rest in a hospital during the final months of her second pregnancy. This was the same clinical recommendation that she had received during her first pregnancy when the fetus went into distress and a successful cesarean delivery was performed.

Corcoran's employer had engaged United Healthcare as the MCO to review all medical care. United denied Corcoran's request for hospitalization. Her physician wrote to United regarding Corcoran's medical problems and high-risk pregnancy. Unknown to Corcoran's physician, United internally sought a second opinion that advised United that "the company would be at considerable risk denying her doctor's recommendations" (*Corcoran v. United Healthcare, Inc.*, 1992, p. 1323). Despite this warning, United rejected the physician's advice and ordered nursing care at home. While at home, the baby went into distress and died.

The Corcorans sued United under a Louisiana law for wrongful death of their child. The Corcorans argued that United was responsible for making the incorrect medical decision; United argued that it makes benefit determinations, not medical decisions (*Corcoran v. United Healthcare, Inc.*, 1992, p. 1330). The federal court, in an extensive decision, held that

> United makes medical decisions incident to benefit determinations. We cannot fully agree with either United or the Corcorans. Ultimately, we conclude that United makes medical decisions—indeed, United gives medical advice—but it does so in the context of making a determination about the availability of benefits under the plan. Accordingly, we hold that the Louisiana tort action asserted by the Corcorans for the wrongful death of their child allegedly resulting from United's erroneous medical decision is preempted by ERISA. (*Corcoran v. United Healthcare, Inc.*, 1992, p. 1332)

Essentially, the court found that Corcoran was denied hospitalization, a benefit due under the plan, and ERISA preempted the tort claim for wrongful death. According to the court, this result was mandated by the broad and sweeping language Congress used in writing ERISA, which indicated that Congress intended ERISA to preempt state laws. In a thoughtful commentary, the federal court reflected on the fact that "ERISA compels us to reach [this result and therefore] the Corcorans have no remedy, state or federal, for what may have been a serious mistake. This is troubling for several reasons" (*Corcoran v. United Healthcare, Inc.*, 1992, p. 1338). First, there is no check or accountability for the "medical decisions" routinely made by MCOs. In effect, there is a weaker deterrent to substandard medical decision making. Second, ERISA enhances the tension between the beneficiary's interests in obtaining quality care and the plan's interest in cutting costs. This tension may be eased in a system that "compensates the beneficiary who changes course [of treatment] based upon a wrong call [for future treatment] for the costs of that call" (*Corcoran v. United Healthcare, Inc., 1992*, p. 1338). Third, the cost-containment features of MCOs, as applied to ERISA plans, did not exist at the time Congress enacted ERISA. This type of fundamental change "would seem to warrant a reevaluation of

ERISA so that it can continue to serve its noble purpose of safeguarding the interests of employees" (*Corcoran v. United Healthcare, Inc.*, 1992, p. 1339).

ERISA preemption in the behavioral health area, as declared in *Corcoran*, is demonstrated by the case of *Lafoy v. HMO Colorado* (1993). Melissa Lafoy suffered from a multiple personality disorder. For many years, she had been treated by her personal psychiatrist and psychotherapist. When she required hospitalization, she was admitted to Cedar Springs Hospital, where her psychiatrist and psychotherapist had privileges. Although her HMO had paid for her hospitalization in prior years, in 1991 the HMO refused to pay for care at Cedar Springs and directed her to St. Francis Hospital for her disorder.

Lafoy sued the HMO for irreparable psychological injuries because she was not treated by her regular therapist. She alleged that under state law and ERISA, the HMO as a fiduciary was required "to act solely in a beneficiary's interest" (*Lafoy v. HMO Colorado*, 1993, p. 100), and this duty was breached when the HMO refused to authorize her admission to Cedar Springs. The HMO filed a motion to dismiss the case, in part, because ERISA preempts Lafoy's state law claims for negligence. The district court granted the HMO's motion, and this decision was affirmed on appeal.

In contrast, some courts have refused to preempt state tort suits challenging the quality of care. An important case is *Dukes v. U.S. Healthcare* (1995). There, a patient died as a result of high blood sugars levels, which could have or should have been diagnosed through a timely blood test that was not ordered. His widow commenced a state court malpractice suit and joined the HMO. In a companion case, Mr. and Mrs. Visconti sued the same HMO on similar theories of malpractice arising from their obstetrician's failure to diagnose preeclampsia, which killed their unborn daughter. The court joined both cases and reasoned that these complaints about the quality of care were not claims for benefits. The HMO did not deny any "benefits" in the sense of refusing to authorize or pay for tests and procedures. Instead, it delivered shoddy medical care. "Quality of benefits, such as the health care benefits provided here, is a field traditionally occupied by state regulation ... and we interpret ... that it remain as such" (*Dukes v. U.S. Healthcare*, 1995, p. 357). From the practitioner's perspective, if the MCO utilization reviewer makes a benefit plan treatment decision critical to the health and welfare of the patient, then the MCO should be legally accountable for its clinical decisions. However, this frequently is not the case. Instead, whether a patient can proceed to sue the MCO turns on the facts of the case, the jurisdiction where the claim is filed, and whether the court determines that the claim is one for denial of benefits or one for the quality of the benefit provided.

When a court determines that the claim is preempted by ERISA, the patient can only recover from the MCO the value of the denied benefit. For example, in the *Salley* case, Salley won damages that compensated him for his daughter's third hospitalization. Although, Salley (an attorney) could afford to litigate with DuPont over the value of the benefit, most patients or family members cannot. Instead, they seek compensatory damages under tort theory from the clinical practitioner whose malpractice insurance coverage benefit serves as a potential source for damages.

State and Federal Law Developments

As previously discussed, although the courts are divided over MCO liability, increasingly, patients have been successful in advancing their cases on the basis of not only denial of benefit decisions but also for the delivery of quality health-care services related to practitioners in the MCO network. Unfortunately, this expanding area of MCO liability does not bring relief to the practitioner because the MCO's liability is generally based on conduct that also results in the liability of the practitioner.

Regulatory actions. In 1995, the Rhode Island Department of Health (DOH) levied fines and penalties against United Behavioral Systems (UBS), an MCO, for failing to abide by the DOH's regulations regarding utilization review (*Rhode Island Department of Health v. United Behavioral Systems*, 1995). Among the many violations cited by the DOH, UBS allowed an agency, which was not certified by the DOH, to provide utilization review services under UBS's direction; UBS did not adhere to its own policies and procedures as presented in its utilization review application to the DOH; UBS did not permit patients and physicians access to the required complaint resolution process; UBS did not use proper utilization review procedures; and UBS did not offer employees financial incentives on the basis of the number of denials or approvals made by such employees (*Rhode Island Department of Health v. United Behavioral Systems*, 1995).

Breach of fiduciary duty. MCOs that administer employee benefit plans are increasingly being held accountable for benefit plan decisions that treat patients inconsistently with ERISA fiduciary standards. Specifically, ERISA was intended to require plan administrators to provide a "full and fair review of claims."

Abuse of discretion by utilization reviewers. In the *Salley* case, the federal court ruled that DuPont was liable because DuPont's MCO abused its discretion when it terminated benefits for Danielle Salley's inpatient hospitalization. According to the court, the MCO

> may rely on the treating physician's advice or it can independently investigate the treatment's medical necessity. In the present case, the [MCO] apparently relied on [Salley's psychiatrist's] description that Danielle was no longer suicidal or out of control. The administrators, however, cannot rely on part of [the psychiatrist's] advice and ignore his other advice. (*Salley v. Dupont*, 1922, p. 10)

In a similar case, *Sansevera v. DuPont* (1994), a federal court once again rejected DuPont's decision to deny benefits because the plan's physician lacked expertise in chronic fatigue syndrome and did not consult an expert. Other cases have overruled plan administrators because those decisions were held to be arbitrary and capricious (see Morreim, 1995).

In *Weaver v. Phoenix Home Life, Life Mut'l Life Ins. Co.* (1993), the Weaver family admitted their son to a hospital for alcohol addiction. Phoenix Home, the MCO, contracted with Cost Care, Inc. for utilization review decisions. Cost Care approved 12 days; on the basis of advice of the hospital and their physician, the Weavers had their son stay in the hospital 30 days. The Weavers submitted a claim for the additional 18 days. Cost Care denied, and provided no explanation to the Weavers, even though they formally requested an explanation. The court ruled that

> an ERISA fiduciary must provide the beneficiary with the specific reasons for the denial of benefits, [and] plan administrators may not evade their responsibility under ERISA by contracting to third parties the obligations they have under ERISA. (*Weaver v. Phoenix Home Life, Life Mut'l Life Ins. Co.*, 1993, p. 158)

The court indicated that it was quite permissible to utilize the services of an MCO but that the MCO has the obligation to disclose to the participant the reason for its decisions. The court granted summary judgment to the plaintiffs, foreclosing any further attempt by the insurer to defend its decision after ascertaining the reasons for the MCO's recommendation.

Vicarious liability. Under the doctrine of vicarious liability, legal responsibility can be imposed on a person or entity for the negligent acts or omission of another because of a special relationship between the two of them, even if the first party's conduct was blameless. Under the theory of *respondeat superior*, an employer may be held vicariously liable for the negligence of employees acting within the scope of their employment. Using this doctrine, a staff-model HMO may be held liable for the malpractice of its employee physicians and health-care professionals. The doctrine of respondeat superior does not apply to independent contractors, who by definition are not employees, such as health-care professionals who contract with an MCO but who are not employees of that MCO.

Under the doctrine of *ostensible agency*, however, an entity can be held liable for the acts, errors, and omissions of independent contractor physicians and other health professionals (such as pathologists, radiologists, and medical directors) if, considering all the facts and circumstances surrounding a case, a patient reasonably believes that the physician is an employee of the hospital. This doctrine was applied to an HMO in *Boyd v. Einstein* (1988). In *Boyd*, the failure of the primary care physician to refer a patient back to the patient's attending surgeon after developing complications from a breast biopsy led to the patient's death from pneumothorax. The *Boyd* court established the legal principle that an HMO could be liable for a bad outcome on the basis of the theory of ostensible agency by the actions of the primary care provider acting as gatekeeper. Similarly, in *Pacificare of Oklahoma v. Burrage* (1995), a United States Court of Appeals determined that a claim of vicarious liability could stand against an HMO in a case in which the HMO held out a negligent doctor as its agent.

Corporate negligence. Under the doctrine of corporate responsibility, courts have long held that hospitals are responsible for the competence of their medical staffs. A hospital has an independent, direct duty to its patients to assure that medical staff membership is granted only to qualified, competent physicians. Using this reasoning, many courts have concluded that MCOs have the same duty and responsibility to their plan participants (see *Harrell v. Total Health Care*, 1989; *McClellan v. Health Maintenance*, 1992). For example, MCOs may be held liable for the negligent selection, credentialing, or monitoring of the practitioner (*Harrell v. Total Health Care*, 1989) and for negligent management or design of the utilization review system, which could be based on a finding of financial incentives to underserved members–enrollees (*Dukes v. U.S. Healthcare, Inc.*, 1995).

Conclusion

The most important lesson for the practitioner to learn from this discussion is that he or she must always provide the proper level and amount of care to his or her patient, regardless of the directives received from MCOs and utilization reviewers. Although the MCO will determine whether certain treatment is medically necessary, the participating provider agreement with the MCO does not establish the standard of care owed by the practitioner to the patient. This standard is determined by the law of the state. The dichotomy between the state standard and the MCO-created standard will inevitably lead to conflicts. The practitioner must apprise her- or himself of the varying standards and practice from a position of knowledge.

References

American Psychological Association. (1992). Ethical principles of psychologists and code of conduct. *American Psychologist, 47,* 1597–1611.

Appelbaum, P. S. (1993). Legal liability and managed care. *American Psychologist, 48,* 251–257.

Barnett, J., & Sanzone, M. (1995). Managed care's impact on treatment termination. *The Maryland Psychologist, 41*(2).

Bennett, M. J. (1988). The greening of the HMO: Implications for prepaid psychiatry. *American Journal of Psychiatry, 145,* 1544–1549.

Black's law dictionary (5th ed.). (1979). St. Paul, MN: West Publishing.

Boyd v. Einstein, 542 A. 2d 1229 (1988).

Corcoran v. United Healthcare, Inc., 965 F. Supp. 2d 1321 (1992).

Dukes v. U.S. Healthcare, 57 F. Supp. 3d 350 (1995).

Employment Retirement Income Security Act, 29 U.S.C. § 1001 *et seq.* (1974).

Gousse v. Cassel, 615 A. 2d 331 (1992).

Harrell v. Total Health Care, W.L. 150239 (Mo. Ct. App. 1989).

Lafoy v. HMO Colorado, 988 F. Supp. 97 (1993).

McClellan v. Health Maintenance, 604 A. 2d 1413 (1992).

Morreim, E. H. (1995). Moral justice and legal justice in managed care: The ascent of contributive justice. *Journal of Law, Medicine, and Ethics, 23.*

Muse v. Charter Hospital of Winston-Salem, 452 S.E. 2d 589 (N.C. Ct. App. 1995).

Pacficare of Oklahoma v. Burrage, 59 F. 3d 151 (10th Cir. 1995).

Post, B. L. (1984). *The law of medical practice in Pennsylvania and New Jersey.* Rochester, NY: The Lawyers Co-Operative Publishing Co.

Rhode Island Department of Health v. United Behavioral Systems, No. 95–19 (Filed in R.I. Ct. June 8, 1995).

Salley v. DuPont, 966 F. Supp. 2d 1011 (1992).

Sansevera v. DuPont, 859 F. Supp. 106 (S.D. N.Y. 1994).

Varol v. Blue Cross and Blue Shield of Michigan, 708 F. Supp. 826 (E.D. Mich. 1989).

Weaver v. Phoenix Home Life, Life Mut'l Life Ins. Co., 990 F. Supp. 2d 154 (1993).

Wickline v. State of California, 192 Cal. 3d 1630 (Cal. Ct. App. 1986).

Wilson v. Blue Cross of Southern California, 221 Cal. App. 3d 660 (1990).

Appendix

Recommendations for Operating in a Managed Care Environment

1. *Read your agreements*. Dr. A. Varol and the other psychiatrists (*Varol v. Blue Cross and Blue Shield of Michigan,* 1989) apparently did not read their agreements. It is very unlikely that a court will forgive you for signing an agreement. As a solo, you probably will not be able to revise, but you should try to modify egregious terms (e.g., indemnification provisions, payment terms, and ability to bill patients under certain circumstances).

2. *Walk away*. No court has held that a participating provider agreement is a contract of adhesion and the practitioner was forced to sign it. If the agreement is unacceptable, then you should reject it.

3. *Set up a matrix summary of your MCO contracts*. Use your computer to outline key terms and conditions: terms of the contract, compensation, utilization review appeal mechanisms, and delivery of non-covered services.

4. *Develop convenient forms*. These forms should allow patients to consent to continued treatment if utilization review says no.

5. *Confirm in writing to the MCO that services are denied*. Be professional. Confirm that the issue has been communicated to the patient.

6. *Do not blindly accept MCO decisions at the expense of legal, moral, or ethical obligations*. When concern is raised about a denial of benefits, consult with a colleague to confirm that a denied treatment is also in his or her estimation medically necessary. Appeal the decision and document your efforts. When professional judgment determines that treatment is required, then treat; failure to do so may result in ethical violations and liability.

7. *Obtain informed consent*. Document the full scope of your discussions in your clinical notes. Use a standard form to memorize the time, place, and general scope of your discussion.

8. *Develop a working relationship with the utilization review*.

9. *Work with your national and state psychological associations*.

10. *Legislative*. Identify the appropriate state regulatory agency charged with managed care duties, educate regulators to patient care issues, and meet with legislative representatives.

11

Legal and Practice Concerns in Organized Systems of Care

Shirley Ann Higuchi and Billie J. Hinnefeld

In the United States, clinical psychology in any organized fashion arguably dates from the time in 1896 when Lightner Witmer first established the psychological clinic at the University of Pennsylvania. In 1905, the first form of the Binet–Simon test was published, and in 1910 the second psychological clinic in a university setting was organized at the University of Iowa. Government officials used psychologists to assist in the selection of armed services recruits during World War I (Prysevansky & Wendt, 1987). World War II further extended psychological research into widespread clinical practice (Napoli, 1981). The importance of mental health status for members of the military and the necessary treatment for mental health problems that resulted from the trauma of combat and separation from home and family became salient practice issues for clinicians. Interest turned to diagnosis, assessment, and treatment of adults. Although clinicians had performed most of their professional activities before the war in child guidance clinics, both group and individual psychotherapy with adults became legitimate activities of clinical psychologists after World War II (Strickland, 1988).

Impressed by the results of the early interventions on the battlefield and faced with a continuing shortage of psychiatrists to deal with the chronically disturbed veterans of World War II, the Veterans Administration (VA) established not only clinical-counseling psychology positions but also training programs to fill the vacancies in these newly created positions (Cummings, 1990). The National Institute of Mental Health (NIMH), which was established immediately after World War II, soon followed the lead of the VA and created a series of training stipends for graduate programs in professional psychology. Both the VA and the NIMH sought to

We would like to dedicate this chapter to Russ Newman, Executive Director of the American Psychological Association's (APA's) Practice Directorate, who is the founder of the Practice Directorate Office of Legal and Regulatory Affairs, as well as the Office of Managed Care. Dr. Newman's visions and leadership for the practice of psychology served as an inspiration for this chapter. We wish to thank the following people: Richardo Guerrero and Cherie Jones, for their research and editorial assistance; Elizabeth Cullen and Eric Harris, for their research on behalf of the APA's Office of Managed Care; and Stanley Jones for his contribution to the case scenarios.

train psychologists for the public sector, but more and more professionally trained psychologists began entering the arena of private practice (Cummings, 1990).

The first licensing law for psychologists was passed in Connecticut in 1945, beginning the regulation of the profession. Licensing laws began to develop, which not only set entry requirements for the profession but also created licensing boards that could serve as a mechanism for disciplinary action. Typical grounds for disciplinary complaints in the past have included (a) fraud, deceit, or misrepresentation in procuring a license or attempting to procure a license; (b) conviction of a felony or crime involving moral turpitude; (c) being habitually intemperate or addicted to alcohol or narcotic substances; (d) illegal, incompetent, or habitually negligent practice; (e) dishonorable, immoral, or unprofessional conduct; (f) violation of the rules and regulations of the board; (g) fraudulent or dishonest conduct; (h) sexual relations with clients; and (i) violation of a specific code of ethics (Reaves, 1984).

As noted previously, a common disciplinary complaint might be based on a violation of a code of ethics. As with licensing, the need for an ethical code was also recognized closely following World War II, probably because of psychology's greater involvement with the public. In 1947, the American Psychological Association (APA) established a Committee on Ethical Standards for Psychologists, and a set of provisional ethical standards was adopted by its Council of Representatives (Council) in 1952. The Ethics Code has undergone a series of revisions since that time, with the most recent version being adopted by the Council in 1992 (APA, 1992).

After its emergence from the universities and armed forces, and until fairly recently, the practice of psychology has mainly been performed by individuals in private settings. Thus, disciplinary issues have revolved around decisions made or actions taken by psychologists independent of the types of obligations that are now incurred in managed care settings. The advent of managed care organizations (MCOs) has introduced a third party into the relationship between the psychologist and his or her client.

In the 1960s, HMOs started including mental health care on an optional basis. New HMO plans that emerged in the late '60s included substantial mental health care as a basic benefit (Bennett, 1988). In 1976, the HMO Amendments were enacted. These amendments, among other things, authorized HMOs to use the clinical expertise of "other health-care personnel." This included psychologists for the first time. The HMO Amendments of 1986 explicitly included psychologists in the list of authorized HMO professionals.

With psychologists' inclusion in managed care, a new set of potential legal and practice issues has been introduced into the psychologist–client relationship. As Simon (1994) stated, psychologists in the past have been accustomed to

> setting our own standards for how we work: fees, referrals, consultations, and so on. But, with the advent of managed care along with a far more litigious public, we practitioners must learn to change in order

to protect both ourselves and our patients. We must protect ourselves from charges that jeopardize our licenses . . . and we must protect our patients from inappropriate care. (p. 121)

One of the primary aims of managed care systems is to control costs, by such mechanisms as caps on benefits, utilization review, and "gate-keeping." The introduction of these factors into the psychologist–client relationship can raise significant legal and practice questions that have not arisen in the past. We address these legal-practice issues in this chapter.

To appreciate the challenges that providers face, we have organized this chapter by sections according to these challenges, which are as follows: The first section provides an overview of managed care arrangements, the second section discusses problematic managed care contract provisions, the third section sets forth specific case scenarios involving psychologists, and the final section provides a summary of the issues presented in this chapter.

Overview of Managed Care Arrangements

The health-care marketplace in the United States is rapidly evolving into complex business arrangements that often seem to promote saving costs before saving lives. Increasingly, the Practice Directorate's Office of Legal and Regulatory Affairs (LRA) of the APA receives requests for assistance by practitioners on how to survive in today's health-care marketplace. In response to this demand, LRA established the Office of Managed Care (OMC) in 1992 to specifically handle any issues relating to managed care and third-party reimbursement. Members' comments, questions, and complaints are recorded in the OMC's Managed Care Analysis and Tracking System (MCATS). Thus, the MCATS data are valuable in determining what issues are most important to the APA membership.

Since its inception, the OMC has monitored and analyzed state managed care laws for the purpose of developing model legislation and assisting state psychological associations with legislative efforts. To date, the OMC has conducted state-by-state legislative analyses and surveys of HMO, PPO, utilization review, parity, and consumer protection laws and has responded to thousands of calls and letters requesting information, aid, and intervention.

Health Maintenance Organizations

Fifteen years ago, the term *health maintenance organization* was a relatively new concept to most patients and practitioners, and few were actually aware of how this system functioned. Now, however, the HMO is perhaps the most well-known of the managed care models. For a predetermined, capitated premium, the HMO delivers, or arranges for the delivery of, carefully managed and controlled health-care services to a set number of individual clients (Boochever, 1986). This unique combination in which the insurer or the arranger of health care is also the provider of health-care services raises some inherent conflicts that can be problematic for professionals contracting to provide services in such MCOs.

For example, marketing materials developed by HMO recruiters frequently stress to consumers that the care being provided by an HMO is of high quality, which leads consumers to believe that the care is complete and comprehensive. The HMO, through its coverage agreement with the enrollees, basically guarantees the quality of the care provided to them.[1] As is becoming more and more apparent, however, especially for mental health care, the level of coverage actually provided sometimes differs significantly from what is promised.

Furthermore, vague and confusing definitions of terms in managed care contracts can affect the provider–patient relationship. For example, a well-known MCO defines an HMO as "an entity that provides, offers, or arranges for coverage of designated health services needed by plan members for a fixed and prepaid premium" ("The Language of Managed Health Care," 1992). What the MCO fails to explain to the beneficiary is that those services that are "needed by plan members" are those services that are in advance approved by the MCO and that may be further limited during the request for treatment by the MCO's utilization review process. In addition to this, the fixed-and-prepaid premium clearly gives the managed care entity a financial incentive to withhold care. As a result of these and other contractual problems described more fully later, HMOs have proven to be less than optimal for participating providers and their patients.

Preferred Provider Organizations

The PPO has historically proved less problematic for participating providers because in most instances benefits tend to be more generous than in the HMO model. Specifically, however, the PPO lacks the prepaid mechanism inherent in the HMO system. PPOs are broadly defined as health-care financing and delivery programs that provide financial incentives to consumers to use a preselected group of providers of health care. Payment to providers is typically on a fee-for-service basis, with discounts offered by the provider in exchange for guarantees of increased patient volume and reimbursement. Consumers are usually not locked into receiving services from these preferred providers but have financial incentives to do so (Higuchi, 1994). Higher levels of coinsurance or deductibles routinely apply to services provided by nonparticipating providers. PPOs, however,

---

[1]It is important to note that under breach-of-contract theory, managed care entities have been held liable for not living up to what they promised in their enrollee contracts or marketing materials. In *Boyd v. Albert Einstein Medical Center* (1988), the court ruled that an HMO might be liable for the acts of contracting physicians, in part, because the HMO had advertised that its providers were competent and that they had been evaluated by the HMO.

still pose significant challenges to providers. Certain practices and policies of PPOs may restrict the delivery of mental health care. An emerging area of concern centers around provider contracting issues in which the PPO requests that participating providers sign contracts that may restrict a provider's ability to deliver patient care by requiring the provider to adhere to certain managed care protocols. This issue is discussed in detail in the Problematic Managed Care Practices and Possible Solutions section.

Utilization Review and Employee Assistance Programs

Other managed care entities and arrangements that have created conflicts for providers include UR and employee assistance programs. Utilization review involves the evaluation of the necessity, appropriateness, and efficiency of the use of health-care services and resources. According to proponents of UR, its purpose is to improve cost-effectiveness while maintaining high quality of care and reducing abuse of services. However, many providers believe the artificial limit on the number of sessions available for therapy and the elimination of covered services because they are viewed as not "medically necessary" by the MCO present an unworkable environment for the provider.

Under an employee-assistance-program system, the provider may be an employee of a corporation that offers a counseling and a referral service to other employees of the corporation. An employee assistance program is set up for employees to seek help for personal or work-related problems and to seek assistance and a possible referral to an outside provider. Conflicts emerge when the provider feels he or she owes a duty to both the employer (corporation) and to the patient, but the loyalties to these two parties are in conflict.

Consistent with the APA Ethics Code (APA, 1992) and the law, as part of the informed consent process, the provider should review with the patient the proposed treatment and any procedures contractually agreed on by the provider in the managed care arrangement or the employee assistance program. Also consistent with Ethical Principle 1.21,

> When a psychologist agrees to provide services to a person or entity at the request of a third party, the psychologist clarifies to the extent feasible, at the outset of the service, the nature of the relationship with each party. This clarification includes the role of the psychologist . . . the probable uses of the services provided . . . and the fact that there may be limits to confidentiality. (APA, 1992)

Problematic Managed Care Practices and Possible Solutions

In this section we explore some of the typical dilemmas faced by providers operating under a managed care arrangement, and we suggest some possible solutions to these dilemmas.

Provider Contracting Issues

Since 1992, the OMC has witnessed a sharp increase in complaints concerning managed-care-provider contracting issues. The OMC has reviewed a number of managed-care-provider contracts and has concluded that many provisions adversely affect the provider–patient relationship. Many practitioners are faced with the challenge of deciding whether they should sign such egregious contracts or whether they should complain about the provisions and potentially risk being rejected as a panel provider. It is important to note that as a practical matter, to challenge legally a managed care contract, the provider must execute the contract with the MCO; a contract provision must be breached; and the MCO must seek to enforce the relevant provision. Once this sequence of events occurs, the legality of the provision could be questioned in a court of law. Therefore, the provider must breach a contract and risk the consequences of challenging an unfair provision. Moreover, as a practical matter, if the provider is unhappy with a particular contract, the provider can always sign the contract and later terminate it without cause by giving the required notice to the MCO. However, many providers hesitate to sign a contract with such provisions because of ethical, licensure, and moral concerns.

No-cause termination provisions. The earliest reported provider contracting provision brought to the OMC's attention was the so-called *no-cause* termination provision. This type of provision is standard in the industry, and the OMC has observed that such a provision has historically been part of the provider contract. A typical provision would in essence state that either party could terminate the agreement by giving the other party 30 days written notice. At first blush, a provision such as this appears to be quite innocent and is quite common in standard, independent contracting arrangements. However, immediate termination of a provider for any reason can be viewed as disruptive to the provider–patient relationship.

The prospects for successfully challenging a no-cause termination provision is particularly troubling for psychologists who contract with managed care companies, because psychologists are often placed in a position of having to negotiate with the company to allow for additional therapy sessions for their patients. There is concern, and perhaps justifiably so, that managed care companies could arguably use the no-cause termination provision as a means of eliminating those psychologists who frequently contest decisions made by the managed care company or its claims reviewer. This issue will be all the more critical as the number of managed care plans increases and psychologists become increasingly dependent on managed care companies for obtaining clients. Nonetheless, challenging no-cause termination provisions appears to be gaining support as the managed care industry evolves. It is important to keep in mind, however, that this issue has not been extensively litigated. Therefore, the information presented here represents prospective theories upon which a claim may be successfully pursued.

There are several arguments that can potentially be used to challenge a managed care company's decision to terminate a psychologist without cause. Because managed care companies, like hospitals, have legal responsibilities, certain due process rights currently afforded to providers in a hospital setting might also be guaranteed to managed care providers. For example, it is well established that hospitals sustain liability for failing to obtain and evaluate information regarding the training and experience of medical staff members and applicants before granting privileges. This liability may also apply to managed care companies and their credentialing procedures. Recent experience has made clear that managed care companies will have to intensify their credentialing procedures or face potential liability similar to that of hospitals (Curtis, 1990). Accordingly, it can be argued that managed care companies, like hospitals, should be required to provide basic due process appeal rights to a provider who is terminated.

Several court cases (e.g., *Hackenthal v. California Medical Association*, 1982; *Pinsker v. Pacific Coast Society of Orthodontists*, 1969; *Salkin v. California Dental Association*, 1986) can be used to strengthen the argument for the right to appeal no-cause termination. Courts have recognized that medical professional associations and other entities related to the provision of health care are of "quasi-public" significance (Curtis, 1990); entities considered to have quasi-public significance cannot expel or discipline members, so as to adversely affect their substantial property, contract, or other economic rights, without fair proceedings. Because expulsion from a managed care plan also involves judgment by his or her own profession and such plans serve the quasi-public function of providing health care, it could be argued that in no-cause termination cases, certain property and economic rights are at risk.

It can also be argued that managed care companies have a duty to show good faith in terminating a contract. It appears that managed care companies believe that a contract between a health-care provider and a managed care company should be treated by the courts like a standard business contract in which no-cause termination provisions are prevalent. Although such provisions found in contracts have traditionally been held to be valid, courts have increasingly implied a duty of good faith that is intended to protect the "reasonable expectations of the parties" (Curtis, 1990). In effect, contracts with managed care companies should be treated as agreements to provide health services rather than as simple agreements to provide business arrangements.

The New Hampshire Supreme Court recently relied on both public-policy concerns and the duty of good faith and fair dealing in ruling that a physician is entitled to review the decision of a managed care company to terminate him or her with or without cause. In *Harper v. Healthsource New Hampshire, Inc.* (1996), the Supreme Court analogized the physician's relationship with the managed care company to an employer–employee relationship. In traditional employment law, a contract providing for termination by either party is an employment-at-will contract. The Court noted that "at-will" contracts are unenforceable if they contravene public policy. The Court further noted that an employer has an implied duty of good faith and fair dealing, which is violated if the employer terminates an employee "out of malice or bad faith in retaliation for action taken or refused by the employee in consonance with public policy." The court observed that "the public has a substantial interest in the relationship between health maintenance organizations and their preferred provider physicians as well." The court concluded that "the public interest and fundamental fairness demand that a health maintenance organization's decision to terminate its relationship with a particular physician provider must comport with the covenant of good faith and fair dealing and may not be made for a reason that is contrary to public policy."

Adhesion contract theory can also be used to argue against no-cause termination. According to this theory, when a contract appears to be one-sided and unfair, particular provisions will be construed against the drafter of the contract to the extent necessary to alleviate the unfairness. Adhesion contracts are commonly found when (a) a standardized agreement is prepared by one party for the other; (b) the preparer wields superior bargaining power; and (c) the contract is offered on a take-it-or-leave-it basis, with no opportunity to bargain. These elements may be applicable to the contractual relationship between a provider and a managed care entity because a court may find the no-cause termination provision to be so unfair and one-sided that the provision would be void and hence unenforceable.

The following are recommended steps that can be taken by a psychologist–provider who is terminated without cause:

- Carefully review the provider contract to determine the circumstances under which a managed care company can effectively terminate the relationship with the provider.
- If the managed care company is able to terminate the relationship, determine whether the company has complied with the termination procedures set forth in the contract.
- To challenge a termination, on receiving notice, contact the managed care company's director of provider relations by phone to explore what alternatives (for redress) exist. Be as congenial as possible.
- If the telephone call is positive and feasible alternatives exist, send a written confirmation of the conversation to the managed care company.
- In the event that the conversation with the managed care company director is negative and the provider wishes to pursue the issue further, file an official complaint with the managed care company. Duplicate complaint letters could be sent to the state's department of insurance, which is responsible for regulating the activities of most managed care companies.
- When appealing a termination decision in writing, the provider should cite specific reasons as to why he or she is uniquely qualified (e.g., cite a successful treatment history, successful working

relationship with the managed care company, and specific experience and training).

- When consulting with the utilization review agent either to appeal a decision or to provide information to the managed care company in support of a complaint, it will be helpful to supply well-kept records and documentation of therapy.
- Be particularly sensitive to the use of the no-cause termination provision by the managed care company as an excuse to get rid of a provider whom it may view as a troublemaker. The OMC has received reports, based on circumstantial evidence, alleging that a psychologist was terminated from a panel merely for vigorously opposing a utilization decision.

A "good plaintiff" (one with a greater chance of success) in a no-cause termination case is one who has historically had a good relationship with the managed care company but whose relationship has soured because of the plaintiff's repeated attempts to appeal or complain about a decision made by a managed care company. Furthermore, evidence of a substantial caseload at some point during the relationship is significant, especially if the MCO has now "dropped" the provider by failing to make additional referrals. The existence of solid documentation of the circumstances leading up to termination is essential.

No-disparagement ("gag") provisions. Another provision that has created much concern in the provider industry is the no-disparagement or gag provision. The OMC has reviewed and analyzed gag clauses in provider contracts, which are intended to prohibit providers from "disparaging" the MCO to patients or other individuals. Such clauses are problematic because they may conflict with other provisions in the contract, such as requiring providers to act in accordance with their professional judgment (e.g., explanation of treatment alternatives to patients). As gag clauses may be interpreted as prohibiting providers from speaking to their patients about decisions by the MCO to deny benefits and the provider's attempt to appeal, such clauses may also deter providers from appealing denial of coverage decisions. Some MCOs have agreed to drop gag clauses after negotiation because the MCOs say they did not realize that the clauses could be interpreted as prohibiting full disclosure to patients.

The issue of abolishing gag provisions in provider contracts has been addressed on a variety of fronts. Provider groups are increasingly claiming that MCOs are limiting their ability to talk freely with patients about treatment options and payment policies, including financial bonuses for providers who save the MCO money by withholding care ("HMO Gag Rules," 1996). It is argued that such restrictions interfere with the provider's ethical and legal duty to provide patients with information about the benefits, risks, and costs of various treatments. For example, the American Medical Association (AMA) Council on Ethics and Judicial Affairs (CEJA) declared that gag rules are an "unethical interference" in the doctor–patient relationship. CEJA, therefore, requested that physicians strike such clauses from their contracts. According to CEJA, "The physician's obligation to disclose treatment alternatives to patients is not altered by any limitation in the coverage provided by the patient's managed care plan. Patients cannot be subject to making decisions with inadequate information. This would be an absolute violation of the informed consent requirements" (Council on Ethical and Judicial Affairs [CEJA], American Medical Association, 1995). CEJA's statement on gag rules follows the 1994 report, "Ethics in Managed Care," which outlined all of the ethical duties of physicians practicing in managed care plans (CEJA, 1994). CEJA's (1995) report said that "the duty of patient advocacy is a fundamental element of the physician—patient relationship that should not be altered by the system of health-care delivery in which physicians practice" (p. 334).

With respect to legal and legislative responses to the gag provision issue, a New York physician group (Choice Care) filed a lawsuit against the New York Department of Health because the department failed to review HMO contracts containing gag provisions. The suit alleges that the state agency should not have approved the contract offered to physicians by Choice Care because of a physician gag rule and a lack of appeal rights in the contract ("Physicians Sue NY Health Department," 1996).

A new Massachusetts law (*Massachusetts General Laws Annotated*, 1995), championed by the Massachusetts Psychological Association, bars MCOs from imposing rules that limit providers' ability to speak freely with patients about all aspects of their health insurance, including alternative treatments that may or may not be covered under the patients' policies. In addition, the new law seeks to protect patient confidentiality by prohibiting MCOs from demanding information about prospective patients' life histories and mental health status before covering them for state-mandated mental health benefits. It can be expected that state psychological associations should monitor closely how the new law will be interpreted and enforced.

These efforts by various entities are laudable, but unfortunately they do not completely solve the problem for providers. The AMA's declaration may be helpful to physicians, but physicians are certainly in a better position to declare an MCO provision to be unethical. MCOs obviously view physician services as less interchangeable with other services than psychological services. If the profession of psychology were to declare a certain provision of an MCO contract unethical, the likelihood, based on past performance, is that MCOs would simply not contract with psychologists and instead would deal with counselors, social workers, or psychiatrists. However, because the AMA has taken the first step in dealing with this ethical conflict, it is hoped that psychologists will be able to follow along with other providers in attempting to standardize all provider contracts to eliminate gag provisions.

Legislative and regulatory initiatives are likewise helpful. Legislation sets the stage and can be used as a model for other state and federal efforts. Any legislation, however, may have its limitations. For example, certain MCOs operating in Massachusetts may be exempted from the recent law (e.g., those self-insured plans governed by the Employee Retirement Security Act of 1974, and those operating under Medicaid managed care). The ERISA law prohibits states from regulating the health benefit plans of companies that self-insure. Medicaid managed care may have a separate set of operating guidelines from the private sector.

The APA has been successful in negotiating with two behavioral MCOs to remove gag provisions from their provider contracts with psychologists. The MCOs have generally been receptive to meeting with both the APA and the state psychological associations because they prefer to deal with a larger group than with individual providers.

"Hold-harmless" provisions. Many managed care entities ask providers to sign contracts that contain hold-harmless provisions. Along with the other provisions in the contracts, these clauses are designed to ensure that the provider and the managed care company are viewed as separate and independent entities, each of which is solely responsible for damages resulting from its own negligence. Essentially these provisions state that liability for a provider's services is covered under the provider's own malpractice policy. Under such a provision, the payer, managed care entity, or any of its agents or representatives shall not be held liable for any cause of action or liability arising out of, or in connection with, services rendered by the provider. Some contracts only hold the provider liable for damages due to the provider's actions, whereas other contracts could be interpreted in such a manner that the provider assumes all liability.

An example of such a provision is as follows. Under the indemnification provision, a contract states that

> providers shall indemnify and hold [the MCO] harmless from any and all claims, lawsuits, settlements, and liabilities incurred as a result of professional services provided or not provided by a provider with respect to any covered person. Relatedly, [the MCO] shall indemnify and hold the provider harmless from any and all claims, lawsuits, settlements, and liabilities incurred as a result of actions taken or not taken by [the MCO] in the administration of the employer's group health benefit plan.

The intent in this provision appears to be that the provider agrees to indemnify the MCO for negligence in providing or not providing services, and the company agrees to indemnify the provider for negligence or other damages in connection with administration of the plan. Requiring the provider to assume responsibility for his or her own negligent conduct, to insure him- or herself against that responsibility, and to protect the managed care company through indemnification for liability does not seem to be an unreasonable contractual arrangement. However, hold-harmless agreements need to be carefully reviewed to ensure that this appropriate intent is realized, especially in light of *Wickline v. State of California* (1987) and its progeny, which suggest that both the managed care company and the provider can be held liable, either separately or jointly when a cost-containment strategy results in negligent care. One also needs to make sure that his or her malpractice insurance not only covers suits with the provider but also covers suits with the MCO due to the provider's alleged malpractice.

For example, one problematic clause that was brought to the attention of the OMC was a provision in a contract that reads as follows:

> Liability for provider services are covered under provider's own practice liability. The payor or managed care entity or any of their agents or representatives shall not be liable for any cause of action or liability arising out of or in connection with services rendered by the provider.

This contractual provision was, in the opinion of the OMC staff, poorly drafted and raised interpretative questions. The provision did not appear to create a true indemnity relationship, because it disclaimed liability rather than requiring the providing psychologist to indemnify against it. A court could construe the clause as an intended agreement to indemnify. However, a potential counterargument is that the agreement to indemnify was intended to cover damages that arose not only from the provider's own negligent conduct but also damages that arose from the managed care company's negligent conduct, so long as that liability arose "in connection with services rendered by the provider."

In the foregoing examples, the hold-harmless provisions appear to set forth a subcontracting relationship between the managed care entity and the provider. Such a relationship would limit each party's liabilities to its own respective actions. Other provisions have been brought to the attention of the OMC that are even more ambiguous. For instance, one MCO's plan contained a provision that stated the following:

> The specialist–provider will hold the managed care organization harmless due to any malpractice litigation and will have a minimum of one million dollars worth of professional liability insurance. Providers shall notify the managed care organization within 48 hours of loss of insurance.

If one were to read this provision literally, any malpractice claim that arose could be seen to be the responsibility of the specialist–provider. In other words, the provider would be required to indemnify the MCO, even if the organization were partially at fault. Clearly, these hold-harmless provisions are unreasonable because malpractice liability insurance typically covers only those specific acts arising out of the conduct of the provider. Typically, the provider cannot assume liability for other parties unless the provider directly arranges for such liability and agrees to take it on. The primary purpose of psychology malpractice liability insurance is to insure against damages resulting from the psychologist's negligence, not from the negligence of entities with which the psychologist engaged in business.

Release of records provisions. Another problematic provision in managed care contracts is the requirement for a broad release of records in exchange for payment. In the absence of state law, there is little check on such requests for information. It may be possible for a provider to limit MCOs' access to information indicating the assessment, diagnosis, and treatment plan for a patient. In this way, MCOs would be permitted to determine the nature of the services while confidentiality is somewhat protected. The laws of New Jersey and the District of Columbia, however, expressly restrict the release of patient information to MCOs (e.g., treatment notes, session notes).

Increasingly, MCOs are asking practitioners to open up all of their patient records for review by the MCO. State laws, however, require that patients give informed consent to the release of their records, thereby prohibiting practitioners from releasing information of non-MCO patients. A practitioner could be subject to disciplinary proceedings by the state licensing board for allowing an MCO to have access to the records of patients with whom the MCO had no contractual arrangement. In this area, clients must give full and knowing consent to the disclosure of this information, and clearly, non-MCO patients have not given such consent for the release of their information. It could be argued that any action taken by an MCO against a practitioner who refuses to release such records is unlawful because the MCO is asking the practitioner to break the law.

Other Conflicts Faced by Providers

Verifying contractual definitions and provisions. Many managed care entities, through contractual arrangements, limit reimbursement to the therapist for services that are deemed medically necessary. These entities typically do not provide a definition of what constitutes a medically necessary service, and, as a result, the therapist is not given a sense, in advance, of what services are and are not covered.

An illustrative case that came to the attention of the OMC concerns an MCO whose actions may have unfairly denied necessary mental health services to a patient who was insured under the company's plan. It was alleged that the MCO had reduced the patient's benefits on the basis of its determination that the current treatment provided by the attending psychologist did not constitute a covered benefit under the plan. Although the psychologist appealed the MCO's original decision, a second denial was issued after an evaluation. The purpose of this evaluation was to provide a second opinion in order to review more thoroughly the basis for the denial of benefits. A medical examination was arranged by the MCO and was performed by a certified psychiatrist chosen by the MCO. After the medical evaluation, the MCO determined that there was not sufficient information to support the medical necessity of care at a frequency of three visits per week. On the basis of its predetermined criteria, the MCO concluded that the benefits would continue for two visits per week and would be reduced to a 1-hr session per week within a couple of weeks. Subsequent to this reduction, the MCO would perform a follow-up review.

One of the issues raised by this case was that the MCO misquoted its own benefit package to the provider and the patient. The MCO had stated in a letter to the provider that services that are recommended by a physician only, and are essential for the necessary care and treatment of any illness or injuries, would be covered. However, this policy was not found in the benefit documents. It is important, therefore, that psychologists and their patients carefully review the written benefits plan and not rely solely on the payer's interpretation. As noted previously, in addition to advertising and marketing materials, benefit summary plans provided to the patient or insured constitute a contract between the patient or insured and the insurance company. It may need to be brought to the MCO's attention by the psychologist that, essentially, any deviation from these contractual obligations could constitute a breach of contract between the patient or insured and the MCO.

Conflict of interest. Conflict-of-interest concerns have also commonly come to the attention of the OMC. For example, when a psychologist is working for a corporation under an employee assistance program, what happens if the psychologist owes both a duty and a responsibility to the corporation that employs the psychologist and to the client? In one case, this issue arose when a psychologist, who was working in an employee-assistance-program setting in a corporation, was informed by the employer that the provision of information or resources to employees on possible issues such as legal referrals, further mental health treatment, or tax assistance was appropriate. However, the corporation also informed the psychologist that in the event that the employee was contemplating legal action against the company, or if an issue such as sexual harassment in the workplace arose, then the psychologist was not to provide resources to the patient regarding legal assistance. The APA Ethics Code (APA, 1992) addresses this issue. Principle 8.03 states,

> If the demands of an organization with which psychologists are affiliated conflict with this Ethics Code, psychologists clarify the nature of the conflict, make known their commitment to the Ethics Code, and to the extent feasible, seek to resolve the conflict in a way that permits the fullest adherence to the Ethics Code. (p. 1610)

Principle 1.21 states,

> (a) When a psychologist agrees to provide services to a person or entity at the request of a third party, the psychologist clarifies to the extent feasible, at the outset of the service, the nature of the relationship with each party. This clarification includes the role of the psychologist (such as therapist, organizational consultant, diagnostician, or expert witness), the probable uses of the services provided or the information obtained, and the fact that there may be limits to confidentiality. (b) If there is a foreseeable risk of the psychologist's being called upon to perform conflicting roles because of the involvement of a third party, the psychologist clarifies the nature and direction of his or her respon-

sibilities, keeps all parties appropriately informed as matters develop, and resolves the situation in accordance with this Ethics Code.

The Ethics Code clearly indicates that in this situation, the psychologist has an obligation to approach the corporation and seek clarification on what his or her obligations are to the corporation and to the client. Furthermore, it appears that the psychologist has a duty to discuss with the patient, at the beginning of the relationship, the potential conflicts or compromising situations that can or will arise. For example, if the company states that the psychologist cannot provide referrals for legal assistance if the patient wants to sue the company, then such a provision should be disclosed to the client. Incidentally, as an employee of the organization, a psychologist would be in an excellent position to assist the company in developing standards in this area, as well as to clarify them for both the corporation and its employees.

Other issues that may need to be clarified at the outset of therapy in order to avoid conflict often revolve around confidentiality. For instance, will the company expect a progress report or access to the patient's records? Will the therapist be expected to report to the company problems such as drug abuse that might affect the employee's ability to perform the duties of a job? Is the nature of the interaction between the client and therapist an evaluation for the company's knowledge or therapy for the client's benefit?

Consumer Protection Legislation

Many state legislatures have introduced "patient protection" legislation that generally regulates MCOs, particularly by establishing consumer protection standards designed to regulate or to prohibit certain managed care practices. Presently, a total of six states (California, Connecticut, Maryland, Massachusetts, New Hampshire, and New Jersey) have enacted patient protection legislation or regulations that affect psychology, either by amending state HMO and PPO laws or by enacting *free-standing* legislation.[2] More states are considering such legislation, and it is expected that more legislatures will successfully pass consumer protection laws in their prospective states.

Until recently, state regulation of managed care concentrated primarily on what benefits were being provided (e.g., parity between physical and mental health benefits guarantees) and who provided them (e.g., antidiscrimination provider laws). A new generation of consumer protection initiatives is, however, beginning to surface, focusing instead on the manner in which services are being provided. These new measures seek to (a) mandate disclosure to consumers of financial arrangements between MCOs and providers, (b) prohibit interference by MCOs with communi-

---

[2]For example, Maryland's Patient Access Act (*Annotated Code of Maryland,* 1997) is a free-standing managed care law, whereas New Hampshire's law (*New Hampshire Revised Statutes Annotated,* 1997) amends an existing managed care law—the state's HMO law.

cations between providers and their patients, (c) protect the confidentiality of patient records, (d) prohibit the termination of providers from managed care panels for appealing treatment decisions made by MCOs, and (e) prohibit MCOs from imposing their own financial and legal risks on providers.

Case Scenarios

The following scenarios are examples of potential conflicts for psychologists in attempting to balance ethics, quality care, and managed care.[3] These scenarios are based on ongoing research performed by the OMC.

> **Scenario 1.** A managed care group has a practice of asking psychologists to perform "blind" psychological evaluations (i.e., write psychological reports based only on raw test data). When a psychologist expresses concern about the legality and the ethics of such a practice, he is told that this a "relatively well-established practice within certain parts of the managed care service community."
>
> **Scenario 2.** A psychologist is asked to join an MCO. However, before being accepted as a provider, the psychologist is informed that a nurse from this organization would need to come to the psychologist's office and review several current patient records. After informing the MCO that this would be a violation of patient confidentiality, the psychologist was informed that the MCO commonly makes such requests throughout the country.
>
> **Scenario 3.** A managed care organization attempts to dictate which tests should be used in the assessment of a patient.
>
> **Scenario 4.** After completing the assessment of a patient and after beginning treatment, the MCO insists on the psychologist sending all test results, including raw data, to their reviewer to determine if treatment should continue. The reviewer is not a psychologist, is not a physician, and is not, in the psychologist's opinion, trained to interpret the data.
>
> **Scenario 5.** A psychologist has been treating a client for anxiety and panic attacks for 10 sessions following the death of her husband. The client is responding to treatment but is still experiencing severe symptoms. The managed care company to which the client belongs has a 10-session limit and will not continue to pay for sessions. The managed care company's physician reviewer suggests medication instead.
>
> **Scenario 6.** A psychologist wishes to solicit a client's action in appealing the decision of a managed care company.

Some licensing boards viewing Scenario 1 may view such blind evaluations as violating conventionally accepted standards of practice. Depending on how the interpretation was to be used and how the data were

---

[3]The analysis and the response to these case scenarios are the opinion of the authors and in no way reflect the opinions or policies of the APA. It is also advised that individual psychologists seeking ethical and legal approaches to their conflicts consult with a local attorney trained in both legal and ethical issues because responses could vary depending on the individual facts of each case and on local, legal, and ethical practices.

collected, some psychologists might argue that test-taking attitude, test-taking surroundings, or other factors could have influenced test results, thus making it difficult to draw conclusions without having a relationship with the test taker.

Other psychologists might argue that psychologists have professional relationships that are not directly with patients. For example, attorneys frequently retain forensic psychologists to reexamine raw test data provided by a psychological expert retained by the other side, to determine whether that expert's conclusions are accurate. In this instance, the professional relationship is with the attorney.

However, even if there is no absolute prohibition against the kind of blind evaluation described here, it does seem that the Ethical Code would require that the psychologist determine for what purposes the blind evaluations would be used and would evaluate, in accordance with Principle 2.02, that those purposes "are appropriate in light of the research on or evidence of the usefulness and proper application of the techniques." Also, Principle 2.05 requires that psychologists state any "significant reservations they have about the accuracy or limitations of their interpretations."

If indeed the MCO, described in Scenario 2, is actually asking the psychologist to allow it to view records of nonmembers, then clearly this would be a violation of Ethical Principles 5.02 and 5.03 concerning confidentiality. It may be possible to mask identifiers in records in a way that might not violate confidentiality, but a psychologist would need to check with local licensing boards and ethics committees to seek their opinions on these steps. Although Section 5.05 does provide that information can be released for billing purposes (e.g., to insurance companies), it can only be done with the consent of the patient. It should also be noted that in this situation, "disclosure is limited to the minimum that is necessary to achieve the purpose." Therefore, even if the MCO were asking for records of one of its members, the psychologist may want to oppose turning over any more of the record than is "necessary."

As presented, this scenario would also violate national Utilization Review Accreditation Commission certification guidelines and all state laws regulating utilization review because such guidelines and state laws do not permit the release of records without the client's consent. The psychologist in this scenario may want to clarify exactly what the MCO wants. A number of MCOs request that providers allow them to see records of patients who are served by their network as part of their utilization review or quality assurance process. They believe they are justified in doing this both by their contract with the payer and by the signature of the client giving the company the right to access any information necessary in the processing of claims. It may be questionable whether a quality assurance review of a provider is really part of the processing of claims. However, one way of dealing with this problem may be for the provider to clearly state, in the informed consent process, the possibility that information may be requested by the MCO for a number of purposes. This solution may not be ideal in certain situations in which the provider believes the MCO is overstepping its bounds. However, it is a protective measure.

Scenario 3 depends on the specific facts of a given situation. If the tests suggested by the MCO are not appropriate for the situation involved, obviously it would not be good practice to give them. However, if the suggested tests are appropriate, even if they are not exactly what the treating psychologist would suggest as optimal, it may not be substandard practice for a psychologist to use them. If the psychologist believes that other instruments would produce better results, a clear case should be stated. However, if these instruments require more time and are more expensive, the MCO may reject these suggestions. Also, if the tests suggested by the MCO psychologist are ones with which the treating psychologist is not familiar and he or she does not feel competent to administer, it would then be inappropriate for the treating psychologist to use them. It may help in such a situation to discuss the alternatives with the MCO psychologist. It also may be useful for the treating psychologist to inquire as to whether the person making suggestions about testing is someone trained and licensed to do the testing.

In Scenario 4, Ethical Principle 2.02 may come into play. This principle states that

> psychologists refrain from misuse of assessment techniques, interventions, results, and interpretations and take measurable steps to prevent others form misusing the information these techniques provide. This includes refraining from releasing raw test results or raw data to persons, other than to patients or clients as appropriate, who are not qualified to use such information.

A psychologist in this situation may want to propose to the MCO that it appoint a psychologist or other qualified provider for the psychologist to send the raw data. However, if the client agrees and the MCO presses for the data, the psychologist may have to comply with the request because Principle 2.02 does seem to permit release of the data to "patients or clients as appropriate." Some states, like Illinois, actually have laws that preclude the release of raw data to those not qualified to interpret it. Obviously, such a law would strengthen the psychologist's position not to release the data to unqualified individuals.

Psychologists, in situations similar to the one presented in Scenario 5, wrestle with seeing that the client's welfare is attended to while also dealing with financial realities. Informing clients before beginning therapy about the limitations on benefits that their MCO may impose is a crucial and necessary element of risk management. However, even with prior knowledge, the patient is still potentially in a situation of needing care. Ethical Principle 4.09 and the law mandate that a psychologist may not abandon a client. Exactly what actions a psychologist must take in order not to be seen as abandoning a client may vary from place to place and from situation to situation. If the MCO makes an inappropriate decision with regard to patient care, the provider may be responsible for appealing that ruling (*Wickline*, 1987). Also, the psychologist has a responsibility to help the client secure alternative health-care services if additional treatment is necessary. The psychologist may need to continue seeing the client until such a referral is possible. If the psychologist continues to treat the client while the client appeals the limitation on benefits, that psychologist may assume some financial risk. If the psychologist's contract with the MCO does not prohibit it, the psychologist may wish to enter into an express agreement with the client as to who is responsible for charges not covered by the MCO.

In Scenario 6, there are important legal and ethical considerations to address if a psychologist encourages a client to appeal an adverse decision made by an MCO. In general, there do not appear to be absolute ethical or legal prohibitions against enlisting a client to appeal an adverse treatment decision by an MCO when a psychologist reasonably believes that benefits are being prematurely terminated or that the proposed treatment plan is inappropriate. Relevant ethical standards, as listed in the Ethical Principles, include Standard 1.25, Fees and Financial Arrangements, and Standard 4.08, Interruption of Services. Standard 1.25 (e) states that "if limitations to services can be anticipated because of limitations in financing, this is discussed with the . . . client . . . as early as is feasible." Standard 4.08 (b) states,

> When entering into employment or contractual relationships, psychologists provide for orderly and appropriate resolution of responsibility for patient or client care in the event that the employment or contractual relationship ends, with paramount consideration given to the welfare of the patient or client.

In 1991, the APA Ethics Committee discussed whether a psychologist would be engaging in an unethical "dual relationship" by encouraging a patient to pursue a formal complaint against an insurance company. In an unpublished opinion, the Ethics Committee determined that "a psychologist would not be unethical encouraging action believed to be in the client's best interest." The Ethics Committee further commented that "the issues in dual relationship are exploitation or loss of objectivity." Although this opinion was delivered under a previous version of the Ethics Code, the issues appear to be similar. Of course, the facts in any situation are unique, and a particular case must be examined on its own merits.

A psychologist must take into consideration a variety of additional factors when deciding what is appropriate in a given situation, including, for example, the mental stability of the client and his or her ability to make independent choices, the "emotional" overtones of any discussion about the actions of the managed care company, and the context in which the discussion takes place. In addition, there may be some potential for a managed care company or a client to bring a claim of financial coercion against the psychologist, because obviously, the psychologist stands to gain from continued reimbursement by the managed care company. Therefore, psychologists should take into consideration issues of client welfare, coercion and exploitation, and disruption of the treatment relationship. Specifically, standards that may be relevant are 1.17, Multiple Relationships;

1.19, Exploitative Relationships; 1.14, Avoiding Harm; and 1.15, Misuse of Psychologists' Influence.

As noted in the Overview of Managed Care Arrangements section, many psychologists sign contracts with MCOs in which the psychologists agree not to discuss company actions with clients. These gag provisions may be interpreted to prohibit psychologists from speaking to their clients about adverse treatment actions and from encouraging clients to make calls, write letters, or advocate for themselves in appealing the decision. Psychologists, however, have a duty under Standard 1.02, Relationship of Ethics and Law, and Standard 8.03, Conflicts Between Ethics and Organizational Demands, to attempt to resolve conflicts between their obligations with these managed care companies and their ethical duties in a responsible manner. Standard 1.02 states that "if psychologists' ethical responsibilities conflict with law, psychologists make known their commitment to the Ethics Code and take steps to resolve the conflict in a responsible manner." Standard 8.03 states that

> if the demands of an organization with which psychologists are affili-
> ated conflict with this Ethics Code, psychologists clarify the nature of
> the conflict, make known their commitment to the Ethics Code, and to
> the extent feasible, seek to resolve the conflict in a way that permits
> the fullest adherence to the Ethics Code.

In addition to those previously listed, ethical standards that may have special relevance include the following: Standard 1.07, Describing the Nature and Results of Psychological Services; Standard 1.21, Third-Party Requests for Services; Standard 4.01, Structuring the Relationship; and Standard 4.02, Informed Consent to Therapy.

Typically, contracts entered into with the MCO by both psychologists and clients contain provisions describing the appropriate procedure for appealing adverse decisions. Some managed care companies as a result of negotiations have agreed to eliminate these gag clauses upon realizing that such clauses could be interpreted to prohibit full disclosure of treatment risks to clients.

If the psychologist's actions are contested by the MCO, however, there are other potential legal avenues to pursue, which are currently the subject of a legal memorandum being researched by the OMC. For example, there may be First Amendment protection for conversations between a provider and a client in the course of their professional relationship. In addition, there may be state constitutional arguments governing freedom of speech in this context. Finally, there may be relevant state or local ethical codes that should be considered in these situations. The psychologist must balance compliance with contract provisions with the managed care company against the legal and ethical obligations owed to the client.

In summary, enlisting client action in appealing adverse treatment decisions of managed care companies is not inherently unethical or illegal. However, a careful consideration of ethical standards and standards of practice, as well as a thorough legal analysis of any gag provision at issue, should be made before action is taken.

Conclusions and Perspectives for the Future of Psychology

It is clear that the evolution of health care in the United States has placed psychologists and all providers in a different arena than the one in which they acted 10–20 years ago. Psychology licensing laws and ethical principles have not fully evolved along with the drastic changes in the health-care delivery system. Relatedly, the health-care laws themselves that are responsible for regulating the conduct of managed care companies have not fully evolved. As mentioned earlier in this chapter, many of the managed care laws currently on the books are "enabling" statutes; that is, laws that allow for the creation of the managed care entity. Much more needs to be done on the state and federal level to regulate the manner in which services are delivered.

With this constant evolution in the health-care arena, it is imperative that legislators responsible for the welfare of consumers of health care aggressively implement consumer protection laws to increase the regulation of managed care entities. The profession of psychology, and other health-care professional groups, must ensure that their licensing laws and ethical principles continue to preserve the integrity of the professions while evolving to reflect the changes in the industry. There is a need to strike a balance, albeit a difficult one, to ensure that the laws and principles governing the health-care profession demand the highest degree of integrity while keeping current with changes in the health-care delivery system.

References

American Psychological Association. (1992). Ethical principles of psychologists and code of conduct. *American Psychologist, 47,* 1597–1611.

Annotated code of Maryland (Vols. 1 & 2). (1997). Charlottesville, VA: Lexis Law Publishing.

Bennett, M. F. (1988). The greening of the HMO: Implications for prepaid psychiatry. *American Journal of Psychiatry, 145,* 1544–1549.

Boochever, S. (1986). Health maintenance organizations. In J. M. Johnson (Ed.), *Introduction to alternative delivery mechanisms: HMOs, PPOs, and CMPs* (pp. 5–10). Washington, DC: National Health Lawyers Association.

Boyd v. Albert Einstein Medical Center, 547 A. 2d 1229 (Pa. Super. Ct. 1988).

Council on Ethical and Judicial Affairs, American Medical Association. (1994). Ethical issues in health care system reform: The provision of adequate health care. *Journal of the American Medical Association, 272,* 1056–1062.

Council on Ethical and Judicial Affairs, American Medical Association. (1995). Ethical issues in managed care. *Journal of the American Medical Association, 273,* 330–335.

Cummings, N. A. (1990). The credentialing of professional psychologists and its implication for the other mental health disciplines. *Journal of Counseling and Development, 68*(5).

Curtis, T. (1990). Fair hearings for physicians denied participation in managed care plans. *Medical Staff Counselor, 4,* 45–47.

Employment Retirement Income Security Act, 29 U.S.C. § 1001 *et seq.* (1974).

General laws of Commonwealth of Massachusetts (chapters 175–176). (1995). St. Paul, MN: West Publishing.

Hackenthal v. California Medical Association, 187 Cal. Rptr. 811 (Cal. Ct. App. 1982).

Harper v. Healthsource New Hampshire, Inc., 674 A. 2d 962 (N.H. 1996).

Higuchi, S. (1994). Recent managed care legislative and legal issues. *The mental health professional's guide to managed care.* Washington, DC: American Psychological Association.

HMO gag rules. (1996, January 6). *New York Times.*

The language of managed health care. (1992). *The managed care resource.* Minnetonka, MN: United Health Care Corporation.

Napoli, D. S. (1981). *Architects of adjustment: The history of the psychological profession in the United States.* Port Washington, NY: Kennikat Press.

Massachusetts general laws annotated (chapters 175–176). (1995). St. Paul, MN: West Group.

New Hampshire revised statutes annotated. (1997). Charlottesville, VA: Lexis Law Publishing.

Physicians sue NY Health Department over HMO contracts. (1996, January). *Managed Care Law Outlook, 8*(1), 2.

Pinsker v. Pacific Coast Society of Orthodontists, 460 P. 2d 495 (Cal. 1969).

Prysevansky, W., & Wendt, R. (1987). *Psychology as a profession.* New York: Pergamon Press.

Reaves, R. P. (1984). *The law of professional licensing and certification.* Charlotte, NC: Publications for Professionals.

Salkin v. California Dental Association, 224 Cal. Rptr. 352 (Ct. App. 1986).

Simon, N. P. (1994). Ethics, psychodynamic treatment, and managed care. *Psychoanalysis and Psychotherapy, 11*(2), 121.

Strickland, B. R. (1988). Clinical psychology comes of age. *American Psychologist, 43,* 104–107.

Wickline v. State of California, 239 Cal. Rptr. 805, 741 P. 2d 613 (1987).

12

Risk Management Realities Surface in New Practice Environment

Barbara Eileen Calfee

The growth of managed care in the field of mental health has forced practitioners to consider some special lawsuit prevention techniques to combat a variety of newly perceived risks (Harper & Veach, 1990). The term *risk management* refers to the task of protecting a clinician's financial assets from a variety of potentially negative events. This chapter[1] is designed to provide clinicians with broad guidance as well as accurate information on how they might minimize their financial risks in the new mental health marketplace. The first part of this chapter defines key terms involved in risk management issues, the second relates these concepts to current risks that clinicians encounter in the present managed care system, the third examines a number of case studies and discusses strategies that all clinicians working in a managed care environment should be familiar with, and the fourth relates to minimizing liability.

Risk management can be differentiated from *quality assurance* in that the former is proactive, whereas quality assurance remains a more reactive review of practice successes and failures (Bittle & Bloomrosen, 1990). In addition, quality assurance managers are interested in exceeding the needs and expectations of clients, whereas risk managers are typically more concerned about avoiding litigation from dissatisfied clients. *Utilization review* refers to the task of making certain that professional resources are prioritized correctly (Bittle & Bloomrosen, 1990). Typically, a utilization professional will be busy looking for ways in which treatment can be done fast, more efficiently, less expensively, or in a more frugal setting. Although it sounds paradoxical, if discharge can be achieved earlier, patient health may actually be enhanced. For example, it is often said that the quicker a patient can get released from a hospital, the less chance

---

[1]This chapter is designed to provide accurate and authoritative information on risk management, but it is not intended to impart legal advice to any specific reader. Although the author is a health-care attorney, this chapter is intended to offer broad guidance and may need to be supplemented by a thorough evaluation of specific state laws, which can be accomplished by seeking the services of a competent legal professional. In addition, all cases discussed throughout this chapter have been presented in national legal reporters. The factual descriptions used are taken from court documentation; therefore, the author is limited in discussing the facts from that perspective.

he or she will have for nosocomial infection. Working concurrently, these concepts greatly enhance the legal posture of the therapist's practice. When all three concepts come together, the therapist will aim for the provision of safe care, in a timely manner, without adding additional risk to the client, and, if possible, will strive to continually improve his or her techniques and client outcomes as well.

Risk management is typically approached in a four-step process (Richards & Rathbun, 1983). The first step expects the professional to identify the events that could compromise his or her practice. Identification in the small private practice can best be accomplished by reviewing current litigation (which is often reported in professional journals) and patient satisfaction surveys. Those working in agency–institutional settings also have the advantage of risk identification through a program of *incident report trending*,[2] *closed claims surveys*,[3] *accreditation and licensure surveys*,[4] *safety committee meetings*,[5] and *occurrence screening*[6] in conjunction with an ongoing quality assurance plan.

The second step mandates that the clinician analyze each identified problem. Typically, the professional will review each potential risk and determine its likely frequency and severity. For example, if a clinician identified the risk of client abandonment that may cause serious injury, he or she would have to take a look at the mix of his or her current client base. If the clinician's practice specializes in the treatment of schizophrenic patients, the risk of abandonment injury would certainly be greater than in a practice concentrating on anxious consumers suffering from acute adjustment disorders. The risks associated with heightened severity or frequency are, naturally, going to merit additional attention.

The third step, which is defined by this "additional attention," helps the professional develop techniques designed to either control the chance

---

[2]Incident report trending is a process whereby incident–accident reports are periodically studied (quite often on a quarterly basis) to determine if certain client injuries are repetitive. When a "trend" of such accidents can be identified, action can be taken to focus on eliminating such problems in the future.

[3]Closed claims surveys are prepared by national malpractice insurers and researchers. These surveys identify the percentage of claims filed nationwide against therapists in a variety of areas (breaches in confidentiality, suicides, medication errors, etc.). Often the nationwide number can help individual therapists and institutions identify the "climate" of litigation brought by clients.

[4]Accreditation and licensure surveys are reports prepared by organizations asked to credential an institution's practice. For example, most hospitals seek accreditation from the Joint Commission on Accreditation of Healthcare Organizations. After an inspection board has surveyed an institution, it will publish a listing of ideas for improvement and outright administration errors.

[5]Safety committee meetings are typically held in facilities providing health care and are attended by the risk manager, safety manager, security representative, maintenance team members, and others whose input is considered valuable in attempts to lessen patient–staff injuries.

[6]Occurrence screening is a process whereby adverse incidents are discovered and flagged through a review of the client's medical files. This system requires trained personnel to screen the records thoroughly, which tends to limit its effectiveness to the larger facility with financial resources available for such employees.

of loss or transfer the chance of loss to another party. *Risk-control* techniques are specifically intended to eliminate completely the risk or greatly minimize it (Youngberg, 1990). For example, some gynecologists no longer deliver babies—a complete elimination of a very high-risk medical practice. Of course, not all risks can be eliminated entirely. Risk minimization can be accomplished by increasing the knowledge of safe practice and defensive documentation techniques. *Risk transfer* is typically accomplished by the purchase of appropriate professional and comprehensive liability insurance coverage (Youngberg, 1990). In addition, the therapist is urged to review contracts for indemnification language that can transfer risk to the professionals' employers and managed care organizations. Because the language of these documents is often difficult to interpret, the clinician needs to consult a contract lawyer for a full review of such "promises."

The fourth step requires the therapist to monitor his or her choice of risk control and to transfer these techniques to determine whether they continue to serve the therapist's present practice profile. At a minimum, it is recommended that a monitoring review be completed annually or anytime there is a substantial change in the practice. With these four steps in mind, let us explore the way in which risk management techniques can be applied to managed care mental health services.

Risk Identification and Managed Care

It appears that the changing landscape of service provision will also affect the nature of risks the professional can expect to identify. In addition to "traditional" risks (such as dual relationships, sexual misconduct, breaches in confidentiality, misdiagnosis, medication dosage errors, etc.), the professional can now expect to encounter some new problems. For example, a therapist whose practice is increasingly involved with managed care may encounter additional risks in the following areas.

- *Client abandonment.* I predict that clients may claim injuries due to insufficient treatment and may initiate disputes regarding the medical necessity of continued treatment. In addition, clients are becoming more aware that some managed care organizations offer financial incentives to providers who have limited the amount of treatment available for clients (Health Insurance Portability and Accountability Act of 1996).
- *Lack of informed consent.* Clients may also have grounds to argue that the treatment they had received was provided without appropriate information. For example, clients may allege that they were denied accurate details of the limitations of their insurance plan or restrictions on types of treatment available (American Medical Association, 1996).
- *Inappropriate access to client data.* Clients may complain that they were unaware that details of treatment would be shared with managed care insurers and certifying agents in order to obtain payment for professional services (Pelletier, 1996).
- *Delayed treatment.* Consumers may claim injuries because of de-

lays in and denial of psychological testing and other diagnostic methods because of the need to wait for managed care organization approval.[7]

- *Practicing without proper licensure.* With increasing frequency, managed care agreements require that providers communicate with enrollees and peers by means of telecommunication (telephone, fax, or electronic mail). Unfortunately, providers may be unaware that such communication is coming from across state lines. Therefore, a counselor in Washington could find him- or herself offering client services to an enrollee in Idaho. If the Washington counselor does not have an Idaho license, it is possible that he or she could be offering professional services without state permission.[8]

A study of managed care agreements entered into by the counselor is another method that will help in the risk identification process. Specifically, the professional needs to gather the following information before entering into managed care contracts.

- Who owns the plan, and how long has it been in business?
- How many enrollees does the plan have, and what are enrollment projections?
- How does the plan select providers, and what other mental health providers have already been chosen?
- What type of advertising does the plan use? What materials and information about the plan are given to enrollees?
- How does the plan monitor quality? Have any liability claims been made against the plan? How are quality assurance documents protected from discovery in court?
- What type of utilization review is conducted, and how responsive is the plan to a provider's request for additional benefit provisions? What definition of care must be met (i.e., medically necessary), and how is that standard determined? Are utilization review professionals available 24 hr a day?
- What services is the provider expected to extend to plan enrollees? If the provider cannot offer all services expected, who must pay for the care?
- How will confidentiality of client information be maintained?

---

[7]See, for example, *Pappas v. Asbel* (1996). The plaintiff became a quadriplegic after an epidural abscess compressed his spine. He claimed that he would not have suffered this injury if his HMO had not forced him to lose valuable time by transferring him to an HMO-approved hospital.

[8]Telemedicine and Interstate Licensure has published *Center for Telemedicine Law: Findings and Recommendations of the CTL Licensure Task Force,* which can be accessed at http://www.arentfox.com/clt/ctlwhite.html or e-mail: telemedlaw@dgs.dgsys.com. The Physician Insurers Association of America (PIAA) has published *Telemedicine: An Overview of Applications and Barriers,* a 15-page document with answers to questions about telephone malpractice. A copy can be obtained by calling PIAA at (301) 947-9000.

With answers to these questions, the potential service provider will be much better prepared to determine whether the agreement is in his or her best interest.

Risk Analysis and Managed Care

These new risks (as well as twists developing on the more traditional practice hazards) will also merit analysis to determine their degree of danger and likelihood. To evaluate the risks fairly, the professional will have to consider three factors together: (a) the nature of his or her practice and the scope of illnesses treated, (b) the number of clients whose insurance coverage is governed by managed care organizations, and (c) any managed care providership agreements entered into by the professional. I provide three case samples to help illustrate these factors.

Case 1: Marilyn

Description. Marilyn is a psychiatrist whose caseload is filled with seriously ill clients. Some are hospitalized, others have tried to commit suicide, and still others are expected to comply with daily medication routines to maintain their mental health. Marilyn estimates that approximately 50% of her patients have mental health insurance coverage provided by managed care organizations. To date, she has chosen not to participate in any PPOs.

Analysis. In reviewing her practice, Marilyn recognizes that, in addition to the typical risks she has long realized, she will have additional risk issues to deal with given her clients' connection to managed care. First, it is clear that a portion of her population requires immediate, long-term intervention. She will risk claims of abandonment if her patients do not receive the length of treatment required to stabilize their conditions. Second, Marilyn may also recognize that her patients who are covered by managed care plans may not have a full understanding of the limitations of the benefits offered for mental health treatment. These "misunderstandings" could lead to allegations that treatment was rendered without proper informed consent. Both risks appear serious and need appropriate treatment. In addition, although Marilyn is currently not under contract with a managed care organization, she may eventually be "forced" to increase participation because of the changing mental health care climate.

Case 2: James

Description. James is a licensed independent social worker who specializes in relationship counseling. Most of his clients are upper-middle-class married couples. About 30% are covered by managed care insurance contracts. To increase his "client appeal," James has become a preferred provider in one of the largest PPOs in the area—an organization designed to "sell" health-care services to local employers. About one quarter of his current clients are referred to him through this PPO network.

Analysis. When James joined the PPO, he did so because so many of his colleagues were involved in such ventures. Although presented with a lengthy contract of participation, James signed the document without really understanding the "fine print." In performing his risk management audit, he now finds it necessary to grasp the details of the arrangement. While reading the document, he comes across several interesting clauses that could affect the "riskiness" of his practice. For example, clients covered by the program must show "medical necessity" for the treatment. However, the plan language is quite ambiguous in defining medical necessity. Will James have to fight the plan's medical director to prove the necessity of his services? James also discovers that the plan's quality assurance director has full and open access to all of the records compiled on plan clients. Some of the information James collects on his clients is very sensitive, to say the least. What happens when this material becomes known by the quality assurance director? In analyzing these risks, James realizes that possible confidentiality issues are probably more troublesome than treatment access because of the relative stability of his client base—but both challenges will have to be addressed.

Case 3: Alonzo

Description. Alonzo, a psychologist, is considering joining a small group practice. Although Alonzo is familiar with two of the other therapists, he does not know about Eileen, a social worker, and Douglas, a child psychologist. Alonzo feels that a group practice would be in his best interests because he could save some money in support services and rent. He also believes that the group may be able to approach insurance companies and offer services to their enrollees.

Analysis. If Alonzo is simply sharing office space, it is highly unlikely that he would ever be held liable for any of his colleagues' malpractice.[9] However, if the individuals are advertising themselves as a group practice, it is more likely that they could share liability for each other's errors. If this practice group begins approaching potential managed care clients, it is quite likely that the courts would interpret their action as implying a contractual tie, thus resulting in shared liability. When deciding whether to join such a group, Alonzo needs to (a) check the licensure status of the others, (b) make certain that each individual has personal malpractice insurance or that the group agrees to purchase a policy that covers all, and (c) have each group member submit three reference letters from

---

[9]Unless practitioners sharing office space are also incorporated or are tied together through a practice contract, it is highly unlikely that "office mates" will be held liable for the malpractice of any one individual.

professionals—these would be shared with all members so that each could contact references, if needed. With these steps in place, Alonzo should be well protected in the event that one of the other therapists encounters legal difficulties.

Minimizing Liability

Once the therapist has analyzed his or her unique practice, clientele, and involvement with managed care, it is time to determine which strategies would be best used to minimize liability. Again, the two major categories of risk treatment are risk control (the complete elimination or minimization of liability) and risk transfer (spreading one's liability to another party, usually by means of a professional liability insurance policy).

The managed care treatment environment offers some distinct risk-control options not available in traditional fee-for-service counseling. For that reason, in this section I have listed and described some ideas for inclusion in the professional's practice.

Controlling Client Abandonment Claims

The counselor is going to have to do some research here—and it might be painful. Risk managers would strongly suggest that a professional become intimately familiar with the insurance contracts covering his or her clients.[10] Once you have identified any limitations in treatment days or sessions, it is your duty to share that information with your clients. This discussion should take place near the beginning of treatment so that discharge-from-insurance-coverage planning can begin immediately. Clients will have to be aware that a variety of options might be available after the insurance coverage ceases. Some will become self-pay clients, some may be transferred to low-cost community treatment, some will choose to leave treatment, and others will remain in lowered cost treatment as part of a select portion of clients treated as "indigent." So as to minimize confusion, the counselor is well advised to put any information about insurance coverage and limitations in writing, both for his or her client care documentation and for dissemination to the client. Likewise, any discussions with representatives from the insurance company should also be documented and explained to the client.

If a client chooses to leave treatment entirely after insurance coverage ceases, the therapist is urged to document this discharge as "against therapist advice," if it is believed that the client requires further treatment in

---

[10]The practitioner is urged to have clients seek insurance information from their employers' benefits administrators. Two pamphlets that can help clients, *Bill of Rights* and *7 Questions to Ask Your Employer's Benefits Manager*, are available from the American Psychological Association, 750 First St., N.E., Washington, DC 20002.

order to prevent mental health decompensation.[11] It is also advisable to write a brief letter to the client, suggesting that although he or she has made a decision not to continue with treatment, further therapy is medically recommended. These two documentation strategies will help transfer abandonment liability directly to the client under the legal theory known as *contributory negligence*,[12] which is designed to assign blame to clients who are not cooperating with the therapist's advice.

Controlling Lack of Consent Claims

Review of clients' contracts will help out with this control technique as well. To defend successfully claims in which the client is alleging that treatment was given (or denied) without client knowledge, the counselor will have to produce evidence that sufficient insurance information was shared with the client. In looking at this type of claim, I suggest that insurance coverage become an integral part of history taking in initial visits. For example, it has long been suggested that mental health professionals find out what physical illnesses and medications currently affect the client. Professionals do this to make certain that treatments suggested are in sync with all aspects of the client's profile. If a client were to indicate that he or she was taking the prescription drug Temazepam, a mild sedative, the professional should take into account the medication's reported side effect of depression when advising this client about his or her mental health condition. Although insurance contractual language and limitations are the primary responsibility of the client, if a therapist determines that a client's insurance package limits his or her outpatient coverage to $500 per year, it is imperative that this fact be shared with the client and weighed when planning for any care required after the coverage has been used. Although those in the various helping professions typically want to help all people without focusing on money, the present health-care system has forced clinicians to view financial resources as an essential ingredient of the informed consent duty.

Controlling Inappropriate Access to Information Claims

When insurance companies are determining whether to pay a claim, it goes without saying that they will request documentation of the need for services and the care actually given (Pelletier 1996). The rule of thumb here is that "less is better." When asked for information, limit your initial

---

[11]Perhaps the clinician can have his or her client sign a form with wording such as "This is to certify that I am leaving the care of Lisa Johnson, PhD, because I have been advised that my health care plan has denied coverage for any further mental health treatment. I am making this decision although I have been informed by Dr. Johnson that I would benefit from further treatment."

[12]Contributory negligence is defined as conduct by a plaintiff that is below the standard to which he or she is legally required to conform for his or her own protection (*Black's Law Dictionary*, 1979).

offering to the insurance company to a brief sketch of the client's diagnosis (according to the *Diagnostic and Statistical Manual of Mental Disorders*, 4th ed.; American Psychiatric Association, 1994) and dates of treatment. Some (although the number grows smaller every day) insurers will find this information sufficient. If a request is made for additional information, carefully share small bits of the information to avoid disseminating nonessential confidential information. By all means, let each client whose treatment is being funded by a third-party payer know that information will be shared with the company in order to provide this coverage. If a client indicates that his or her employer is self-insured, this may signal that the insurance questions will come directly from his or her employer's human resources department. This means that employees at the client's own worksite may be privy to sensitive data. Although it is hoped that personnel officers maintain confidentiality of employee health data, there are no guarantees, and it is advised that the client be made aware of this possibility. Some self-insured individuals may choose to pay out-of-pocket for treatment to keep such information from their employers.

Controlling Delayed-Treatment Claims

The counselor may actually have some help from the legal system with regard to the most serious delayed-treatment situations. If the client is believed to be in need of hospitalization to prevent serious harm to him- or herself or to others, by all means utilize your state's involuntary commitment process. Do not wait for third-party approval—act now. It is almost guaranteed that the clinician hesitating to hospitalize the dangerous client will garner little jury sympathy. For less serious treatment situations, the professional is urged to make notes of conversations with insurance claims managers, proving his or her attempt to provide timely treatment and the payer's denial of need.

Besides control measures, the other treatment option is the transfer of risk—usually interpreted as a transfer of injury cost to an insurance company. Of course, professional liability insurance will still be necessary to provide full coverage in times of managed care debate. However, one risk transfer that will benefit the counselor may be inflicted by the court itself. Mental health professionals are beginning to see more courts impose professional liability responsibility on the insurance companies themselves.[13]

[13]See, for example, the following court cases: (a) *Pacificare of Oklahoma v. Burrage* (1995). The court ruled that the Employee Retirement Income Security Act (ERISA) of 1974 does not preempt liability claims involving physician compliance with standards of care or the relationships between HMOs and physicians. (b) *Jackson v. Roseman* (1995). The court held that ERISA (1974) did not bar a medical malpractice action against health-care providers and their HMO on the basis of the plan's vicarious liability for the negligence of the providers. Because the claim did not involve a direct effort to recover benefits or enforce an employee's rights under the plan, the court would not apply the ERISA preemption. (c) *Woolfolk v. Duncan* (1995). The court ruled that a patient could sue a health plan for discriminating against him or her because of the patient's HIV status.

The message is clear: "If a managed care organization is going to take on professional decision making, it will be held liable for professional practice within appropriate standards of care."

For example, in *Dunn v. Praiss* (1995), the Supreme Court of New Jersey ruled that an HMO could be held liable for failing to properly co-ordinate a member patient's overall care. Several courts have also found that HMOs can be held vicariously liable for the negligent acts of their approved providers (*Schleier v. Kaiser Foundation Health Plan of the Mid-Atlantic*, 1989; *Sloan v. Metropolitan Health Council*, 1987). Although courts agree that admitting a provider to a managed care network does not render the provider an "employee" of the HMO, the organization may still have partial responsibility for the provider's negligence—although the clinician will always be held liable for any client injury his or her conduct directly caused.

The manner of advertising utilized by the organization may also come under court scrutiny. For example, in *Boyd v. Albert Einstein Medical Center* (1988), the court reviewed the HMO's advertising pamphlets disseminated to members. The advertisements claimed that the providers were "competent" and had been "evaluated" for periods "up to 6 months" before having been "selected" as providers. In addition, other member documents provided that the HMO "guaranteed the quality" of the care provided and "assumed responsibility" for such quality. Given these statements of "endorsement," the court found that the provider could, indeed, impute negligence to the HMO.

Other courts have viewed such claims differently in light of the Employee Retirement Income Security Act (ERISA) of 1974. ERISA was intended to preempt lawsuits that employees might be tempted to bring against employee benefit plans. For example, if a person is employed by a steel company, he or she probably was offered health insurance as an employment benefit. ERISA may prohibit the employee from bringing a suit against the steel company for malpractice committed by his or her physician, who was paid by the employer-sponsored plan. For that reason, some defendant HMOs have successfully claimed ERISA exemption.[14] However, courts have started to erode this exempt status by distinguishing the form of such lawsuits. For example, plaintiffs couching their allega-

---

[14]For example, see *Dalton v. Peninsula Hospital Center* (1995). The estate of a deceased patient brought a malpractice claim against a hospital, a physician, and an HMO through which the patient received medical care. The patient was a dependent minor who was covered by her parents' health-care plan. Under the plan, the parents selected a primary care physician for their daughter but later argued that the HMO doctor was incompetent. In its defense, the HMO raised the ERISA (1974) preemption; however, the parents claimed that their negligent hiring and retention claim was beyond the scope of ERISA. The court dismissed the claim against the HMO, stating that the claim related to an employee benefit plan—exactly the kind of claim designed to be preempted by ERISA. See also *Pomeroy v. Johns Hopkins Medical Services* (1994) and "ERISA Preemption of Medical Negligence Claims Against Managed Care Providers: The Search for an Effective Theory and an Appropriate Remedy" by G. J. Minc (1996).

tions as "negligent credentialing,"[15] "negligent supervision" (*Independence HMO v. Smith*, 1990; *Kearney v. U.S. Healthcare, Inc.*, 1994), and "negligence related to financial incentives"[16] have been able to shift at least a portion of provider liability to the third-party-payer organizations. In the previous example, the steel company employee might very well be able to hold the company liable if it entered into an insurance agreement with a company known for hiring unlicensed doctors. For all of these reasons, risk transfer will continue to be an area of growing interest in the years to come.

Conclusion

Risk management techniques continue to play an important role in the professional's arsenal of lawsuit prevention strategies. Coming to terms with the changes brought about by managed care will only serve to enhance and strengthen a therapist's posture in the courtroom. If applied appropriately, the courtroom may be avoided altogether.

References

American Medical Association. (1996). *Update—State PPA activities* (AMA Special Report, March). Chicago: Author.

American Psychiatric Association. (1994). *Diagnostic and statistical manual of mental disorders* (4th ed.). Washington, DC: Author.

Bittle, L., & Bloomrosen, M. (1990). QA, RM and UM functions require coordinated information management. *Journal of Quality Assurance, 12*(1), 9–14.

Black's law dictionary (5th ed.). (1979). St Paul, MN: West Publishing.

Boyd v. Albert Einstein Medical Center, 547 A. 2d 1229 (Pa. Super. Ct. 1988).

Dalton v. Peninsula Hospital Center, 626 N.Y.S. 2d 362 (Ny. Super. Ct. 1995).

Dunn v. Praiss, 139 N.J. 564 (1995).

Employment Retirement Income Security Act, 29 U.S.C. § 1001 *et seq.* (1974).

Harper, L., & Veach, M. (Eds.). (1990). *Risk management handbook for health care facilities.* Chicago: American Hospital Publishing.

Health Insurance Portability and Accountability Act, Pub. L. 104–191 U.S.C. § (1996).

Independence HMO v. Smith, 733 F. Supp. 933 (E.D. 1990).

Jackson v. Roseman, 878 F. Supp. 820 (D.C. Md. 1995).

Kearney v. U.S. Healthcare, Inc., 859 F. Supp. 182, 186–87 (E.D. Pa. 1994). [Published in *Hospital Manual Law Bulletin*, 1994, October, *3*(10), 3]

McClellan v. Health Maintenance Organization of Pennsylvania, 442 Pa. Super. 504, 660 A., 2d 97 (1995).

---

[15]For example, *McClellan v. Health Maintenance Organization of Pennsylvania* (1995). The estate of a deceased patient sued his HMO after the man died of malignant melanoma when it was discovered that his doctor failed to conduct tests on a removed mole. The appellate court ruled that the family could sue the HMO under the theory that it had not carefully selected its physicians.

[16]See, for example, *Smith v. HMO Great Lakes* (1994). The plaintiff claimed that her physician suffered financial penalties when he referred him HMO clients to specialists and that this penalty deterred him from advising the plaintiff to seek a consultation with a high-risk obstetrician.

Minc, G. J. (1996). ERISA preemption of medical negligence claims against managed care providers: The search for an effective theory and an appropriate remedy. *Journal of Health and Hospital Law, 29,* 97–106.

Pacificare of Oklahoma v. Burrage, 59 F. 3d 151 (10th Cir. Ct. 1995).

Pappas v. Asbel, 675 A., 3d 711 (Pa. Super. Ct. 1996).

Pelletier, M. (1996). Confidentiality within managed care settings. *Confidence, 4*(4).

Pomeroy v. Johns Hopkins Medical Services, Inc., 868 F. Suppl. 110 (D. Md. 1994).

Richards, E., & Rathbun, K. (1983). *Medical risk management.* Rockville, MD: Aspen Systems.

Schleier v. Kaiser Foundation Health Plan of the Mid-Atlantic States, 876 F. 2d 174 (D.C. Cir. 1989).

Sloan v. Metropolitan Health Council, 516 N.E. 2d 1104 (Ind. Ct. App. 1987).

Smith v. HMO Great Lakes, 852 F. Supp. 669 (N.D. Ill. 1994). [Published in *Medical Liability Report,* 1994, November, *16*(11), 270–271]

Woolfolk v. Duncan, 872, F. Supp. 1381 (E.D. Pa. 1995).

Youngberg, B. (1990). *Essentials of hospital risk management.* Rockville, MD: Aspen Systems.

13

Practicing Without Third Parties: How Private Pay and the Development of Basic Business Skills Solve the Ethical Problems of Managed Care

Dana C. Ackley

The managed care community tells us that their services became necessary because our practice patterns led to too much treatment, at excessive prices. These assertions are wrong. We have been making some basic mistakes, but not in our practice patterns. Our mistakes have been in the way we have approached the business of practice.

We provide services in exchange for money. This is how we make our living. Rather than learning how to market our services on their merits, we relied on third-party reimbursement as the bedrock of our financing structure. This was passive dependency. It allowed those on whom we depended to take control of our income stream. As their control of our income stream increased, their power to control our behavior automatically grew as well. In handing over control of our income, we overlooked the fact that we also handed over control of the way we provide services. Few of us seem happy with that part of the bargain.

If this is our problem, then the solution is not to find ways to maintain or deepen our dependency on third-party financing structures, as many colleagues suggest. The answer is to shift from a dependent business stance to self-determination. Self-pay is not proposed as a nice "add-on" for a few therapists lucky enough to attract rich clients. Rather, it is proposed as the best financing approach for the vast majority of current and potential users of our services. Private pay immediately solves the vast array of growing ethical dilemmas created by third-party reimbursement.

Creating a viable profession that relies primarily on direct payment by clients will require that we learn to practice effective business behaviors. Integrating business into practice has not been typical of our approach.

An extended discussion of these and related topics may be found in *Breaking Free of Managed Care: A Step-by-Step Guide to Regaining Control of Your Practice* (Ackley, 1997).

239

Why Did We Ignore Business Issues?

We avoided learning business issues for three reasons. We feared that business would have a negative impact on ethics, we believed that we were simply not "cut out" to learn business skills, and our profession never confronted the emotional conflict about taking money for helping. Let us examine each briefly in turn.

First, many of us have avoided learning about business because of concerns that it would negatively affect our professional ethics. We seemed almost proud of not being "business people." Yet, many of our clients are business people. Do we automatically regard their behavior as unethical? In truth, ignorance and passivity about the business of practice are responsible for creating the most serious ethical dilemmas in the history of our profession. Actively developing and using good business practices, rather than creating ethical problems, will help solve them. However, therapists' concerns about business ethics are not totally unfounded. Business practices can certainly be misused, but then so can therapy processes. It is difficult to think of any human activity that cannot be perverted. However, just because business practices can be misused does not mean that they are evil in and of themselves. The only way we can ensure that the business part of our practice is conducted ethically is to do it ourselves. With a better understanding of what business is really about, we will see just how feasible this is.

Second, we have tended to view business skills as alien to what we knew or could comfortably learn. This was based on ignorance, not truth, but the perception has, of course, guided our behavior. Few of us took business courses to help guide our practices. We spent our time and energy learning clinical skills, as if we had to choose between one set of skills and the other. The fact that we were not mandated to take business courses in graduate school, and were even discouraged from doing so, helped cement the idea that they were neither necessary nor helpful.

Third, there is the emotional conflict we have about making money from helping. Our profession has yet to face that conflict in a systematic way. Profit is the central requirement of every business. Without it, no business can survive, whether it is a hardware store, a major corporation, or a professional practice. All of us, even helping professionals, need to make a profit of some dimension. Otherwise, how can we support ourselves and our families? Yet, it is hard to talk about profit among ourselves. When we are seen as being interested in profit, we run the risk of incurring raised eyebrows, which seem to say, "Don't you really care about people?"

However, profit and caring are not mutually exclusive. If we face the problem squarely, we can deal with our clients on this issue much more straightforwardly than we have thus far. Caring about our clients is not about inappropriate self-sacrifices. These days such behavior is called codependency. As we know, with codependency, nobody benefits. Making a profit while delivering an effective human service provides an example of self-care for our clients, who often sorely need such a model.

We cannot escape dealing with business issues. Even if you work for a nonprofit agency, business issues exist. The agency must find a way to take in enough money to pay its bills, including your salary. The money may be generated by grants, donations, subsidies from business or tax revenues, insurance payments, or private pay, but it must be generated. Likewise in private practice, you have to generate enough income to pay your office expenses and to support yourself and your family in a manner that is commensurate with your skill level and experience, and that does not leave you feeling angry, victimized, and burned out.

What Business Issues Did We Ignore?

Essentially, there are four business-based principles and practices that we have largely ignored: marketing, the relative impact on the buying decision of value versus cost, the issue of money and control, and the negative impact our attachment to the medical model has had on our credibility in the marketplace.

Marketing

Building a market for products or services is a business necessity. An ethical business with no market is soon out of business. We have been uncomfortable about marketing, thinking of it as telling slick lies on glossy paper. It can be that. It does not have to be.

Marketing is a two-step process of education. That is all it really is. The first step in marketing is to educate ourselves about what people want or need. The second step is letting people know that we have it. There is nothing inherently unethical about that. In fact, it seems more unethical for societal resources to have been used to provide us with our education and skills so that we can develop services that no one wants or needs. It also seems unethical to have something that people want or need and keep it a secret.

Value Versus Cost

As therapists, we have tended to believe that purchasing decisions are primarily a function of cost. Successful business people know that most buying decisions are made on the basis of value. Cost is secondary. Its importance varies inversely as the value of the good or service in question. The greater the perceived value, the less cost enters into the decision-making process.

Except for the super rich, people must establish priorities to guide their buying decisions. These priorities are based on the value that a good or service has for them. When people increase their perception of the value of a product or service, it moves up on their list of priorities. They are then more likely to buy it.

This means that there are two fundamental ways to build a market.

One is to increase the perception of value. The other is to lower the cost of the product or service so that people will buy it even though it may be low on their list of priorities.

For example, at one time people did not value car phones. They saw them as a gimmick. Car phone companies could have lowered the price of their product to build a market. This would have been risky because unless demand exploded, the profit margin might not have been large enough to keep the companies in business. Instead, they educated consumers about the potential value of car phones. Women driving alone long distances, parents of teenagers with new driver's licenses and old unreliable cars, and people with older parents still driving were encouraged to think about how a car phone could mean increased safety. Business people for whom a missed call could mean a missed sale were shown how a car phone could be a means to increased accessibility and greater income. Such marketing (education) allowed potential consumers to visualize how car phones might be of value to them, allowing them to make an informed purchasing decision. Sales went up.

Instead of helping people to understand the value of our services, we chose to lower cost as our primary marketing strategy. It was not an informed choice on our part because we had not learned to think through these sorts of business decisions. Our way of lowering cost was to win third-party reimbursement, thereby reducing out-of-pocket costs for consumers. We did not try to sell our services on their merits, despite the high merits they have to offer. As a result, the vast majority of the general public without experience with therapy, and thus unaware of its value, hold it in low priority. Those who experience therapy tend to hold it in high value. When more of the general public comes to understand therapy's value, it will move up on their list of priorities. It is our job to help them develop this understanding. Then cost (and insurance) will become secondary.

Twenty years ago most therapists, including me, welcomed third-party reimbursement with open arms. It was a mistake. Arthur Kovacs and George Albee (1975) were lonely voices in those days, trying to help our profession see the dangers inherent in this process. Most of us thought third-party payments would expand our market considerably. They did. More people came to see us than ever before. The bad part was that reliance on third-party payments kept us from finding superior ways of expanding our markets that would have served even more people in better ways, and left us in control of our services.

Before we attempt to educate potential clients about the value of our services, we will need to think clearly about it ourselves. Unfortunately, we have lost sight of that value. This has happened for two reasons. First, for 20 years we have thought in terms of cost. This focus gradually eroded our focus on our value. Second, managed care has been able to create serious self-doubt among us, as we are a group of introspective people prone to such doubt. This makes us vulnerable to believing the twin charges of managed care: that we keep people in therapy too long and that we charge too much for it.

My first response to the charges and expectations of managed care was severe self-doubt. If managed care clinicians could get results so fast, what was wrong with me? After a period of depression, anxiety, and shame, I began to question the assumption that managed care services were really so much better. As a clinical psychologist, I was trained to look at the data. Therefore, I made it my business to review the data on therapy outcome and cost effectiveness.

What I found was that the data did not support managed care claims (Ackley, 1993, 1997). The data showed that therapists have a long history of providing tremendous clinical value while responding to a variety of client needs. Even prior to managed care, on occasions when short-term therapy worked best, most of us used it. When more was needed, more was given. What our services contribute to quality of life is more than comparable to the contributions of traditional medical care. Therapy services also provide tremendous economic value in at least four areas:

- significant reductions in general health-care costs (Berkman, Leo-Summers, & Horowitz, 1992; Borus et al., 1985; Brody, 1980; Cummings, Dorken, & Pallak, 1990; Fiedler & Wight, 1989; Gonik et al., 1981; Hankin, Kessler, Goldberg, Steinwachs, & Starfield, 1983; Jones, 1979; Kessler, Cleary, & Burke, 1985; Kessler, Steinwachs, & Hankin, 1982; Kiecolt-Glaser et al., 1993; Massad, West, & Friedman, 1990; Mumford, Schlesinger, Glass, Patrick, & Cuerdon, 1984; Orleans, George, Houpt, & Brudie, 1985; Schlesinger, Mumford, & Gene, 1983);

- large cost reductions for business by improving productivity while reducing accidents, grievances, and other on-the-job problems (Broadhead, Blazer, George, & Chiu, 1990; Dobson, 1989; Harrison & Hoffman, 1989; Hayashida et al., 1989; Holder, Longabaugh, Miller, & Rubonis, 1991; Jansen, 1986; Kamlet, 1990; Kronson, 1991; McClellan, Luborsky, O'Brien, Woody, & Druley, 1982; McDonnell Douglas Corporation and Alexander Consulting Group, 1990; Michelson & Marchione, 1991; "More Than 2 Million Workers," 1993; Pelletier, 1993; Rice, Kelman, Miller, & Dunmeyer, 1990; Robinson, Berman, & Neimeyer, 1990; Steinbrueck, Maxwell, & Howard, 1983; "Spotlight: Managing Stress in the Workplace" 1991; Vaccaro, 1991; Walker, 1991);

- better financial futures for children and adolescents who use our services (see Kazdin, 1993, for a review); and

- reduced costs to society for those clients who learn alternatives to "acting out" (see American Psychological Association Practice Directorate, 1995; see also the special section "Prediction and Prevention of Child and Adolescent Antisocial Behavior" in the *Journal of Consulting and Clinical Psychology* [Tolan, Guerra, & Kendall, 1995] for a series of articles on the effectiveness of psychological interventions on antisocial behavior in children and adolescents).

In terms of our "excessive" charges, our premanaged care fees put us in the low average range of earnings when compared with others of similar educational levels.

When I recognized that our services had the high value I had originally believed they had, my professional self-esteem was restored. That helped me take a proactive frame of mind. I then could recognize that managed care is a reduction in employee benefits sold as an improvement in therapy. Employees receive coverage for a much narrower range of services but are led to believe that they are getting better service.

If our profession succumbs to the pressures of managed care to "play ball," one result, I fear, is that people who need more services than the impersonal, crisis-oriented approach now offered through third-party reimbursement will say, "I tried therapy and I failed." They will not recognize that therapy has failed them.

Money and Control

Just as there are basic laws of the science of psychology, there are basic laws of money. The one most relevant here is this: "When you invite other people's money, you automatically invite their control." Imagine going to the grocery story with money in hand. You give the grocer your money, and he selects the groceries you will take home. Satisfied? Of course not. He could easily have picked out a big thick steak, while you are a vegetarian. Third-party payers want as much control over the services they pay for as you want over the groceries you pay for.

This means that there is no way to have any form of third-party reimbursement without also having third parties control the way we practice. The only reason insurance companies left us somewhat uncontrolled for so long was that outpatient therapy represented a very small pot of money to them. With the explosion in the use of inpatient mental health care, the mental health pot in general grew large enough to interest third parties (see Ackley, 1997).

Managed care companies need to do two things to earn the business of an employer: cut health-care costs and make them predictable. Predictability of costs is even more important than relative cost because predictable costs can be handled by adjusting the prices a company charges for its products. Unpredictable costs can ruin companies. To achieve control of health-care costs, managed care companies must have control over treatment delivery.

Contrary to what many people believe, the therapist and the managed care company are equally trustable when it comes to looking out for the client's interest. The difference is that the managed care company's client is the employer.

During seminars on building a managed-care-free practice, I ask therapists who they believe should control treatment. Thus far, the universal answer from the thousands of therapists I have asked is that the two people sitting in the room involved in the therapy process, client and therapist, should control it, because that is when therapy works best. By coming to understand the law of money and control, we can now recognize that for control to reside in the consulting room, only the client's money can be involved. Third-party-supported therapy, by definition, will always be second rate.

There are a number of creative efforts under way to reshape third-party reimbursement systems to make them more humane and more responsive to the needs of therapy users. For the people who still choose to use insurance, more humane systems are certainly preferable to the managed care systems we have now. My concern, even with reformed systems, however, is that they do not eliminate third-party money, which means that third-party control cannot be eliminated. In addition, even if we are successful in swinging the pendulum back toward what we consider to be reasonable, we make ourselves vulnerable to the strong possibility that the pendulum will shift yet again 5 or 10 years from now. We will then have to fight the same battles all over again.

Our Reputation and the Medical Model

If you want people to buy a product or service from you, you must be seen as credible. In other words, your reputation is crucial. In linking our services to the medical model, a natural consequence of getting into the third-party reimbursement system, we enhanced our reputation with a few people but did great damage to our reputation with most people in our society. We believed that using the medical model made us seem more professional, borrowing on the prestige of "real doctors." However, borrowing on this prestige inextricably linked us with the concept of "mental illness." This concept drives people away from our doors in droves.

The use of the medical model not only hurts our reputation, but can actually do damage to some of the people whom we are trying to help. The following material shows that although the medical model was a step forward from what preceded it, when applied to psychological problems, it can actually do much unintended harm. There are at least six serious problems with the medical model.

Our market. From a business point of view, the medical model robs us of 90% of our market. The Rand Corporation did a wide-ranging series of studies on psychotherapy. Among the issues examined was the effect of the size of the copay on utilization of outpatient therapy (Manning, Wells, Duan, Newhouse, & Ware, 1984). In this study, the size of the copay varied from 0% to 100%. Thus, when the copay was 0%, therapy was free. As predicted, more people sought therapy when the copay was smaller. However, even when therapy was free, only 10% of the people studied were willing to avail themselves of the service.

Although estimates vary widely, those who use the medical model tell us that the percentage of people with diagnosable mental disorders is well in excess of 10%. Depressive disorders alone are said to affect 10% or more of the population at any one time. If we let go of the premises of the medical model, it is not hard to see that all of us, that is, 100% of us, have problems in living from time to time, and that we might benefit from expert consultation.

Why won't more people come for therapy? One answer, which we have already discussed, is our failure to educate people about its value. Another is shame. People feel shame if they see themselves as mentally sick. Fifty years of telling people that "mental illness is an illness just like any other illness" has not had much impact on our society. One person looks at another, sees clear evidence of physical problems, and says, "You're sick," in tones of caring and concern. One person looks at another and sees evidence of emotional difficulties or behaviors that they do not endorse and says, "You're sick!" in tones of disgust.

Up to 90% of our population is unwilling to call themselves sick in this way. Perhaps their self-esteem is too intact. What should we do? Batter their self-esteem until they see what wretched wrecks they are? Our job is to present a more reasonable, less damaging model for them to use to access our services.

One hundred percent of the population has problems. Thus far, we have been serving only about 10%. If we see ourselves only as helpers of the "mentally ill," then we have a serious market saturation problem, as managed care has been saying. The value of our services must be seen as high enough to overcome not only issues of cost but also issues of stigma. As an alternative, if we see ourselves as specialists in helping people learn and change, our market is limitless. Not only can we continue to help those with whom we already work, but we can begin to reach many others as well. Our expertise becomes much more widely accessible and acceptable to people who really need it.

Health-care reform. For financial reasons, all health-care providers today are experiencing intense pressure to change the way they practice. To the extent that we call ourselves health-care providers, we too will continue to be dragged through health-care reform. This will continue to have a devastating effect on our profession and cannot help but have a devastating effect on the services we provide. By shifting away from calling what we do health care, we can continue to provide all of the same services we do now but without having to distort them in the unhelpful ways that are demanded by third parties.

The destruction of privacy. With the advent of managed care, and its need for high levels of accountability to outsiders, our clients' secrets no longer stay "locked in our drawer." Highly personal information is sent to a variety of people. Reports, at least of the fact of consultations, are routinely sent to many employers. Ellen Schultz (1994) of the *Wall Street Journal* reported that once this information is in the hands of employers, they find it difficult not to use it for their own purposes, which are not always in their employees' best interests.

Then there is the Medical Information Bureau (MIB). According to

Kiplinger Magazine ("What Insurers Are Saying About You," 1995) and the *Family Therapy Networker* (Freeny, 1995), almost all individual life, health, and disability policies that are sold in the United States and Canada are sold by companies that belong to the MIB. According to these articles, the MIB collects medical and credit histories on applicants and, when requested, passes that information along to member firms that use it to help determine whether to cover an applicant, and, if so, what premium to charge. The Freeney article is a chilling account of what happens to information revealed in therapy, once that information escapes into cyberspace, even beyond the MIB. I fear that unless we warn clients about what happens to this personal information when they sign releases, we could begin to face lawsuits for failure to provide them with the facts they need to give informed consent.

Of additional concern is the fact that managed care companies are going through great upheavals in ownership. Suppose you are sending confidential material to the XYZ Managed Care Company, which has convinced you it knows how to handle such material appropriately. What happens to this information when that managed care company is purchased by the ABC Managed Care Company, perhaps with different standards or practices?

As clients come to understand the privacy risks they are taking, they are increasingly likely to hold back information. You may never know that they are doing so. You do know, however, the impact that this withholding will have on outcome. In fact, as therapy becomes less private, people are unlikely to come at all.

Clients must be ill. Because health insurance will reimburse only for the treatment of illness, we must declare our clients to be ill. Declaring that someone has a mental illness has increasingly serious effects on the therapeutic process.

Even before managed care, these effects existed, though to a lesser extent. Third parties asked less of us, which meant that the kind of thinking that they want us to do intruded less into the consulting room. This made it easier for all involved to deny that we were, to some degree, using a medical model approach. Yet we were already on the slippery slope leading to our current predicament. Had we not made those earlier compromises, we might not have been willing to make the ones now being demanded of us.

Today, to gain reimbursement, it is no longer enough just to list a diagnosis on the insurance form. We must document that illness in detail. To document illness, we must focus with the client on pathology. To do that, we must pay a great deal of attention to symptoms. The more serious the symptoms, the more likely, up to a point, that we will win reimbursement. If we do not spend considerable time focused on symptoms during our sessions, we will not know how to fill out the forms or answer the reviewer's questions. A comparison can be made between therapists doing therapy to satisfy reviewers and teachers who teach "to the test."

Most psychological symptoms can best be understood as an attempt, or the result of an attempt, to solve some problem in living. Usually this attempt is manifestly unsuccessful, or the person would not be sitting in our office. Our job is to help clients solve their problems in better ways. The more attention we pay to symptoms, the less time we can spend dealing with the underlying life issues that create these symptoms.

Furthermore, as we focus on pathology, we lead our clients into focusing on it as well. The greater attention they pay to how "messed up" they are, the less they can focus on their internal resources for change and growth. This is consistent with Milton Erickson's thoughts about selective attention. None of us can focus on everything at the same time. If we, as experts, convince our clients that the truly relevant material is their pathology, they are likely to believe us. If we point them toward their strengths, they are more likely to find them. It is their strengths that will solve their problems, not their "pathology."

Finally, third-party reimbursement controls the very goals of our work. Today, "medical necessity" usually involves getting rid of the symptoms and not much else. Our natural talent is the nurturing and fostering of health and well-being. We, like the entire health-care system, have become distracted by illness, because that is where the money is. Our task is to develop a model that associates money with well-being.

Medical model and personal responsibility. The medical model promotes a lack of personal responsibility for behavior: "I can't help it! I'm sick!" A recent cartoon notes that the mantra of the 1990s is, "I'm a victim of _____" on T-shirts. Just fill in your choice of mental disease. Another version is, "Maybe it's chemical."

Of course it is chemical. It is always chemical. However, it is always other things too. People exist on many levels: biological, psychological, emotional, spiritual, social, cultural, behavioral, and chemical. What we do, think, or feel affects the chemicals within the synapses in the brain. In addition, the particular chemical mix within the synapse can affect our mood, and thus our behavior and thoughts as well. In other words, it is an integrated system, not a linear series of events. All of the elements are always involved.

A mistake of the medical model is to encourage thinking in linear rather than systemic terms. One result is the belief that as soon as we find a physical correlate for an undesirable feeling or behavior, we have found the cause. People jump to the conclusion that every biological problem needs a biological intervention. These assumptions excuse people from any responsibility for the origin of the problem or for taking care of it.

Consider how different that mode of thinking is from what we find within the theoretical models that we favor when actually conducting therapy. List in your own mind the models you use in your daily work. Which of these models does not encourage clients to take responsibility for their behavior? Each, in its own way, searches for methods to empower people to gain greater control over their lives. That outcome demands personal responsibility. It is personal responsibility that gives people freedom and dignity.

The elimination of medical model thinking does not eliminate biological or chemical issues as factors in human problems. Nor does it invalidate biological or chemical interventions. It simply puts them in their proper perspective. People may be born with the life problem of having a body that is excessively attracted to alcohol or one that is excessively impulsive. Contrary to popular thought, this does not excuse them from having to learn how to control that aspect of their being or controlling the consequences of that element of who they are. To excuse people from this responsibility is the ultimate act of disempowerment. The medical model, with its linear focus on biology and chemistry, disarms people in ways from which many never fully recover.

It may help to recall the genesis of the medical model for emotional problems. In the early 1800s, people whom we may now describe as schizophrenic were often thought to be possessed by the devil. In other words, they were considered to be evil. Sometimes their "treatment" was to get stoned to death because their bizarre behavior scared people. Calmer, more humane individuals, appalled by such cruelty, responded that these people were not evil; they were sick. They chose a different cause, one that seemed to eliminate blame. As a result, these individuals were given what passed in those days for humane psychiatric care.

This is consistent with a recent article by Weiner (1993) in the *American Psychologist*. Weiner noted that people are quite willing to help others who have a problem through no fault of their own, but are not willing to help people who are responsible for their dilemma. This is evident in the way people respond to a family whose home accidentally burns down versus the way they respond to an arsonist who burns his own house.

What is needed is a model that holds people responsible for their behavior without calling them either evil or sick, a code word for incompetent. Fortunately, we already have many of these models. They are the therapeutic theories we use in the office. We just have done a poor job of helping our society understand them.

Status differential. The medical model creates an inappropriate status differential between client and therapist. If there are "sick" people and "well" people, and there are only two people in the consulting room, it rapidly becomes clear who is supposed to play what role.

Identifying oneself as mentally sick interferes with a sense of general competence. When we do not feel reasonably competent, the resulting discomfort usually makes it hard to think clearly. This hinders the ability to learn. In other words, by using the medical model, therapists hinder the learning that they are paid to facilitate.

The truth is, of course, that we are all struggling. We live in a highly demanding, fast-changing, stressful culture. None of us are born with all of the skills we may need. None of us have had broad enough life experiences to prepare us sufficiently for everything life may throw at us. Being therapists does not mean that we are better adjusted in every way than our clients. What we do have to offer is our knowledge about the laws of human behavior, development, and change. The potential power of that knowledge becomes actualized when mixed with genuine interest in and respect for the person sitting across the room.

We all need to engage in lifelong learning. Different people need to learn about different things at different times. Someone currently labeled as schizophrenic may need to learn more about distinguishing between reality and nonreality. Someone currently labeled as depressed may need to learn more about the kinds of thinking that generate hopeful feelings. A company CEO may need to learn more about how to handle power in a way that draws the best performance from his people. A mother may need to learn how to access her patience in dealing with an impulsive, demanding child. A person who has used alcohol for anxiety control may need to learn alternative anxiety-control mechanisms.

Lifelong learning is a value. The medical model defines this "need to learn" as a disease. That is crazy.

An Alternative Approach

Solving our current ethical dilemmas requires a number of changes. One key change is in the way we think, shifting from the medical model to a more inviting, empowering approach to human problems. This shift prepares us for other changes in our thinking and in our business practices that will offer higher value for both client and therapist.

Changing Our Conceptual Base

Over the past few years I have had the chance to ask thousands of therapists about the theoretical models they use when actually working with a client. Thus far, not one has answered that he or she uses the medical model. Instead they talk of cognitive–behavioral therapy, psychodynamic theories, family systems, solution-focused, and a long list of other models. That suggests that therapists did not endorse the medical model because it was intellectually compelling or clinically useful. We endorsed the medical model for business reasons. It gave us access to third-party reimbursement.

Let us now do business differently. Not only will we gain control of our business, and thus its ethics, but we will also be able to clean out of our therapy behaviors some of the unnoticed and unhelpful effects of medical model thinking.

Let us begin with a different general model. All of the theoretical models that therapists report using when actually with clients can be subsumed under the rubric *the problem-solving/skill-building model*. Theoretical orientations may differ from each other widely, but they all share two features. Each identifies problems people struggle with and suggests ways that therapists can help people build their skills to solve those problems. Of course there is wide variety—both of problems seen and of therapeutic activities—that helps strengthen skills. Great! This gives real diversity to the marketplace, allowing people, both therapists and clients, with their own diverse styles and needs, all to find a place to be.

All people have problems. Recognizing this fundamental fact does a great service for people by solving the blaming problem. Up to now, people have had two choices: They could be evil (and run the risk of getting stoned or shunned) or they could be incompetent. Neither choice is helpful. That is one reason why denial of problems is so popular. The choice we could now offer is that people can be competent and develop new skills at the same time.

With this choice, the barrier of shame is eliminated. If everybody has problems, then having problems is normal. The false distinction of illness–wellness is eliminated. The kinds of services we can provide to people multiply, making our expertise much more accessible to the public. I look to the day when consulting a therapist will be as much a part of life as consulting one's dentist, attorney, or accountant.

Changing Our View of Our Opportunities

Having decided not to work for managed care, I have spent the last several years researching alternatives. My income dropped during the first 3 of those years by about 20%, the same amount it would have declined had I joined managed care panels. However, without contracts to struggle through, telephone calls to make to reviewers, and endless forms to complete, I had hours free to invest in research that has now paid off. I had decided to leave the profession if good alternatives could not be found. What I discovered, to my surprise and delight, is that managed care represents less than 10% of our opportunities.

It is my belief that the best alternative to managed care, for both clients and therapists, is a practice based on private pay, marketed not just to the traditional 10% of the population willing to call themselves mentally ill, but to the other 90% as well. This is far more feasible than "conventional wisdom" has led us to believe. Our profession has drastically underestimated the proportion of the population willing to forgo insurance benefits when they have been properly educated about problems in using them. It has drastically underestimated the number of people who will see us if we can operate outside of a mental illness model.

On the basis of my research, I began my own transition from a heavily third-party-dependent practice to a cash practice. Within 2 years, 93% of my income was free of third-party reimbursement. My income increased significantly, more than recapturing that "lost" 20%. Much of this change resulted from the simple step of educating clients about the pros and cons of using third-party reimbursement. When people are armed with the facts, the majority prefer not to use their insurance "benefits." (My office continues to file for those clients who choose to use their insurance. If clients ask me to make out-of-panel reports to their managed care companies, I do so. Few ask.) My therapy clients continue to represent a broad range of the economic spectrum, including single mothers and young adults with low-paying jobs.

Some therapists believe that clients will demand that we deeply discount our fees, essentially matching the managed care rate, if we want them to pay out of pocket. That has not been my experience. Clients can see the difference in value between what their insurance coverage makes available and what can be provided when external constraints are eliminated. I offer a small ($5) administrative discount for not using insurance if the client pays in full at the time of the visit. This makes sense, as my secretary is saved the time and trouble of filing. Although I also offer two other payment options for private-pay clients, 90% of them choose the small discount option.

If we match the managed care rate, we are implicitly suggesting that our services have the same value that managed care services have. We may not mean to say this, but that is the message that results. Private-pay services, using the problem-solving/skill-building model, have much greater value in terms of privacy, client−therapist control of the process, elimination of the damage done by the requirement to carry a psychiatric diagnosis, and elimination of the shame long associated with "needing therapy." They put the client and therapist on an equal footing, eliminating the status differential. By making room for client self-esteem within the business structure of therapy, private-pay therapy has a better chance of succeeding in reaching the client's goals from the beginning.

We are told that people will not pay out of pocket for services that their insurance will cover. That is true. However, insurance no longer covers the kinds of service I offer: private, client-directed, non-illness based. Furthermore, the costs of therapy to clients are less than often imagined. Research shows that 90% of episodes of outpatient therapy last less than 25 sessions (Bak, Weiner, & Jackson, 1991). Assume that a therapy session costs $100. This means that the total cost is under $2,500 for most people. By stretching out payments, just one of many financing alternatives, this service comes within reach of the vast majority of people. This is increasingly true as people reorder their priorities about how to spend their money in response to our doing a better job of educating people about the value of therapy.

Insurance rarely covered 100% of therapy costs anyway. By shifting to private pay, people are not going from $0 to $2,500. They are only increasing their out-of-pocket costs over whatever their copay was, often as much as 50% after an initial deductible. A great many insurance policies require huge sacrifices of quality and privacy for relatively few dollars.

Just how much money is available for private pay? Is it worth pursuing? In 1992, $800 billion was spent on traditional, reimbursable health care. However, an additional $114 billion was spent on health services not reimbursed by third parties (Pelletier, 1993). This is the money we are told no one will spend. Many people see some of these services, such as acupuncture and other forms of alternative medicine, as valuable. Other services for which people paid out of pocket are well out of the mainstream. The point here is that people spent money on services that they perceived to have value. There is at least $114 billion available for health care outside the insurance system.

However, these are just medical dollars. We can compete for other dollars as well. For example, many people spend money on divorces—a lot of money. Marital therapy might be a better choice. People, including older adults and the less well-to-do, also spend money on such things as

- pets, pet food, and veterinarian bills;
- sound systems, television, and computers;
- college and adult education activities;
- self-improvement through Dale Carnegie courses; private music and dance lessons; aerobics classes; Weight Watchers; and tennis, golf, and fitness coaches;
- recreational activities such as golf and tennis;
- home remodeling and redecorating; and
- alcohol, drugs, and cigarettes (a household with two people, each of whom smokes one pack per day, spends $1,600/year on cigarettes).

Where should therapy fit within a set of priorities? Should it always be after all of these items?

On the basis of my experience thus far, it appears that private pay can work for about 80% of the population. People within this economic range reorder their priorities to make room for their therapy bills, once they are convinced of the value.

Changing the Way We Think About and Work With the Economically Disadvantaged

People on the lowest end of the economic scale must use most of their limited financial resources to meet their basic needs, as defined by Maslow's pyramid. Yet these people need therapy services too. Finding a way to meet their needs has been a dilemma that has eluded a fully satisfactory solution by any system yet designed.

The economically disadvantaged will suffer the same ill effects from using insurance and buying into the medical model as everyone else. Furthermore, great numbers of the economically needy do not even have insurance. Remember, to have insurance you either have to have a full-time job with decent benefits or the money to pay the monthly premiums on your own.

Pro bono services. Professionals in private practice are expected to provide some services for the public good, or "pro bono." However, it does seem that in trying to meet this need some important issues need to be fully considered. Unfortunately, pro bono services alone cannot satisfy all of those in need of therapy. Private practitioners, unlike community agencies and free clinics, do not receive donations, grants, or subsidies to supplement their fee incomes. Therefore, clinicians in private practice cannot afford to see large numbers of people for much less than full fee and still pay their own bills without, in effect, charging their other clients for the needy person's therapy. If full-fee clients are told that they are subsidizing other clients' therapy and choose to do so, there may not be a problem. However, full-fee clients might prefer to make their charitable contributions through other mechanisms.

Agencies and free clinics. Because agencies and clinics are subsidized, they are in a position to serve people of lesser means for a reduced fee. In fact, community agencies have been the first line of defense for providing therapy to the economically needy. However, in recent years, as some of their funding has dried up, many agencies have begun to move toward a private practice, insurance-dependent model of service. One means of providing pro bono services might be for therapists who wish to do so to donate some of their free time to such agencies, just as lawyers and business people work with the United Way, Boy Scouts, and the American Cancer Society, especially if funding for these agencies can once again come through taxes and charitable contributions. Unlike insurance money, which is designated for individuals who, to get the money, must be branded with a diagnosis, subsidies are earmarked for the clinic. Individuals can pay a reduced fee out of pocket and still receive the benefits of the private-pay and problem-solving/skill-building model if the clinic chooses to operate on that model.

Of course, clinics are supported by third-party money, and the third parties, such as local governments or the United Way, will still want some outside control. However, that control can focus on overhead, not on individual treatment plans. There is room for therapists to influence the philosophy, mission statement, and values of the clinic. They can make it their business to be involved with local government or the United Way to make sure that these values are understood up front and to assure continued adequate funding.

Medicaid. You may wonder about Medicaid. Medicaid is not an insurance program, even though it looks like one in some ways. It is an entitlement program much like Aid to Dependent Children and food stamps. Medicaid is not based on premiums people pay but rather is money that comes from tax dollars—it is a government subsidy. The difference between this subsidy and other subsidy money agencies might receive is that this money is earmarked for the individual rather than for the agency.

The advantage of Medicaid is that there is no charge to the patient for covered services. It allows recipients to go either to clinics or to those private practitioners who are willing to accept Medicaid reimbursement rates. The disadvantages of Medicaid are the same as the disadvantages of indemnity insurance programs: psychiatric diagnoses are required, privacy is sacrificed, and number of sessions is limited. In addition, many Medicaid programs today are being shifted over to managed care/HMO-based models. Those programs will suffer from all of the disadvantages managed care has to offer.

Some clients and practitioners may be willing to endure these disadvantages, feeling that such services are "better than nothing." However, the agency model suggested here seems to have significant advantages in that clients can have access to the problem-solving/skill-building model, privacy can be better assured, and access to seasoned private practitioners can still exist to the extent to which those practitioners donate some of their time to these facilities, whether in direct client contact or in supervision. The agencies could continue to employ a mix of new graduates, those who are more experienced but who prefer not to go into private practice, and those who are especially trained to work with the economically disadvantaged, or who find such work uniquely fulfilling and satisfying.

Changing the Way We Think About Marketing

By using appropriate marketing techniques, we can educate the public about our value. This will move therapy up the list of priorities people have, which will increase the size of our market. Within that context, we can offer services that are controlled only by the participants, that are private, that are individually tailored, and that are nonshameful.

How do we educate ourselves about what the community wants and needs from us, and how do we let them know what we have to offer? How do we communicate the value of our services? These are marketing questions.

For a service to be perceived to have value, it must speak to real questions that potential clients have. Therefore, as we plan our marketing efforts, we must figure out what questions people in our area have about problems in living. There are many inexpensive ways for us to learn this information. We can listen to those who already visit us, reframing our description of their concerns from DSM-IV-relevant language to the language of ordinary people. In addition, we can learn which self-help books people buy, because in making each of those purchases they tell us about the problems that are on their minds. We can look at magazines that feature self-help articles to see what topics are written about, because publishers have already done market studies to determine what people are most concerned about. Finally, we can read the newspaper, which is a daily accounting of problems with which people struggle.

How can we educate people about our value? Although the full answer to this question goes beyond what can be discussed here (see Ackley, 1997), some introductory comments can be made. Business people know that potential consumers determine value primarily on the basis of anticipated benefits, not on the basis of methods used to get those benefits. Yet when we attempt to communicate to people about our services, we tend to do so in terms of our methods instead of the outcomes or benefits that people can expect to obtain.

For example, our Yellow Pages ads tend to use words like *psychotherapy* and *assessment*. People do not want psychotherapy, they want the benefits therapy may offer. It is an extra step, requiring additional knowledge most people do not have, for people to discern potential benefit from an ad that talks about our methods. Do you suppose that anyone ever wakes up, turns to his spouse, and says, "Honey, I think I'll go get a dose of biofeedback." Nobody wants biofeedback in and of itself. What people want is freedom from various forms of pain.

People do not want marital therapy, they want improved marriages. People are not interested in psychoanalysis, they are interested in not hating themselves. Our services can deliver these benefits. We should talk to people on their terms about benefits so they can make an informed decision.

If we want people to come to see us, we need to take down some barriers we have inadvertently erected over the years. When we talk to people, let us talk to them in English. Too often, our attempts at communication have relied on jargon, which to most people is a foreign language. This is a difficult and unnecessary barrier for us to erect against potential clients. We will increase our success by taking it down. In addition, we may even increase our own understanding of what we do. In my experience, I know that I have really mastered a new psychological concept when I can explain it in nonprofessional language.

Another barrier for many potential clients is the initial commitment they believe must be made before a therapist will see them. Many people believe that they must be willing to commit to a several-year process before they can even begin therapy. This is somewhat akin to being willing to marry someone on the first date. Most people are unwilling to make such a commitment.

We can increase our potential market by making it easy and attractive for people to start seeing us. Many businesses begin relationships with people through "entry-level services." These are typically short, low-cost services that allow someone to experiment with those particular goods or services. We can reach a larger part of society by offering a variety of well-targeted, useful entry-level services.

Most smoking cessation programs, for example, last just a few sessions. However, this need not be the end of the relationship, if you offer a genuinely helpful service. Now the client knows you. The client may have other issues he or she would like to examine. The brief, initial experience gives the client an opportunity to try therapy and you. This overcomes the barriers of ignorance and prejudice many people have about "shrinks," because these initial sessions have given them more accurate information about you, who you are, and what you do. If the experience is positive, people are likely to return with other issues that could benefit from your attention.

The example of smoking cessation is used here because it is so accessible to so many therapists. It is not, however, particularly creative. One of the exercises in my seminars on building a managed-care-free practice asks participants to design some possible services along the lines discussed here. The creativity, ingenuity, and enthusiasm they demonstrate in this exercise give me great faith in our future. Furthermore, the services developed in these exercises speak to genuine needs of people in great pain who are largely ignored by our current service delivery system. Not only that, but many of the services would reach people much earlier in the problem cycle than our current delivery system allows. Through them, much unnecessary suffering and damage could be avoided.

Let us find ways to tell people that we are available to work with them on issues that matter to them. Let us speak their language and offer them services that will allow them to get to know us before they make a larger commitment.

Concerns about professionalism. As we move into marketing activities, there is the realistic danger that we could fall prey to being glitzy, getting so caught up in the marketing process that we forget our professionalism. Although we do need to help people understand the realistic benefits of therapy, we need to avoid overpromising. Thus far, our strategy has been to underpromise, which undereducates potential clients. I have found that as therapists experiment with the appropriate language in which to present their services to prospective clients, they do an excellent job of presenting realistic outcomes that most people can achieve.

Concerns about competition. A second danger has to do with how we compete with each other. We do compete, and we always have. In my community, even though we are in competition, therapists from different practices still consider one another friends and refer clients when another therapist has the needed skills. In some communities, I am hearing that competition has become increasingly cutthroat. That is not good for anyone. As we educate clients about our services, it remains unprofessional for us to say that we have an answer that is superior to all others. It is still unprofessional for us to try to win by tearing others down. Not only is it unprofessional, it is bad business. We will win few clients with negative advertising.

In presenting our services, we need to talk about the value they have to the people who use them. This is the cornerstone of our strategy in regaining control of our profession and its ethics. Our failure to present our value to the public in intelligible ways has left us vulnerable to external controls. In addition, as we expand our market to 100% of the population, there will be plenty of business for everyone. As more therapists shift to a private-pay model, their natural process of educating people will create additional demands for services. The more of us who are operating a private-pay, problem-solving/skill-building practice, the more normal and desirable our services will become for the public. In this way, competition breeds more business.

Changing the Way We Think About Money

Although people will come to us feeling less shame and with more of a sense of an empowered equal status, they will still come to us feeling emotionally vulnerable. We have worked hard to avoid taking financial advantage of this vulnerability. Sometimes, however, this has led us to make business decisions about payments which are bad for us financially, and which, ironically, may create unintended problems in terms of the emotional price clients pay in lieu of money.

Therapy is a professional transaction that involves the exchange of money for service. Although we get uncomfortable with money sometimes, it really is an excellent exchange medium. For one thing, money is quantifiable. People know when they have paid the right amount. When we rely on client gratitude rather than on money, it is hard to know when enough "units of gratitude" have been paid. The use of gratitude as the primary currency also distorts the therapeutic process.

In addition, using money as the mechanism of payment helps maintain the boundaries between therapy and other kinds of human transactions that can sometimes bear a superficial resemblance to therapy. Many ethical violations committed by therapists involve boundary issues. Clearly establishing the business aspects of the therapeutic relationship can help client and therapist alike to avoid becoming friends, business partners, and sexual partners. Essentially, money legitimizes the relationship.

Conclusion

At the beginning of this chapter, I made the point that we avoided developing our business skills partly out of fear that using business principles would lead to ethical problems. By now, I hope that you can see the ethical advantages of being good therapists and good business people. These identities are not mutually exclusive.

Many therapists view our professional future with despair. I believe that our best days lie ahead. By adding good business practices to our mix of skills, we can regain control of our profession and can solve many of the serious ethical problems that currently exist. Our services to those whom we already serve will be even more effective than they currently are. Beyond that, we can provide services to people who would never see us under the old ways of practicing. We can develop services that are more creative, speak to a wider range of issues, and allow people to solve problems far earlier in their development. Ultimately, opportunities to help our society to become increasingly human will multiply. And for all this, we can still get paid what we are worth.

References

Ackley, D. C. (1993). Employee health insurance benefits: A comparison of managed care with traditional mental health care: Costs and results. *The Independent Practitioner*, *13*(1), 33–40.

Ackley, D. C. (1997). *Breaking free of managed care: A step-by-step guide to regaining control of your practice*. New York: Guilford Press.

American Psychological Association Practice Directorate. (1995). *Violence in the workplace*. Washington, DC: Author.

Bak, J. S., Weiner, R. H., & Jackson, L. J. (1991). Managed mental health care: Should independent private practitioners capitulate or mobilize? *Texas Psychologist, 43*, 23–37.

Berkman, L. F., Leo-Summers, L., & Horowitz, R. I. (1992). Emotional support and survival after myocardial infarction. *Annals of Internal Medicine, 117*, 1003–1009.

Borus, J. F., Olendzki, M., Kessler, L., Buens, R. J., Brandt, U. C., Broverman, C. A., & Henderson, P. R. (1985). The offset effect of mental health treatment on ambulatory medical care utilization and changes. *Archives of General Psychiatry, 42*, 573–580.

Broadhead, W. E., Blazer, D. G., George, L. K., & Chiu, K. T. (1990). Depression, disability days, and days lost from work in a prospective epidemiological survey. *Journal of the American Medical Association, 264*(19), 2524–2528.

Brody, D. S. (1980). Physician recognition of behavioral, psychological and social aspects of medical care. *Archives of Internal Medicine, 140*, 1286–1289.

Cummings, N. A., Dorken, H., & Pallak, M. S. (1990). *The impact of psychological intervention on healthcare utilization and costs*. San Francisco, CA: Biodyne Institute.

Dobson, K. S. (1989). A meta-analysis of the efficacy of cognitive therapy for depression. *Journal of Consulting and Clinical Psychology, 57*, 414–419.

Fiedler, J. L., & Wight, J. B. (1989). *The medical offset effect and public health policy: Mental health industry in transition*. New York: Praeger.

Freeny, M. (1995, September/October). Do the walls have ears? *Family Therapy Networker, 5*(19), 37–43, 65.

Gonik, U. L., et al. (1981). Cost-effectiveness of behavioral medicine procedures in the treatment of stress-related disorders. *American Journal of Clinical Biofeedback, 4*(1), 16–24.

Hankin, J. R., Kessler, L. G., Goldberg, I. D., Steinwachs, D. M., & Starfield, B. H. (1983). A longitudinal study of offset in the use of nonpsychiatric services following specialized mental health care. *Medical Care, 21*, 1099–1110.

Harrison, P. A., & Hoffman, N. G. (1989). *CATOR Report: Adult inpatient completers one year later*. St. Paul, MN: Ramsey Clinic.

Hayashida, M., Alterman, A. I., McLellan, A. T., O'Brien, C. P., Purtill, J. J., Volpicelli, J. R., Raphelson, A. H., & Hall, C. P. (1989). Comparative effectiveness of inpatient and outpatient detoxification of patients with mild-to-moderate alcohol withdrawal syndrome. *Journal of Studies on Alcohol, 52*(6), 517–540.

Jansen, M. (1986). Emotional disorders in the labour force: Prevalence, costs, prevention and rehabilitation. *International Labour Review, 125*(5), 605–615.

Holder, H., Longabaugh, R., Miller, W. R., & Rubonis, A. V. (1991). The cost effectiveness of treatment of alcoholism: A first approximation. *Journal of Studies on Alcohol, 52*(6), 517–540.

Jones, K. (Ed.). (1979). Report of a conference on the impact of alcohol, drug abuse, and mental health treatment on medical care utilization. *Medical Care, 17*(Supplement), 1–82.

Kamlet, J. S. (1990). *Depression in the workplace: Issues and answers*. Baltimore, MD: National Institute of Mental Health.

Kazdin, A. E. (1993). Psychotherapy for children and adolescents: Current progress and future research directions. *American Psychologist, 48*(6), 644–657.

Kessler, L. G., Cleary, P. G., & Burke, J. D. (1985). Psychiatric disorders in primary care. *Archives of General Psychiatry, 42*, 583–587.

Kessler, L. G., Steinwachs, D. M., & Hankin, J. R. (1982). Episodes of psychiatric care and medical utilization. *Medical Care, 20*, 1209–1221.

Kiecolt-Glaser, J. K., Malarkey, W. B., Chee, M. A., Newton, T., Cacioppo, J. T., Mao, H. Y., & Glaser, R. (1993). Negative behavior during marital conflict is associated with immunological down-regulation. *Psychosomatic Medicine, 55*, 395–409.

Kovacs, A., & Albee, G. (1975). Comments on "insurance reimbursement." *American Psychologist, 30*(12), 1156–1164.

Kronson, M. E. (1991, April). Substance abuse coverage provided by employer medical plans. *Monthly Labor Review*, 3–10.

Manning, W. G., Wells, K. B., Duan, N., Newhouse, J. P., & Ware, J. E. (1984). Cost sharing and the use of ambulatory mental health services. *American Psychologist, 39*(10), 1077–1089.

Massad, P. M., West, A. N., & Friedman, M. J. (1990). Relationship between utilization of mental health and medical services in a VA hospital. *American Journal of Psychiatry, 147,* 465–469.

McClellan, A. T., Luborsky, L., O'Brien, C. P., Woody, G. E., & Druley, K. A. (1982). Is treatment for substance abuse effective? *Journal of the American Medical Association, 247*(10), 1423–1428.

McDonnell Douglas Corporation and Alexander Consulting Group. (1990). *Employee Assistance Program Financial Offset Study: 1985–1989.* St. Louis, MO: Author.

Michelson, L. K., & Marchione, K. (1991). Behavioral, cognitive, and pharmacological treatments of panic disorder with agoraphobia: A critique and synthesis. *Journal of Consulting and Clinical Psychiatry, 59*(1), 100–114.

More than 2 million workers attacked on job. (1993, October 18). Chicago: Prodigy News Service.

Mumford, E., Schlesinger, H. J., Glass, G. L., Patrick, C., & Cuerdon, T. (1984). A new look at evidence about reduced cost of medical utilization following mental health treatment. *American Journal of Psychiatry, 141,* 1145–1158.

Orleans, C. T., George, J. K., Houpt, J. L., & Brudie, H. K. (1985). How primary care physicians treat psychiatric disorders: A national survey of family practitioners. *American Journal of Psychiatry, 142,* 52–57.

Pelletier, K. R. (1993, August). *Practical strategies for health promotion.* Paper presented at the Albert Einstein College of Medicine Summer Institute Conference on Healthy People, Healthy Business, Cape Cod, MA.

Rice, D. R., Kelman, S., Miller, L. S., & Dunmeyer, S. (1990). *The economic costs of alcohol and drug abuse and mental illness: 1985* (Report submitted to the Office of Financing and Coverage Policy of the Alcohol, Drug Abuse, and Mental Health Administration, U.S. Department of Health and Human Services). San Francisco: Institute for Health and Aging, University of California.

Robinson, L. A., Berman, J. S., & Neimeyer, R. A. (1990). Psychotherapy for the treatment of depression: A comprehensive review of controlled outcomes research. *Psychological Bulletin, 108,* 30–49.

Schultz, E. (1994, May 18). Open secrets: Medical data gathered by firms can prove less than confidential. *The Wall Street Journal,* p. 1.

Schlesinger, J. J., Mumford, E., & Gene, V. (1983). Mental health treatment and medical care utilization in a fee-for-service system: Outpatient mental health treatment following the onset of a chronic illness. *American Journal of Public Health, 73,* 422–429.

Spotlight: Managing stress in the workplace. (1991, March). *Prevention Report, U.S. Public Health Service,* p. 7.

Steinbrueck, S. M., Maxwell, S. E., & Howard, G. S. (1983). A meta-analysis of psychotherapy and drug therapy in the treatment of unipolar depression with adults. *Journal of Consulting and Clinical Psychology, 51,* 856–863.

Tolan, P. H., Guerra, N. G., & Kendall, P. C. (Eds.). (1995). Prediction and prevention of child and adolescent antisocial behavior [Special section]. *Journal of Consulting and Clinical Psychology, 63,* 683–725.

Vaccaro, V. A. (1991). *Depression: Corporate experience and innovations.* Washington, DC: Washington Business Group on Health.

Walker, C. K. (1991, September). Stressed to kill. *Business and Health,* p. 42.

Weiner, B. (1993). On sin versus sickness: A theory of perceived responsibility and social motivation. *American Psychologist, 48*(9), 957–965.

What insurers are saying about you. (1995, December 6). *Kiplinger Magazine.*

14

Ethics and Capitation From a Business Perspective: A Personal Account

Anthony M. Trachta

Like most professionals who have experienced capitated behavioral health care, my first experience took place when a small but vibrant provider company, for which I was working at the time, decided to go at-risk and form a managed care company serving a commercial population. Being new to the field, we, as clinicians, had very little experience upon which to base our initial attempts at setting capitation rates and did so on the basis of information received from the commercial carrier in the area before taking on the contract. Even within our own organization, there was a fair amount of resistance to forming a practice based on a capitation rate and to reorganizing our treatment models to be briefer, more intensive and focused, and under constant utilization review.

We built a capitation rate based on a combination of facts and guesswork, and we decided to try to make the system conform to the rate rather than to build the capitation rate based on a particular treatment model. At that time, in 1987, we felt it more important to get into the managed care market than to worry excessively about a particular level of margin. We were committed, however, to redesigning treatment modalities that would provide a high level of quality of care within a low carve-out capitation rate, and we used our own provider network primarily to provide the treatment indicated for the patients in this population.

The initial contracts were from a carve-out HMO for about 35,000 children's lives, and these contracts were then enlarged by a contract from another commercial HMO in the area for about 50,000 adult and children's lives. Added later to these were some carve-out contracts obtained from a few small area employers. In all, the company eventually managed about 125,000 lives, with an average capitation rate of about $3.50 per member per month. The benefit of this endeavor is that I obtained tremendous experience in running a component of the organization for adults that delivered care that had to be accessible, flexible, and patient focused in order to stay within the cap rate.

The population that we served was made up mostly of working- and middle-class families whose utilization patterns were by and large very manageable within this capitation rate. What made it most manageable, however, was that by contract, high utilizers who used up their benefits bounced into the public system as a default. Therefore, it was much easier to manage the low utilizers and the balance sheet. I realized only later that this was the phenomenon that was occurring in most commercial managed care populations. The commercial managed care carve-out rates were simply not designed to provide services to the high-utilizing population; they were (and are) the public sector's problem.

Capitation in the Public Sector

When I began working in the public-sector population, as managed care began to penetrate Medicaid plans, the rules all changed. In managed Medicaid, especially in the mandatory plans, there is no public default. The plan is responsible for a population that already has a high-service utilization rate, so capitation rates that work in the commercial sector would be far too low. Medicaid enrollees can be system savvy, entitled, and linked to public delivery systems in a long-term way. As Medicaid managed care grows, the rules are being rewritten. In the commercial population, historical trends have shown that spending for mental health and substance abuse services may be in the range of $2–$8 per member per month; whereas for Medicaid-only fee for service, historical trends have shown that spending may be in the range of $40–$50 per member per month (Frank & McGuire, 1995). (In Pennsylvania, spending rates are currently $44 per member per month for Medicaid-only fee for service.)

It is easy to see that the same per-member-per-month capitation goals are not going to be achieved with this population, as was done with a commercial population, no matter how much unnecessary or inefficient services are redesigned or trimmed. Other complications can also occur. Medicaid spending by states is historically divided into at least three funding streams: (a) Medicaid fee for service, (b) county-based dollars often provided by the state to supplement Medicaid fee for service by program services, and (c) spending for state hospitals. In Pennsylvania, these three funding streams contribute about equally to the care of the Medicaid population.

Among Medicaid recipients, the utilization trends indicate that approximately 70% of the money spent for mental health and substance abuse care is spent on about 10–20% of the population, who are the highest utilizers (Frank & McGuire, 1995). Therefore, a great majority of Medicaid users mirror some of the utilization patterns of the commercial population, who are primarily families who receive Aid to Families With Dependent Children. However, a small but significant proportion of Medicaid subscribers are intensive utilizers, who, when funding streams are combined, can use up to $175 per member per month for behavioral health care.

Ethical Considerations

Understanding the critical differences between these two populations is important when attempting to determine not only the setting of capitation rates but also when considering the ethical considerations inherent in how the money is spent. Couple this with a 25-year-old public delivery system that in most states has evolved slowly since its origins, and one can see the dilemma. Though most public providers have historically taken good care of the population known as the *severely persistently mentally ill* (SPMI), in providing these services, they have done so with an "entitlement approach" mentality. In other words, more is better. They have little notion of their existence as a delivery system and do very little on a regular basis to monitor quality control, outcomes, access, or targeted level of care placement. Thus, there is the phenomenon of the permanent patient, who stays in the revolving door of psychiatric and substance abuse treatment, bouncing from inpatient to long-term partial to outpatient and maintenance throughout extended episodes of care.

As Director of Managed Care for Psychiatric Services at the Western Psychiatric Institute and Clinic of the University of Pittsburgh Medical Center, my responsibility over the last 2 years has been to work with the rest of the executive team to understand how to enter the Medicaid managed care market with a population largely made up of a combination of Medicaid subscribers, many SPMI, and a small commercial population base. Historically, as the largest provider of services to the SPMI population in this area, we set about this mission with a firm commitment to working toward the goal of a reasonable capitation rate and a benefit design approach that would allow for the reengineering of the delivery system but that would not allow for the expulsion of our historical population from access to benefits and services. We have jokingly referred to this approach as our *transition tightrope*. The ethical question is how to form a managed care company that obtains business through contracts with Medicaid and still treat the severely mentally ill, who are historically disenrolled from managed Medicaid plans. In other words, can a managed care company be fair and accountable simultaneously? Can an innovative, well-linked delivery system be provided and can the available dollars be spent more wisely? In addition, these goals are further complicated when one considers that included in this planning are provisions for the maintenance of two other central aspects of our mission—namely, research and academics—areas traditionally not funded by managed care.

One ethical dilemma that we had resolved quickly was the determination that we would put a ceiling or limit on our level of profit or margin in this endeavor. Although many commercial managed care companies freely admit to a 20–25% profit from the Medicaid managed care patients, we determined that our level of profit would be capped between 3% and 4% and that much of it would go toward the continued funding of research and care. We believe that this funding is important not only because it is historical but also because it will allow us to train clinicians of the future and to develop the technologies necessary for studying outcomes and patient satisfaction and for maintaining quality of services. Using this strategy, we hope to address these learning and improvement concerns.

In this process, we have also had to grapple with the issues of infrastructure, information systems, and management of the back-office responsibilities (claims adjudication, claims payment, etc.). The easiest decision in dealing with these issues would entail contracting with a company that already provides these services to a large Medicaid population and relinquishing certain aspects of the responsibilities for a price. We have decided, however, that this decision will inevitably take more money away from providing proper health care. Therefore, we will try to build that infrastructure ourselves, bring in external talent that we employ, and be our own self-managers. The risk is greater, but the expenditure of dollars will be more under control. We have realized that as a high-cost academic medical center, we will not be able to use ourselves as providers for many of the patients that we refer. We will absorb too much of the capitated service dollar. We have, therefore, sought to make relationships with other public-provider partners who would furnish better access at lower cost than is possible within this medical center. We are currently working with them to develop provider contracts that will allow them to participate in the provision of care. These partners must agree, however, to perform according to quality and utilization standards and to participate in the development of outcome measurements and quality benchmarks so that all providers will be held to the same standards of quality. Their continued position in the network will be determined by their performance. We are also investigating the possibility of risk sharing with providers who we believe are already in a better position to accept risk because of their efforts to reengineer their delivery systems, and we believe that this risk sharing among public providers is the true way to successful partnerships. This risk–reward relationship will motivate providers to initiate and continue the process of evolving cost-effective, accessible services, thus assuring the survival of our high-cost medical center. This strategy speaks to ethical access by allowing inclusion of willing providers in an incentive-driven system of care.

Another ethical issue that we are considering in this process is confidentiality. Many providers have expressed concern over the open access that managed care companies seem to have to entire patient records throughout the patients' utilization and precertification processes. We believe that an internal infrastructure will be able to better manage confidentiality issues in that there will be less information transfer and more in-house management of sensitive information.

Taking a lesson from my commercial-side experience, the formation of our own managed care company will also allow us to design flexible clinical programs that we can self-monitor and pay for according to patients' needs. The only way managed care can work in the Medicaid population is to have a highly flexible continuum of care made up of the full range of services, including long-term care, inpatient partial, intensive outpatient, 23-hr evaluation, outpatient, and residential, among other modalities. We must also build a network of partners who will share the risk and who will potentially share the reward. We also believe that this will allow us to bring some of the social service aspects into our capitation by partnering with providers of subsidized housing, transportation services, in-home care, and "wraparound" services. All of these services are truly necessary to reduce utilization among the SPMI population and to enhance the continuum of care for better outcomes.

All of this leads to a basic position on the issue of ethics and capitation. We believe that this transition is critical for the Medicaid population, and reorganization of the delivery system should not be done precipitously or in a statewide manner. We believe that health care should be regional and that a pilot or demonstration project approach to setting appropriate capitation rates must be the methodology. We believe that it is ethically necessary with this population to include social service components in the benefits plan, and we believe that these will enhance the overall outcomes and cost management.

Even though an initial approach to this managed care company might be a carve-out of behavioral health care, we believe that eventually a fully integrated approach incorporating the medical side with the benefits plan and managing them together in a more connected way is the long-term goal. We believe that the true savings that can be accumulated in the delivery of health care can be contributed to significantly by offset medical costs. Numerous studies have shown that patients who are high utilizers of behavioral health-care services are also high utilizers of medical services and that the integrated medical–psychiatric approach is the only true long-term solution for this population. We believe that to be truly ethical, we must also build in education and prevention models that promote good maternal–infant health-care approaches to substance abusers. We also believe that it is only ethical to eventually combine all funding streams that relate to the provision of behavioral health care, including county-based monies, state hospital monies, and eventually children and youth and juvenile justice monies so that a true wraparound approach can be accomplished. The SPMI population uses resources from these funding streams concurrently, but their parallel nature prevents true system coordination. We believe that it is only with these considerations that one can truly arrive at a capitation rate that will make sense for Medicaid population.

Summary and Conclusion

I believe that the aforementioned issues speak to the fiduciary–stewardship responsibilities inherent in managed care. Although we as health-care providers are responsible for the welfare of any population, we are also responsible for providing health-care resources in a fair and judicious manner. We owe the public sector nothing less.

Our experience in private- and public-sector capitated services shows increased financial and clinical pressure in clinical services in general, and in public-sector services specifically. Our efforts to address ethical issues as we develop capitated services in the public sector have emphasized that a set of ethical principles must guide the formation of a risk-bearing entity. In our case, these principles must be in alignment with those of an academic medical center with the caveat that cost-effectiveness, quality, and value drive the process of entering the market.

Reference

Frank, R. G., & McGuire, T. G. (1995, Fall). Estimating costs of mental health and substance abuse coverage. *Health Affairs*, 103–115.

Index

About the Editors

Laurence R. Barnhill, PhD, is a psychologist and marriage and family therapist in private practice in Bloomington, Indiana, and is currently president of the Indiana Psychological Association. He is also president and chief executive officer of Alliance Behavioral Healthcare, PC, a multidisciplinary group practice in Bloomington. Barnhill was the founder of the Bloomington Family Institute and was clinical director and chief psychologist of South Central Community Mental Health Center in Bloomington. He has taught in the departments of psychology, sociology, and counseling at Indiana University. He has presented numerous workshops on ethics and managed care, multidisciplinary group practice, business consulting, and family therapy at regional and national conferences and has written numerous articles and chapters on family therapy and family violence.

Richard F. Small, PhD, received his doctorate from the University of Colorado. He is director of Spring Psychological Associates in Sinking Spring, Pennsylvania, is a past president of the Pennsylvania Psychological Association, and is currently on the American Psychological Association Council of Representatives. He has authored several books and numerous articles on insurance, managed care, ethical, and bereavement issues. Small is currently enrolled in the Master of Bioethics program at the University of Pennsylvania.